D1035562

Stapme

The Biography of
Squadron Leader
B. G. Stapleton DFC, DFC (Dutch)

David M. S. Ross

GRUB STREET · LONDON

Published by
Grub Street
The Basement
10 Chivalry Road
London SW11 1HT

British Library Cataloguing in Publication Data
Ross, David
  Stapme: the biography of Squadron Leader Basil Gerald
  Stapleton, DFC, Dutch Flying Cross
  1. Stapleton, Basil Gerald 2. World War, 1939-1945 – Aerial
  operations, South African 3. World War, 1939-1945 – personal
  narratives, South African 4. Fighter pilots – South Africa – Biography
  I. Title
  940.5'44968'092

ISBN 1 902304 98 5

Typeset by Pearl Graphics, Hemel Hempstead

Printed and bound in Great Britain by
Biddles Ltd, Guildford and King's Lynn

CONTENTS

FOREWORD

There are a number of privileges inherent in being a member of the Battle of Britain Memorial Flight, some obvious, such as the opportunity to fly two of the world's most famous fighters and, in the role of Commanding Officer, the opportunity to act as custodian of a large part of the nation's flying heritage. Among the less obvious privileges is the opportunity to meet those heroes, acknowledged or unsung, who fought WWII in the Royal Air Force and survived, unscathed or otherwise. It is largely thanks to the generosity of the 48th Tactical Fighter Wing of the United States Air Force that I have been able to meet men of the calibre of Gerald Stapleton, either as guests of the A10 Squadrons at RAF Alconbury or latterly of the F15 Squadrons at Lakenheath.

As comrades-in-arms those American airmen acknowledge our debt to Gerald Stapleton and his ilk despite the fact that to hear Stapme and his colleagues talk one might imagine no debt was due. It is almost as if WWII was an inconvenience, but worth getting into as the only fight available. Perhaps understandable with the benefit of years of training and hard experience, but we should remember Gerald Stapleton's entry to the fray was backed up by a magnificent 62 hours dual flying and 105 hours solo. Those hours consisted of a motley collection of types including Tiger Moths and Ansons, none of which could be deemed particularly representative of the Hurricanes and Spitfires he was to fly in combat, nor did that training include much in the way of combat skills such as air-to-air gunnery or formation tactics. By comparison, I entered the peacetime frontline in the early 1960s after 250 hours of training, all of it relevant and most of it on aircraft of representative performance. Today's fighter pilot takes at least six years from joining to get to the frontline, enough to miss an entire World War!

Last month the funeral of Her Majesty Queen Elizabeth the Queen Mother was seen as the passing of an era by the majority of the populace; I believe Gerald Stapleton and his surviving comrades represent the last of the 'talented amateurs' whose dedication and resolve forged them into Britain's most vital shield and the instruments of ultimate victory.

Enjoy the book – remember the debt.

Squadron Leader Paul Day OBE, AFC, RAF
Officer Commanding
Battle of Britain Memorial Flight

RAF Coningsby
May 2002

PROLOGUE

During research into the life of Flight Lieutenant Richard Hillary and the history of 603 (City of Edinburgh) Squadron, RAuxAF, I learned much about those with whom Hillary had served during the Battle of Britain. During that period of the Squadron's history there were many abiding characters immortalised in Hillary's *The Last Enemy*. One who was initially quite elusive was Squadron Leader Basil Gerald 'Stapme' Stapleton DFC, DFC (Dutch).

Stapme is one of 2,918* Fighter Command aircrew who fought in the Battle of Britain. Of that number, 544 were killed during the battle (10 July – 31 October 1940) with a further 796 killed in the course of their duties between 1 November 1940 and 15 August 1945 bringing the total to 1,340. Over the years, time has naturally taken its toll and of the 1,578 survivors, the 'Few' are indeed getting fewer. Stapme survived to see peace and was, by his own admission, fortunate to have lived the many years which most of his young colleagues had been denied.

A survivor and an 'ace' of the Battle of Britain, Stapme moved to a Delivery Flight, then to a Merchant Ship Fighter Unit, where he faced the prospect of being launched by rockets off the deck of a merchant 'rust-bucket' in defence of the trans-Atlantic convoys. Next he saw service with 257 (Burma) Squadron before, once again, moving to a Delivery Flight. In 1944, having spent a lengthy period as a gunnery instructor, a job he relished, he took over command of 247 (China-British) Squadron in France. Once again he saw a large number of colleagues killed in action before he was forced to land behind enemy lines and spend the remainder of hostilities as a POW.

Following the end of WWII and on completion of his Short Service Commission, Stapme did not remain in the RAF. He believed he had no future in the force in peacetime. His various jobs will come as a surprise to many and his adventures have left him quietly content with a host of vivid memories.

Having initially made contact with Stapme while he was still living in South Africa, I received a telephone call shortly after he returned to live in England and in his instantly recognisable voice, only slightly tinged with a South African accent, he said: 'Stapleton here. So you want to know more about Richard Hillary? Come on over and we'll have a beer.' On meeting him I soon realised that his was a story in itself and one which was worth telling; a conclusion I have arrived at with many of the 603 Squadron fighter pilots.

To many, the image of 'Stapme' Stapleton with his large handlebar

---

*This number now includes Squadron Leader John Strawson DFC, a recent addition who served briefly with Stapme in 603 Squadron during the battle. Strawson is included in the 796 who did not survive the war.

moustache epitomises the public's perception of what a typical Battle of Britain fighter pilot looks like. The development of this association, albeit an inaccurate one, was nevertheless evocative of the times and due mainly to Stapme's likeness to the wartime caricature of 'Flying Officer Kyte'.

Interestingly, the reason why Stapme and a number of the other younger members of 603 Squadron attempted to grow moustaches was so that they appeared older than they actually were because in their opinion the senior pilots in the Squadron exuded know-how and credibility. Some of those older members had first joined the RAF or AAF as far back as 1931-32 and with war looming the newcomers were keen to be perceived as as experienced as the old hands. In truth, whilst the youngsters looked to their elders for role models, when war came they all shared a natural but common shortfall – a lack of combat experience. When 603 Squadron were sent to relieve one of 11 Group's beleaguered squadrons during the Battle of Britain, Stapme and his contemporaries underwent a shocking baptism as frontline Fighter Command pilots. As eager young men, they bonded quickly, but conditions also required them to learn rapidly as fighter pilots and as a fighting unit. During their initial patrols they attempted to pick up the skills required in order just to survive, before progressing to shooting down an enemy aircraft, if they were lucky. Some lasted a matter of hours whilst others rode their luck and survived the battle only to be killed later in the war.

In this book I hope you will enjoy reading of Stapme's early life, his wartime experiences, and post-war years when the story unfolds of his time spent living in far-off places. With two failed marriages behind him it was during a period of heavy drinking that he met his present wife, Audrey, who quite possibly saved him from an insalubrious future and even an early death. Some years later, Stapme's eldest son, Mike, who has contributed to the story, declared himself an alcoholic. Whilst Stapme had Audrey to help get his life back on course, Mike fought his own battle and has now been free of the habit for a great many years. He is justifiably proud of this, particularly as he is an experienced club/hotel manager and temptation is never far away. Stapme and Mike describe the years spent living and working in Botswana as the happiest of their lives and recall Botswana as being 'God's own country'. Sadly, fate ultimately sought out the Stapleton family when Stapme's youngest son, Harvey, died following a motocross accident. Stapme's life came full-circle when he returned to England where he and Audrey now live their days in quiet retirement in the part of Lincolnshire from where his family originated.

Since our first meeting I have come to know Stapme well, and there have been many memorable moments. We have attended the last five Battle of Britain Fighter Association Reunions at RAF Lakenheath together and while there are many enduring memories, one anecdote is from a poignant 'last' ever function at that venue. After a typically superb evening's hospitality from the 48th Fighter Wing of the USAF we were on the Air Force coach taking us back to our accommodation when Stapme suddenly burst into song (his voice akin to Bud Flannagan). We reached our destination well before he had finished his song but all the Fighter Association members and their wives sat in silence until Stapme had finished, at which point spontaneous applause and cheering broke out. He still enjoys a beer when out at such functions and when questioned about his wartime experiences he typically ponders for a moment before answering in a concise and assured manner. He is most likely to understate rather than overstate. He is a mine of information, is charismatic, charming, a true gentleman with the ladies, and great fun to be with. He is also one of the 'Few' who fought for freedom in the Battle of Britain and who continued to do 'his bit' long after.

A history or biography is just a story about the past. Embroidered in its telling from one person to another over time, the truth is invariably distorted and what we are left with is something which may be more readable, more amusing and more marketable, but in doing so the true story can be lost. This is simply the story of Stapme unembellished by time. I hope you enjoy it. It is an honour to have been asked to write it.

One aspect caused some difficulty during research for this book. Stapme's logbook, along with his medals and other memorabilia, went missing many years ago in South Africa. Therefore, without the logbook, piecing together his flying career proved difficult. In order to provide the reader with an estimation of hours flown by Stapme during training and his time with 603 Squadron, up to and including the Battle of Britain, I've taken averages from the pilot's flying logbooks of Wing Commander George Gilroy and Squadron Leaders Jim Morton and Jack Stokoe, 603 Squadron contemporaries of Stapme. The figures which appear in the text are therefore approximate.

Also, as Stapme contributed so generously to my previous book on Richard Hillary, it is only natural that of his quotes included in that book some appear again here. However, he has once again cast his eye over his words and amended some where necessary.

DAVID M. S. ROSS
MAY 2002

ACKNOWLEDGEMENTS

With thanks to my friends Gerald and Audrey Stapleton who invited me into their home on so many occasions, offering hospitality and kindness. I would also like to thank the proprietors of the Ketton Club for the times when we sought sustenance and good conversation.

I am once again indebted to the Rt. Hon. Lord James Douglas-Hamilton, Lord Selkirk of Douglas, PC, QC, MA, LLB, MSP, for his support and expertise. Thanks also to the following: Stapme's brother, Air Vice-Marshal Deryck Stapleton, sister Marjorie Gétaz, and Stapme's son Mike; the Staff at Air Historical Branch (RAF); Staff at the RAF Museum, Hendon; Ernie Hardy; Nicolas Trudgian for the excellent jacket painting; Robin Elvin who produced the particularly life-like portrait of Stapme, and allowed us to reproduce it for the book; Air Commodore Sir Archie Winskill KCVO, CBE, DFC*, RAF (Ret'd); Mick Rogers and the 247 Squadron Association; Wing Commander John Young AFC, Historian – Battle of Britain Fighter Association; Malcolm Smith, Hon. Secretary of the Fighter Association, and his wife Joyce; Colin and Rose Smith of Vector Fine Art for their support and hospitality; Angus and Ruth Davidson; Betty Johnstone (née Davie); Wendy Roberts; Lyn Deans; Jean Blades; Jean Cunningham; Jean Liddicoat; Lynne Robinson; George Skipper; Mike Craig and Tony Kirk of the Military Gallery; Dr Mark Whitnall; Bill Strawson; Andrew Davies; Steve Read; Ken Layson of the *Daily Mirror* and Squadron Leader Paul Day OBE, AFC, RAF, OC BBMF, for kindly agreeing to write the Foreword.

Group Captain Bob Kemp QVRM, AE, ADC, FRIN, RAuxAF, former Commanding Officer 603 (City of Edinburgh) Squadron, RAuxAF; Serving members of 603 Squadron, in particular the present Commanding Officer, Wing Commander Alasdair Beaton AE; Squadron Leader Barry Greenhaugh; Flight Lieutenants Derek Morrison and Barbara Murray and Sergeant Martin Steele RAF; Members of the 603 Association, in particular: John Mackenzie (Chairman), John Rendall, Arthur Carroll, Alec Mackenzie, Bert Pringle, Jim Renwick, George Knox and George Mullay Jnr. All the above made Stapme and I very welcome during our visits to the 603 Squadron Town Headquarters in Edinburgh.

Fellow historians: Squadron Leader Bruce Blanche RAuxAF, Norman Franks, Christopher Shores, Chris Thomas, Geoff Rayner, Chris Goss, Richard Smith, Andy Saunders, John Maynard, Jack Foreman, David J. Marchant, John Alcorn, John Coleman, Bill Simpson, Henry Buckton, Andrew Jeffrey, and Squadron Leader Peter Brown AFC.

At Grub Street Publishing: John Davies, Anne Dolamore, Dominic Busby and Louise King with thanks for all your hard work.

I apologise in advance for anyone I may have inadvertently omitted.

Finally to my family for their love, support and expertise: My father, Squadron Leader Cliff Ross RAF (Ret'd); mother Maureen Ross; Kerry and George Cathro; and Alison.

All photographs and graphics which appear in this book are from the author's collection, with due acknowledgement and thanks to my sister, Kerry Cathro for the additional artwork; Ron D. Hefer for granting exclusive UK copyright to the author for the portraits of Squadron Leader B.G. Stapleton DFC; Colin Smith of Vector Fine Art; Rebecca Jenkins and the *Leicester Mercury*; Mark Dowie at the *Montrose Review*; photos of Squadron Leader Stapleton whilst with 257 Squadron from Peter Steib via Geoff Rayner; Derek French; Desmond Carbury; John Coleman; Jean Blades; Jean Cunningham; Lyn Deans; R.B. Gardiner; Andy Saunders; Chris Thomas; Mick Rogers and the 247 Association; *The Sunday Post* (Edinburgh); Vic Seymour Photographic Services; illustration of Typhoon 1B ZYY by K. Mallen; the Goss/Rauchbach Collection; and the photo collections of Gerald and Audrey Stapleton, Deryck Stapleton and Marjorie Gétaz (née Stapleton).

A List of Equivalent Ranks which Feature in the Book

Royal Air Force	*Luftwaffe*
Marshal of the Royal Air Force	Generalfeldmarschall
Air Chief Marshal	Generaloberst
Air Marshal	General
Air Vice-Marshal	Generalleutnant
Air Commodore	Generalmajor
Group Captain	Oberst
Wing Commander	Oberstleutnant
Squadron Leader	Major
Flight Lieutenant	Hauptmann
Flying Officer	Oberleutnant
Pilot Officer	Leutnant
Warrant Officer	Stabsfeldwebel
Flight Sergeant	Oberfeldwebel
Sergeant	Feldwebel
Corporal	Unteroffizier
Leading Aircraftman	Obergefreiter
Aircraftman First Class	Gefreiter
Aircraftman Second Class	Flieger

The flying circus was in town and large crowds gathered around the bi-plane and its leather-clad pilot. At five bob a 'flip' the pilot offered a circuit before landing again. Some held back with trepidation, others were keen to fly for the first time but couldn't afford the price. From amongst the crowd, wrapped up against the chill, a young fair-haired teenager emerged and walked towards the aircraft. After a few words the pilot helped the youngster into the front cockpit before donning his helmet and goggles and climbing into the rear compartment. He called out to his ground crewman to turn over the airscrew and the engine spluttered, the wooden blades accelerated momentarily before slowing and then the engine roared into life emitting a cloud of exhaust fumes which billowed over the crowd. The lad sat intently, without goggles or helmet, his hair blowing in the wash from the airscrew. As the bi-plane moved away from the crowd the tail swung round, the blast from the propeller whipping up the dew from the grass and sending the icy moisture swirling over them before it moved away across the field, the wing-tips bobbing up and down as the undercarriage found every undulation. Aligned for take-off, the pilot opened the throttle, the engine revs increased and the aircraft moved across the field, gathering speed all the time until it lifted gently into the air. Once airborne it banked sharply to starboard and flew to the rear of the crowd a few hundred feet off the ground. It then banked to starboard again, lost height and with the engine just ticking over, touched gently down in the field. With intermittent bursts of throttle the pilot taxied back towards the crowd and cut the engine. The airscrew came to a halt, the pilot unfastened his straps, climbed out of the cockpit and onto the wing where he unfastened the youngster's straps. With his face covered in a light film of oil, cheeks ruddy from the cold, but a picture of joy, he climbed from the cockpit. Having experienced flight, he now knew what he wanted to do when he left school. His pilot had been an ace from the First World War and his relaxed attitude and casual yet commanding approach to flying the aircraft inspired his young client. This first experience of flying had been inspirational and something the youngster never forgot.

Night & Day
(Cole Porter)

Like the beat, beat, beat of the tom-tom;
When the jungle shadows fall,
Like the tick, tick, tock of the stately clock,
As it stands against the wall,
Like the drip, drip, drip of the raindrops,
When the summer show'r is through;
So a voice within me keeps repeating, you, you, you.

Night and day you are the one,
Only you beneath the moon and under the sun.
Whether near to me or far,
It's no matter, darling, where you are,
I think of you night and day.

Day and night why is it so,
That this longing for you follows wherever I go.
In the roaring traffic's boom,
In the silence of my lonely room,
I think of you, night and day.

Night and day, under the hide of me,
There's an Oh, such a hungry yearning, burning inside of me.
And its torment won't be through,
Till you let me spend my life making love to you,
day and night, night and day,
Night and day.

CHAPTER ONE

'BAAAASIL!'

Basil Gerald Stapleton was born in Durban, South Africa on 12 May 1920. One of three children; older brother, Deryck (later Air Vice-Marshal Deryck C. Stapleton CB, CBE, DFC, AFC, RAF (Ret'd)*, and younger sister Marjorie. His grandfather owned a local brewery producing Stapleton's Pale Ales and his great uncle, Richard Valentine Stapleton, was one of the partners of a solicitors in Broad Street, Stamford, Lincs. Today, his name still appears on the frontage of the premises. Gerald's father, John Rouse Stapleton OBE, always known as 'Jack', was born in Thurlby, near Stamford on 4 February 1885, and had a distinguished career in marine radio service and broadcasting. He trained at the South London Telegraph Training College from 1901 to 1903 when he joined the Marconi Company in July of that year and was at sea as a radio officer from 1910 until 1912. From 1912 to 1919 Jack Stapleton was in charge of the Government Wireless Station at Welikado, Ceylon, and during WWI was a senior officer of the Ceylon Engineer Corps. In 1920, with the birth of Gerald imminent, his wife stayed with her parents in Durban whilst Jack Stapleton travelled to India where he was involved with early wireless and broadcasting experiments. Stapme's earliest memory was of being on his father's desk in Calcutta aged three. His father's two claims to fame are that he was responsible for the establishment of radio broadcasting in India and for the installation of the Marconi radio set in the RMS *Titanic*. As history records, it functioned perfectly but failed to bring about immediate assistance when the White Star liner sunk with the loss of over 1,500 lives after glancing off an iceberg on 15 April 1912. In 1928 he was appointed director of the Indian Broadcasting Company and in 1930 director of the Calcutta Station for the Government of India. Jack Stapleton was awarded the OBE in the King's Birthday Honours List of 1941, and at the time of his retirement was director of All India Radio in Calcutta and manager for the Marconi International Marine Communication Company Limited and the British Wireless Marine Service. Gerald remembers: 'Later in life he suffered from cataracts, which also afflicted me. Whilst working on his car he had trouble seeing and used to swear loudly in Hindustani, so the rest of us wouldn't understand!' Jack Stapleton made his home in Sarnia in Natal in December 1946 and opened a small leather goods shop in Pinetown, near Durban.

Gerald's mother, Myrtle Natal Borland, was born in Natal on 21 December 1886, and was the artistic member of the family who had a great influence on

---

*See his autobiography *Winged Promises* published by the RAF Benevolent Fund.

the young Gerald. She was awarded a Gold Medal for Piano and Singing at the Royal Academy of Music. A talented pianist and experienced piano tutor, she attempted to teach Gerald to play. Unfortunately, his own artistic inclination was to play by ear rather than by learning to read music. This frustrated the instincts and went against the classical training of his mother and Gerald was told to: '. . . stop being provocative!'

Gerald was only at his first school a short time before being moved to another in Norbury, south London, where he 'won a pen knife for winning the egg and spoon or sack race, I can't remember exactly which.' During one of his school holidays he went to stay with an 'uncle' in Lincolnshire where he earned some pocket money assisting the local milkman on his round.

His father was sent to work in India, initially unaccompanied, but later his wife joined him once the boys had settled in to boarding school. Gerald recalls his early life:

> We had been living in West Croydon for a couple of years when Dad was sent to India with the Marconi Company, as director of the Indian Broadcasting Company. My mother and father decided to put my brother and me into an English school before he departed. Our first school had been Ellaland, on the south-east coast, when I was six, but this closed soon after and we were sent to Norbury College and then King Edward VI School in Totnes. My father then left for India. There, I received my education from about nine years old until the school leaving age. One of the deciding factors for sending us to a school in that part of the country was because my brother had been suffering from double pneumonia and pleurisy and the doctors had advised my parents to send him to a more suitable climate to aid his recovery. Devon was perfect. As it happened, he made a full recovery and he retired from the RAF as an Air Vice-Marshal.
>
> My mother initially stayed locally in a cottage in Torbay called 'Seacroft' and we were week-day borders at King Edward VI School. We enjoyed our weekends at home. Eventually, when my brother was fully recovered she went back to Croydon, before joining my father in India – some three years after my father was first posted overseas. She used to come over from India to visit and, if I remember correctly, she did something like eleven trips across from India to England and back between the wars. Eventually, she went to live in Clarens, Switzerland, where my sister, Marjorie, went to Le Chatelarde school for girls. My brother and I joined our mother and sister for a number of the school holidays. We travelled out by boat and train. It was while I was in Switzerland that I learnt to speak French. Because Dad only took leave once every four years, we really didn't see much of him.

Nicknames were a typical part of school (and service) life and Gerald and his colleagues were no exception. However, on one occasion the older lads called him by his first name but directed it at him in a sheep-like 'Baaaasil'. He responded by punching the nearest senior on the nose. Apart from his immediate family, he was known as Gerald from then on and didn't experience any other problems while at school in Devon:

> We had a very good house mistress called Crawshaw. We had another who we nicknamed 'Hottentot' (I can't recall her real name). We used to have a master who was first-class and we used to call him 'Ghandi' because he was a little fella with a sharp nose and glasses. He gained an MA at Oxford and eventually became a headmaster. I have a photo taken in 1936 of the football team when my brother was captain. I'm standing there as a fifteen or sixteen year old. I didn't have my colours at that time. When you got your colours you got a cap with a tassel and you wore a shirt with light blue/dark blue quarters. If you didn't have your colours you wore a striped jersey, so on the field you could tell who had been awarded their colours for football. My brother became school sports captain. We didn't really see each other, he seemed to live in a different world; the 'big boys' as we called them.

Gerald initially had little understanding of algebra and trigonometry and received extra tuition from his teacher Mr Foster, known as 'Plush'. Although he gained his Oxford Schools Certificate for many subjects including arithmetic, he failed the algebra and trig: 'I really excelled at geography, history, English and later French, passing the Oxford Schools Certificates in each. I loved the required reading.' His strengths lay in his sporting ability, including rowing but in particular football and rugby:

> I was captain of both teams. We had 'fives', .22 shooting, Boy Scouts, tennis, swimming and rowing. I was in the coxless fours. We actually beat Dartmouth once on the River Dart. We competed about fifteen miles up-river from the estuary. The year before, the team went down to Dartmouth where we found the river was particularly rough. I never remember the surface being rough at Totnes. During the race our shell sank and as the naval cadets had a little raised gunwale running around the top edge of their shell, not so much water got in. By the following year our school had made the same modification to our shell and we went down and beat them.

As a senior, Gerald won the cricket 1st XI batting prize: 'Previous winners had received a new bat but I was presented with a leather-bound copy of James Fenimore Cooper's *Last of the Mohicans*. I was furious!'

Sport brought Gerald plenty of enjoyment during his school years, but as a senior he was given an opportunity which was to prove so thrilling, it was to provide a career on leaving school and, ultimately, a place in the history records. Alan Cobham (later Sir Alan Cobham) toured the country from 1932-35 with his National Aviation Day 'flying circus' offering the public the opportunity of what became known as 'the five-bob flip'. He became famous in the twenties and thirties for making epic long distance flights and later for pioneering the development of in-flight refuelling. Gerald recalls:

> My first flight was in an Avro Mongoose in 1935, with the now legendary Ernst Udet, who was then flying with the Alan Cobham

Flying Circus. They came down to our part of the country and from a grass field on the outskirts of Totnes I experienced my first taste of flying. From that moment on I knew what I wanted to do. Stoneham, who was also a pilot with the circus, finished up at White Waltham, arriving as an instructor while I was there learning to fly.

Gerald left school in the summer of 1938. Initially, his ambition had been to pursue his growing love of languages and study Modern Languages at Oxford: 'I held back going to Brasenose College because of the Munich situation. It seemed clear that war was inevitable and I wanted to be part of it.' However, this decision infuriated his father who was deeply disappointed because he was determined Gerald should go to Oxford. Even though his father put pressure on him, hoping he would at least start his course, Gerald remained resolute and on 23 January 1939, he applied for a Short Service Commission for four years active service in the RAF. By that time his brother had already joined the RAF, perhaps adding to Gerald's determination to join up. While he was waiting to hear if he had been accepted, he met Joan Cox, from Chislehurst (now Greater London), whom he later married at Montrose.

Gerald was eventually accepted by the RAF and sent to No.13 Elementary and Reserve Flying Training School (E&RFTS) at the Civil Flying School, White Waltham, Berks, which was privately run by de Havilland. Here he underwent three months *ab initio* flying training (in September 1939, it was re-designated No.13 Elementary and Flying Training School – E&FTS). Gerald lodged with twenty other student pilots in a house (also used as their Mess) in Cherry Tree Lane, which led down to the airfield some 300 yards away. He recalls being paid 16s 6d [82^1/$_2$p] a day during that initial period of training but when his training at White Waltham came to a close his daily wage dropped to 11s 6d [57^1/$_2$p]. He initially learnt to fly the de Havilland Tiger Moth I & II and the Monarch. To this day the Moth is one of his favourite aircraft: '. . . because the wind was in your face.'

Another young pilot that Gerald remembers being on the same course and who later made a name for himself, was Roland Beamont (later Wing Commander R.P. Beamont CBE, DFC*, DL, FRAeS).

The evening before their Air Proficiency Flying Test, Gerald drove into London with two colleagues for a night out. At 02.00 hours the following morning, during the return journey, Gerald lost control of the car and crashed into a telegraph pole. Whilst he and one of his colleagues escaped injury the other was knocked unconscious, receiving a severe cut to the head in the process. He regained consciousness at the scene and, concussed and confused, his first words were: 'Thank God I don't have to take my flying test tomorrow.' 'Oh, but you are.' Gerald quickly informed him. His colleague was left with a scar on his head which was visible for many years. Gerald recalls with amusement:

> The car was my mother's and it was written-off. She received £30 in exchange for the wreck and bought a fur coat. When she returned to India to see my father, he asked her where she got it from!

At the end of the training course, Gerald was 'granted a Short Service

Commission for 4 years Active Service as Acting Pilot Officer, General Duties Branch, Royal Air Force, with effect from 23.1.39.' At White Waltham he had accumulated approximately 28 hours flying dual and 25 solo. RAF No.41879, he was sent to No.1 Depot, Uxbridge, 'Supernumerary Disciplinary Course' on 1 April 1939 and then to 13 Flying Training School (FTS) at Drem, East Lothian, for flying training on the 15th:

> At 13 FTS we flew the Audax, Hart Trainer, Hart, Oxford I & II and Anson. My chief memory of Drem is that it was so very busy. I was already familiar with the aerodrome when I later returned there with 603 Squadron.

The trainee bomber pilots progressed to flying Airspeed Oxfords whilst the potential fighter pilots remained on single-seat aircraft. In May, Squadron Leader John Grandy (later, Marshal of the Royal Air Force Sir John Grandy, GCB, KCB, CB, KBE, DSO) was posted to 13 FTS to take over as Chief Flying Instructor. Gerald reflects on his time there:

> While at Drem I met a South African from Pietermaritzburg. He tried to do a loop in a Hart. Unfortunately, he was too low to the ground, crashed and was killed. His family back home were very well-known. I remember flying down to Southampton to box for the RAF against the Navy. I flew down in an Oxford with a chap called McGillivrey. He was an ex-professional boxer who taught me quite a lot. He was a middleweight, I was heavyweight. We went down to Southampton where we were told 'Sorry, we've got no opponents for you.' So we went 'out on the town,' totally unaware that we had been duped. The next morning we were awoken at eight o'clock and told we now had opponents. McGillivrey won his fight easily, but I climbed into the ring with a twenty stone marine. Each time I hit him I seemed to go backwards. In the third round I couldn't keep my guard up, I'd had it. Out I went, although I have to say, it wasn't unpleasant.

Gerald later fought in an elimination contest which would have brought him up against very much tougher opposition in the next round. Unfortunately, he missed out: 'I tripped into a left-hook and my jaw was broken!'

With training complete Gerald had by that time accumulated approximately 62 hours flying dual and 105 hours solo (day and night). On 21 October 1939, he was posted to recently reformed (4 October) 219 Squadron flying the Blenheim I. Six days after he left Drem 13 FTS was absorbed by 8, 14, and 15 Service Flying Training Schools (SFTS). 219 Squadron was based at Catterick with detached units at Scorton, Leeming and Redhill. Gerald was sent to the latter at Redhill, Surrey, but has no recollection of being there. However, he was not required and the next day was sent to 11 Group Pool (attached) at St Athan for Operational Training where he converted from Hart bi-planes to Harvard monoplanes, and then to Hurricanes, before being sent to a squadron. Gerald was with 11 Group Pool until 20 November 1939, when he was posted to 32 Squadron at Biggin Hill for a brief period of flying duties before being posted to 603 (City of Edinburgh) Squadron, AuxAF, on 16 December. By that time he had added a further six hours flying dual and 60 hours solo bringing his total of hours flown to 233. One aspect that does not appear on his Service Record was recounted by Gerald:

> Following conversion to Hurricanes at St Athan, I was posted to 32 Squadron, a frontline operational squadron equipped with Hurricanes. Although I can clearly recall my time there, it does not appear on my record of service. Nevertheless, with hindsight I was lucky to have flown both the Hurricane and Spitfire.
>
> When landing the Spitfire you put down the undercarriage and flaps to slow the aircraft, it was so sleek, whereas with the Hurricane you just closed the throttle. The Spitfire and Hurricane swung to the left on take-off and, with a bit of practice, could be corrected by use of the rudder; you didn't even know you were doing it, it just became habit. However, during my later experience when flying the Typhoon, I found it swung the opposite way and of course that was trouble because you were in the habit of putting rudder hard on one way when now it was needed on the other. It was quite something because you never used the controls in any ham-fisted way, but gently. With the Typhoon you had to get used to really putting rudder hard-on to counteract the swing. Up to an altitude of 8-10,000 feet the Typhoon was faster than anything the RAF had at that time – I had 400mph on the clock at low level in a Typhoon – beyond that altitude its performance fell away. The Typhoon really was a low-level ground attack aircraft. It was about twice the weight and twice the size of the Spitfire 1a. The Napier Sabre engine had 24 cylinders with 48 plugs and when one required changing, all 48 had to be changed!
>
> I was not with 32 Squadron very long before I was sent to 603 Squadron at Turnhouse in December 1939, when it was decided to send a number of experienced, full-time pilots to the auxiliary squadrons to complete their establishment of pilots. By the time I arrived, there were a number of newcomers.

Gerald is of the opinion that a particular incident led to his name being included for such a posting. On a circuit of the airfield, during a practice flight, he had found that he had a problem with his flaps. The subsequent landing had been fast and deliberately crabwise in order to slow down the Hurricane. Although he managed to get the aircraft down safely he had broken the rule of landing with the canopy shut and his Flight Commander at that time, Flying Officer Michael Crossley* gave him a severe telling off. The next thing he remembers was receiving the news that he was being posted to 603 Squadron. He was later to gain further experience flying Hurricanes which ultimately left him in the position of being able to compare and assess the characteristics of both the Hurricane and the Spitfire.

---

*Later, Wing Commander Michael Crossley DFC, DSO. By the end of the war Crossley had been credited with: 20 enemy aircraft confirmed destroyed, one unconfirmed, two shared destroyed and one damaged.

CHAPTER TWO

SPITFIRE SQUADRON

After reporting to Station Headquarters at Turnhouse, Gerald was immediately sent to Prestwick with the rest of the Squadron which was there to provide protection for the troopships arriving in the Clyde from Canada:

> We were never at Turnhouse for any length of time. We always seemed to be moving somewhere. On arrival at Turnhouse we were sent to Prestwick. From there we were sent (west coast to east coast) to Montrose and Dyce. From there we went to Drem before returning to Turnhouse then off to Dyce and Montrose again before returning to Turnhouse prior to moving south!

Gerald was allocated to B Flight with Flying Officer Fred 'Rusty' Rushmer as Flight Commander. His equally experienced deputy, Flying Officer Laurie Cunningham, who had been with the Squadron since 1935, was in charge when Gerald arrived but handed the reins back to Rushmer on 17 December. Characters in the Squadron who Gerald came to know well include: Pilot Officer Brian Carbury '. . . an excellent role model for fighter pilots' who became the Squadron's highest scoring pilot of the Battle of Britain earning him the DFC and Bar; Sergeant Pilot Ronald 'Ras' Berry '. . . his flying skills were outstanding and seemed to come naturally. He was also a real joker.' A Regular RAF officer, Pilot Officer Noel 'Broody' Benson, (who had joined the Squadron on 18 December) gained his nickname because '. . . he used to sit for ages in the dispersal hut and stare ahead into space ignoring all that went on around him. He was a very good pilot, always well turned-out and very keen to do well as a fighter pilot when the opportunity came.' Also with B Flight was the experienced and dedicated Londoner and Regular RAF officer, Flying Officer John Boulter, nicknamed 'Bolster':

> Boulter was an older chap who I remember having big ears (an observation also made by Richard Hillary in *The Last Enemy*). He used to stand drinking, leaning on the bar all evening, talking and quietly watching the antics of the more active. By the end of the evening, at kicking-out time, he would simply release his grip on the bar and fall flat on his face.

Gerald remembers being totally reliant on his RAF salary whilst others in the Squadron were quite well-off:

> Most of the other chaps in the Squadron were of monied parents, not untypical of an auxiliary squadron. Somebody had to pay for the flying, usually it was Dad. The men that made up the nucleus

of the Squadron were really nice chaps.

There was a mixture of Auxiliaries, 'VR' and Short Service Commission officers in the Squadron. I remember that Carbury and I were short service. Carbury was about six feet two inches tall and very thin. He was an excellent pilot. I used to fly as his No.2.

The two who impressed me most were Bubbles Waterston [Flying Officer Robin McGregor Waterston, known by most as Bubble] and Rusty [Rushmer], my flight commander, the nicest person I knew. Rusty had bright red hair and seemed to be just too much of a gentleman to be a fighter pilot in that he was quiet and quite introverted. It was hard to associate him being in such a profession, it didn't seem to suit him, like so many pilots in 603 Squadron. He didn't seem to handle his authority over us in the usual way. If we said something to him that he didn't agree with he tended just to ignore the comment. Nevertheless, he commanded great respect from us and was a good leader. He was an outstanding pilot and we had great faith in him as a flight commander. He was a lovely chap. We now know of course that he was killed but at that time and for many years afterwards all I knew was that he had just disappeared. I didn't really get to know my colleagues as pilots beyond their general handling skills because you're not flying with them in the same aeroplane, but from the point of view of the elder brother figure and the advice he gave you, Rusty was a great influence. I was nineteen then and probably very full of myself.

My closest friends were Bubbles and Ras Berry. Bubbles was a wonderful happy-go-lucky person who lived life to the full. He was from what I believed to be a wealthy family but never gave any indication that he was from such a background. He was the most popular member of the squadron.

Together, Gerald and Bubble were responsible for creating a legend. For a brief period in July/August 1940, prior to being sent south to where the air fighting was at its most intense, they deviated from the usual pursuits of off-duty fighter pilots and spent their free time away from Montrose aerodrome playing with children at the tiny hamlet of Tarfside, in picturesque Glen Esk.

Although Gerald saw less of the pilots in A Flight, particularly when the flights were detached to Dyce and Montrose, he came to know them also, including another popular and dedicated Auxiliary, Flying Officer Ken Macdonald, who led the Squadron on a number of occasions in the Battle of Britain, Pilot Officer George 'Sheep' Gilroy whom he believes actually looked a little like a sheep and Flying Officer 'Jack' Haig who first joined 603 in 1932. Gerald recalls that he looked '. . . too old to be a fighter pilot', a not untypical reaction from one so young. Haig's nickname was, appropriately, 'Old Gent'. Two others were Pilot Officer Dudley Stewart-Clark who was a member of the wealthy Coates family, manufacturers of fine threads, and Flying Officer Charles Peel who was the first member to die in the Battle of Britain. Peel was quite a character and Gerald remembers one incident:

> Charlie Peel owned a puppy bull-dog called Shadrak, and when
> we had a high-ranking visitor one day (possibly the AOC),
> Charlie got a bit flustered when presented to him and, instead of
> saying 'sit Shadrak' to his excited pup, he said 'shit Sadrak'. The
> pup actually bit one of the visitors!

Other members of A Flight included: Pilot Officer Ian 'Woolly Bear' Ritchie,
so nicknamed because he was a powerfully built but very gentle man; the good-
looking Pilot Officer Jim 'Black' Morton; Regular Sergeant Pilot 'Bill' Caister,
the oldest but most experienced pilot in the Squadron; and Flight Lieutenant
'Uncle' George Denholm who commanded the Squadron throughout the Battle
of Britain. During the years following the end of WWII, Gerald managed to
stay in touch with, amongst others, Berry and Denholm and has retained many
memories of the young men who served with him in 603 at that time.

At Prestwick Gerald met the CO, Squadron Leader Ernest Hildebrand Stevens,
popularly nicknamed 'Count':

> He didn't seem to want to fight in the Battle of Britain. He had a
> medical problem in that his right shoulder would dislocate when
> he opened or closed the canopy of his Spitfire, but he could have
> used his other arm, it didn't require both hands. I think perhaps he
> didn't want to be a frontline fighter pilot.

Whilst Stapme's opinion is one which was shared by other 603 pilots and
ground crew, following the outbreak of war Count Stevens' age, experience and
intellect was put to good use and by the cessation of hostilities he had attained
the rank of Group Captain and been awarded the OBE (Military) for his
outstanding work on fighter tactics at Bentley Priory, Headquarters, Fighter
Command.
    At Prestwick, Gerald also had to convert to type having previously flown
Hurricanes. The Spitfire quickly became his favourite fighter (although he talks
fondly of many of the aircraft he has flown during his career as a pilot). The
squadron pilots had recently completed the process of converting from
Gladiator Mark Is to Spitfire Mark Is which were in full service by the time of
the air raid on 16 October.

> When I first flew a Spitfire after a Hurricane, as I pulled back the
> throttle to land, one of the big differences between the two aircraft
> became obvious, the Spitfire didn't slow quickly. You were going
> around in a circuit and it may have been your first or second spin
> in it, and you pulled back the throttle and the darned thing kept
> going, because you had a certain speed at which you would lower
> your flaps and a certain speed to lower your undercarriage. The
> Spitfire was a useful aircraft in that an idiot could fly it. It took
> very little training. I believe the Me109 was a more tricky aircraft
> to fly, so more training was required in order to get the best out of
> it. The Spitfire used to glide down when it stalled, it didn't drop a
> wing; the Hurricane did. When you consider that the Spitfire had
> an offset radiator it was remarkable that it didn't drop a wing. You
> could make all sorts of mistakes. You could drop the aircraft down

from a height of about six feet onto the airstrip, and it wouldn't do any damage because the aircraft would just sink slowly onto the ground. I think that the Spitfire was such a good aircraft because it was so simple to fly. You still had to be correct on landing though because of the narrow undercarriage, therefore the landing was one of the more tricky parts of flying it, same as the 109. But I have no complaints at all about that aircraft. When you trimmed it to fly hands-off it just went slightly down and then slightly up again. It wouldn't turn. As it gained speed it would gain lift and go up. As it went up it would lose speed and go down again, in a dead straight line.

603 Squadron had been embodied into the RAF on 23 August 1939 and between the declaration of war and the end of the year the existing Auxiliary Air Force personnel had been bolstered by a number of Regular pilots and ground crewmen, sent to provide extra skills and make up the numbers. Prior to their move south during the Battle of Britain there was an additional influx of Regular and Volunteer Reserve (RAFVR) pilots, by which time it could be considered to have become an auxiliary squadron by name only.

It wasn't long after Gerald's arrival that he was participating in intensive flying operations which consisted initially of sector reccos (reconnaissance flights), which gave him the opportunity to familiarise himself with the local terrain, followed by camera gun exercises and 'flying patrols'.

From the outbreak of war and until the Squadron moved to Hornchurch in August the following year, there was plenty of opportunity for the pilots to take leave. There were usually three aircraft at 'readiness' for immediate take-off, and the rest of the pilots were either 'available' (ready for take-off within half an hour) or 'released' (allowed to leave the aerodrome). During the period at Prestwick, the pilots and ground crew were billeted with the locals in their homes with transport arranged to take them to the airfield each morning. The low temperatures at that time of year were unpleasant with severe frosts prior to snow-fall and at dispersal they only had tents in which to shelter. However, the spirit in the Squadron was good and the conditions surmountable. The officers' mess was situated in an old mill and the local inn to the airfield at Prestwick was The Red Lion where the pilots congregated for some serious drinking and a chat about all matters relating to flying. On one occasion Count Stevens led a group of officers on an evening out at the local ice-rink where they watched an ice-hockey match.

Amongst the many characters in the Squadron, one of Gerald's earliest acquaintances was Flying Officer John Young (now Wing Commander John Young MA, AFC, RAF (Ret'd) Official Historian for the Battle of Britain Fighter Association), who had recently joined the Squadron from 41 Squadron at Catterick. His brief was to assess the flying skills of the younger, less experienced members of the Edinburgh Squadron and make recommendations for further training. He recalled: 'I had a great relationship with Gerald but he could be a bit slap-happy.' On 22 December, after only six days with his new unit, Gerald found an area of soft ground on the Prestwick airfield and tipped his Spitfire (K9997) onto its nose. What made matters worse was the fact that John Young had warned Gerald prior to the flight to beware of the only soft ground on the airfield. For this error he felt the wrath of the considerably more experienced (although only slightly senior in rank) Flying Officer Young. As a consequence of John's 'school-masterish' approach to his job of ensuring the younger less-experienced pilots in the Squadron made progress, Pilot Officer Ian Ritchie christened him 'Dobbin', which the youngsters thought most appropriate and adopted it enthusiastically. Interestingly, whilst both pilots confirm the cause of the accident, the 603 Operational Record Book ('Squadron Diary') records that the accident was as a result of the collapse of the undercarriage due to the undercarriage selector lever not being in the locked position. In 1999, at the annual reunion of the Battle of Britain Fighter Association at RAF Lakenheath, Suffolk, these two great characters were reunited, though not for the first time, and reminded of the occasion at Prestwick. John Young, referring to his rank and pre-603 Squadron experience as an instructor, said to Gerald, in his slow deliberate manner: 'Yes, but although I was only a flying officer to your pilot officer, when I shit on you, I actually did it from a great height!'

On 10 January four Spitfires of A Flight, led by Flight Lieutenant George Denholm with Flying Officers 'Jack' Haig and Ian Ritchie, and Pilot Officer Colin 'Robbie' Robertson, were sent to RAF Montrose, home of No.8 Service Flying Training School. There had been an increasing number of air attacks by the Luftwaffe on convoys, fishing fleets and ports, and the Spitfires were sent there to provide protection. On 14 January the Section at Montrose became a Flight when Flying Officers Fred Rushmer and Laurie Cunningham with Pilot Officers Ras Berry, Charles Peel, Noel Benson, Graham Thomson and Gerald were also attached to Montrose. During this period the Squadron operated a rota system with pilots at Prestwick and Montrose and the same system of 'readiness' with the addition of regular night flying at the latter. According to the ORB, 'fighting patrols' and 'flying practice' continued throughout January.

On 17 January George Denholm received orders to move the remainder of the Squadron to Dyce. The entire Squadron was now based at Dyce (A or Station Flight) and Montrose (B Flight). Interceptions and engagements were sporadic but they gave the pilots the opportunity to practice and hone their fighting skills in the Spitfire. It is important to remember that whilst part of 13 Group in the north, they only came up against Luftwaffe bombers and armed reconnaissance aircraft, and their first taste of combat against fighters only came after they moved south to 11 Group. By this time the Battle of Britain had been raging for nearly seven weeks although aerial combat over the south had been occurring for even longer. At Montrose the 'servile demeanour expected in a flying school' was something the pilots of the Edinburgh Squadron paid little heed to and they were tolerated with mixed emotions by the senior officers and instructors of 8 SFTS and the staff of RAF Station Montrose. However, their Spitfires were the envy of the other pilots. The officers mess provided comfortable accommodation for Gerald and his colleagues including good food and Newcastle Brown Ale, which was very popular. Some of the pilots 'milked' a little 100 octane petrol from the bowsers for use in their own cars without which many may have been left stranded if they had relied solely on rationing.

John Mackenzie and Bert Pringle were responsible for Gerald's Spitfire during the time he was in Scotland and have fond memories of their time together. John remembers:

> I gave Stapme a fiver to get me some cigarettes when he was going into Montrose. I never saw that fiver again. He once drove into town for a drink in a bowser full of 100 octane fuel!*

Bert Pringle adds:

> He was a sorry looking sight. Everywhere he went he carried all he owned in a small scruffy suitcase. Eventually the fastening broke and I tied the lid closed for him with a piece of string.

The people of Montrose are remembered as being very hospitable. Dispersal lacked all creature comforts and was a different story, although there were few complaints. The airfield could be particularly muddy following rainfall and for most of the year both pilots and ground crewmen had to endure heavy, cloying mud which got everywhere including the huts and aircraft cockpits. This posed a problem when it dried out. B Flight had a number of wooden huts which were not insulated. In one the flight commander had his office, partitioned from the pilot's locker and ready-room (there was a special operational telephone line in the flight commander's office direct to A Flight at Dyce). In another there was a room for the ground crew and a room in which radio/telephony (R/T) technicians could work on the equipment, out of the cold biting wind and away from the mud. These huts were single-skinned buildings with very basic furnishings and were cold and draughty. The pilots were inclined to move their chairs outside whenever the sun came out. The nearest toilet was a smelly chemical 'Elsen' and quite naturally pilots were seen to slip away on cue with a newspaper or magazine tucked under one arm. It wasn't long before the old huts were replaced by new ones although they were of the same type. The sand dunes on the far eastern edge of the airfield protected the airfield only very slightly from the on-shore winds, which could make flying conditions very tricky. It required a very steady hand to cope with the sudden loss of air speed when an aeroplane passed over the dunes as it approached from the sea, probably caused by the west winds rising over them, leaving a patch of calm

---

*Today, John Mackenzie is Chairman of the 603 Association. He served with the Squadron for the duration of WWII and is the sole surviving member of the ground crew who, as an AC1, also worked on Spitfires flown by Richard Hillary. John recalls him being temperamental and he quickly gained a reputation for finding and complaining about anything which was wrong with his aircraft before reluctantly signing to accept the aircraft as airworthy; a not unreasonable attitude to take as any problems with his Spitfire could put him at a disadvantage in combat and were potentially lethal. But as the years have passed a number of the ground crew recall there were regularly small problems with Squadron aircraft that were not rectified before the next patrol unless, of course, they were particularly serious in which case the aircraft was deemed 'unserviceable'. Despite the best efforts of Freddy Marsland and Tug Wilson, on the morning of 3 September, when Richard Hillary was shot down and badly burned, some ground crew veterans recall Hillary complaining that a number of minor problems with his aircraft had not been fixed; nevertheless, he had signed for it. He later recalled in his book that a replacement canopy had jammed as he tried to exit his flaming aircraft but the problems he had reported did not include any fault with his canopy. Bomb damage to his aircraft which required a replacement canopy had been invented by Hillary for his book. In reality, airflow over his aircraft at high speed would have been enough to cause resistance when trying to slide back the hood.

air below in the area where the aircraft touched down. This caused it to drop
onto the airfield alarmingly with the pilot hoping the undercarriage would take
the force. There were a number of flying accidents for one reason or another.
Gerald reflects on the weather conditions on the east coast of Scotland:

> The weather could be so foul at Montrose and when the wind
> blew in off the North Sea, over the dunes on the eastern, seaward
> side, it was bitterly cold and flying conditions were impossible at
> that time. I once saw an Avro Anson flying backwards! It couldn't
> land going forwards, it wasn't fast enough. Snow was falling and
> in the wind it was blowing almost horizontally. It must have been
> about eighty miles per-hour as all our aircraft were tied down
> otherwise they would have flown away on their own.

The temperatures during winter were extremely low and the pilots found that
the inside of their canopy would freeze up, reducing visibility considerably.
Fortunately, there was no threat from fighters and the high-flying intruders
were easy to spot by the vapour trails. At such low temperatures the .303
machine guns of the Spitfires were also inclined to freeze-up and the pilots and
their ground crewmen quickly devised a system of putting fabric patches
soaked in dope over the gun-ports to prevent icy moisture and (during the dry
weather) dirt and grit penetrating the working parts of the guns. This worked
well and when the Spitfires returned from patrols it also gave the armourers an
indication as to whether the guns had been fired and therefore whether or not
they needed re-arming.

Gerald's rank of Pilot Officer was confirmed in an appointment on 23 January
1940 and on 9 February with fighting patrols and flying training continuing
apace, Gerald made his first claim. The following information is reproduced
exactly as it appears in the Squadron ORB:

Green Section comprising F/O J.L.G. Cunningham, F/O R. McG. Waterston,
P/O B.G. Stapleton intercepted Heinkel 111. Visibility very poor – no
confirmed results.

Sgt/Pilot Caister crashed Spitfire K9998 on Dyce Aerodrome when landing,
mainly due to soft nature of ground.

Details of Work Carried Out
11.37 – 12.50 hours 9.2.40

Aircraft Type and No.	Pilot	Time Up/Down
Spitfire		
L1026	F/O J.L.G. Cunningham	11.37 – 12.50
L1046	F/O R. Mc G. Waterston	11.37 – 12.50
L1022	P/O B.G. Stapleton	11.37 – 12.50

Green Section was ordered off to investigate aerial attack on shipping 10
miles east of Arbroath. Visibility was poor. Heinkel 111 was sighted by
Green Leader who was too close to open fire. Green 2, delivered a No.1
attack and fired 800 rounds before Heinkel 111 climbed into the clouds and
disappeared.

Caister's Spitfire had actually overturned on landing but he managed to escape from the cockpit and was unhurt. Off-duty activities were limited at Montrose. Gerald reflects on the difficulties of not being from the locality:

> Unlike the members of the Squadron whose family homes were within easy driving distance of the airfield, we had no homes to go to during our time off. Therefore, the mess was our home from home, as far as we were concerned anyway. We drank and socialised there. Similarly, while the local Scotsmen could entertain at their own homes, we would get the occasional invitation but we were unable to offer the same in return. We had nowhere to invite them to.
>
> I got married to Joan, my first wife, in Montrose.

At that time, it was illegal for a couple to marry under the age of 21 without written approval from their parents. The vicar marrying the under-age couple would ordinarily require a signed certificate of proof. However, in Gerald's case, as a member of the RAF, he also had to apply to his commanding officer, Count Stevens, for permission, which he duly did. Stevens then instructed his adjutant, Flying Officer Ian 'Shag' Wallace, to contact Gerald's parents in India to get their approval. Gerald remembers his father's reaction:

> Stevens sent a telegram to my father, and he sent a telegram back saying: 'Don't be a blundering idiot!' I was nineteen and my father had told me that I would be mad to get married before I was twenty.

Fortunately, as Jack Stapleton was not in the country at the time, Stevens had the authority to grant approval on behalf of Gerald's father in his absence, even though he had been contacted and refused to sanction the marriage. Gerald recalls the reaction of his CO, a peacetime lawyer: 'Count Stevens kindly offered to deny ever having seen the response and told me to go ahead and get married, which I did.' Gerald's wife to-be, Joan Cox, travelled up from Chislehurst for the occasion. It was a quiet affair with no best man and none of his service colleagues present.

Life was difficult for the newly-married couple. As Gerald was under 25 and, in accordance with Air Ministry rules, he forfeited 'married man's allowance' and a 'married quarter' which put the couple at a considerable financial disadvantage until he reached the required age.

Gerald recalls: By the time I met my father again later in South Africa the marriage was over and he said 'You *were* mad, weren't you!'

Intensive flying practice continued from Dyce and Montrose for those not at readiness with all Squadron night-flying using the airfield at Montrose. 603 also carried out 'co-operation flying' in conjunction with army anti-aircraft and searchlight batteries and operated a system whereby some of the senior, most experienced pilots were attached to RAF Turnhouse in order to familiarise themselves with the job of controller in the Operations Room.

During the working day, each flight operated a system of rotation of its pilots, with the aforementioned three groups of three pilots placed on staggered states of readiness. Uncle George was very keen that those left took part in daily intensive flying exercises which were undertaken, weather permitting, by all but the section at readiness. As a consequence, his pilots accumulated valuable flying hours honing their formation flying, navigation, general flying, and dog-fighting skills in the Spitfire. The most experienced pilots led each section with the next most experienced at No.2 with No.3 being the least experienced. However, their lack of actual combat experience against fighters would prove crucial. On 4 March Gerald was granted twelve days leave, returning on the 15th.

On 9 April the 603 pilots learnt that Germany had invaded Norway and Denmark, and by 15 April 603 Squadron had moved to Drem where Gerald had trained with 13 FTS.

The land on which RAF Drem was established was owned by Dr. Chalmers Watson who produced the very first herd of tuberculin-tested milking cows in Britain. His wife was the former actress, Lily Brayton, who had played the leading role in *Chu Chin Chow* on the London stage during WWI. The couple lived in Greywalls, a large house next to Muirfield Golf Club in Gullane, where many of the officers from Drem were entertained. Today the house is a hotel.

Drem aerodrome with its notorious slope accounted for many accidents. As had been the case with Montrose, many of the buildings at that time were wooden huts, including the watch-office.*

The officer commanding RAF Drem while Stapme was there was Charles Keary, who had been a pre-war member of 603 Squadron but had left at the outbreak of war. Whilst the flying school was *in situ* he ran a very strict environment in accordance with King's Regulations and Air Council Instructions, but that all changed when 602 (City of Glasgow) Squadron moved in and, with Drem becoming an operational airfield, the FTS moved out in October 1939. The pilots of the Glasgow Squadron had little time for the old spit and polish routine and the strict discipline of pre-war establishments and gave the CO a hard time with their own interpretation of the rules and regulations. The arrival of 603 had, in contrast, meant little change for the former member of their unit!

The 26th of April was a significant day in Gerald's life. The ORB records: 'Pilot Officer B.G. Stapleton jumped by parachute from Spitfire L1025 after landing gear had been damaged while attempting a night landing (Unhurt).' The incident occurred whilst he was at Drem. As Gerald approached the airfield after a night patrol, one of the undercarriage legs refused to lower. Squadron Leader Stevens instructed him to head inland over the Lammamuir Hills and jump from the aircraft once he had exhausted his fuel supply. He also sent Rusty Rushmer up to escort him. Gerald recalls:

> I remember I was fortunate in that there was a big harvest moon
> (even though it was April), a huge orange moon hanging in the
> sky. The nearby searchlight battery had been warned of my
> presence and at 7,000 feet I jumped out of the aircraft. My initial

---

*Today, although the surviving cream-coloured aircraft hangars are still standing, they are used to store hay bales and are in a very poor state of repair. Many of the buildings which made up the maintenance and domestic sites still remain, including the art-deco petrol station with original pumps and the station cinema. The airfield was returned to arable crop farming after the war but the problematic slope is very evident.

pull on the ripcord did nothing and I had to give it another violent tug, twisting my body in the opposite direction before it opened, much to my relief. Hanging under the parachute, the silence was remarkable.

We had never been taught to land by parachute and I hit the ground backwards and on the down-slope of the hillside. One of the cartilages in my right knee came out on impact, the crack sounded like a shot from a gun. I gathered my parachute and, as it was cold, wrapped some of the folds of silk around my shoulders and hobbled towards the crash-site of my Spitfire where, I had been told, I would be met. When I arrived I stood over the crater where the aircraft had plunged to earth. There were a number of small fires. As I glanced across, I met the terrified fixed stares of two soldiers from the searchlight team who had just arrived at the site. I was wrapped in the white parachute silk and silhouetted against the moon and they looked at me as though I was a ghost. I said to them: 'I'm the pilot of that.' I apparently gave them the fright of their lives. I never reported the injury – stupidly thinking I would be taken off flying. I paid for that decision with a knee that exceeded its 'sell by' date.

Gerald's deliberate attempt to hide his injury is an example of what many young men were prepared to do in order to oppose the threat from the Germans. In 1998, after years of discomfort and damage to his spine, later requiring surgery, he finally had an operation to replace the damaged knee.

On 5 May 603 left Drem and returned to Turnhouse but to the derision of Charles Keary, 602 moved back in. Whilst at Turnhouse the local lads were able to travel from home each day, as they had during peacetime, but even those who were a long way from home had had a reasonable choice of places to go when off-duty. Apart from the officers mess, the nearest bar was in the Maybury where Gerald spent many a happy hour, a stylish, prominent, art-deco building at the east end of Turnhouse Road which in those days housed a casino. Sometimes the pilots visited some of the bars in Edinburgh itself. Eventually, as the Squadron achieved acclaim in the coming battle, one or two of the more prestigious establishments kept a table permanently reserved for the officers of 603 Squadron. Gerald again:

> In Edinburgh the Squadron had a table reserved for its pilots at the D'Guise, a nightclub in the Old Caledonian Hotel. The 'Cale' (pronounced 'Cally') was a station. It's been closed down now but whereas Waverley served destinations north-east and up the north-east coast, the Cale served the stations to Glasgow. Then there was the Glasgow-Edinburgh connection. Nobody could sit at the table in the Cale, even when the other tables were all taken. It was always reserved for us. You could go in any time and you always had a table.

Although the Headquarters of 603 Squadron was then, as it still is today, at 25 Learmonth Terrace, Gerald never visited the building during his service with the Squadron. However, he managed two visits during 1999, when he was reunited with a number of the veteran ground crew personnel as their honoured guest.

For 10 May 1940, the ORB records: 'All leave stopped. J.C. Boulter and I.S. Ritchie recalled. Holland and Belgium invaded by Germany.' Entries in the Squadron diary prove that leave was still freely granted. The following day A Flight 602 Squadron joined A Flight 603 at Dyce, the first time the two squadrons were based at the same aerodrome. On 14 May, news reached the pilots that Holland had surrendered and fighting in Belgium had intensified. Flying Officer John Young was posted to 249 Squadron at Church Fenton and fought with the unit during the Battle of Britain. It was many years before 'Dobbin' Young and Stapme met again.

On 28 May, Belgium capitulated. Meanwhile, the Squadron continued to spend many hours airborne on fighting patrols, co-operation day and night practice flying. On 2 June the Squadron was presented with its badge by Air Vice-Marshal Richard Saul, Air Officer Commanding No.13(F) Group, which included the Squadron motto 'Gin Ye Daur' (If You Dare!).

On 5 June, 1940, Gerald crashed on landing at Turnhouse in Spitfire N5236 after the failure of the flaps and then the brakes. According to Bert Pringle his fitter:

> He abandoned three previous attempts to land before he finally managed to get down on the fourth. When we examined his aircraft we found the fault. Stapme was lucky. The only injury he received as a result of the crash-landing was a small cut to his forehead.

On 13 June Gerald was granted four days' leave. For 14 June the ORB records: 'Day and night flying practice. Germans entered Paris.' Gerald returned from leave on the 16th. On 26 June, Turnhouse was bombed for the first time. Flying Officer 'Jack' Haig was actually airborne and, following a fruitless search, he requested permission to land, but was refused on the grounds that German intruders were thought to still be in the area and the flare path would not be lit. Running low on fuel, Haig headed for open country, gained altitude and turned towards 'Lang Wang' (the A701 Edinburgh to Moffat road). The engine spluttered and died and he baled out of Spitfire N3190 into the darkness. He sprained an ankle on landing and hobbled towards the nearest farmhouse. With rumours of a parachutist having been seen in the area, the farmer was not very friendly until he realised he was facing a fellow Scot. He then gave Haig a lift back to the airfield but on the way they crashed into a bomb crater.

On 30 June A Flight moved from Turnhouse to Dyce.

CHAPTER THREE

'STAP-ME, WHAT A FILLY!'

On 3 July 1940, flying with B Flight now at Montrose, Gerald shared in the destruction of a Ju88A-2 (4D+IS) of 8/KG30, ten miles north-west of the airfield. The ORB reads:

> 3.7.40
> Green Section:
> Time Up: 13.46 hours. Time Down: 14.50 hours.
> 1. Flying Officer Carbury
> 2. Pilot Officer Berry
> 3. Pilot Officer Stapleton
> Section ordered to investigate aircraft flying over Montrose. Aircraft was a Ju88. Section attacked and Ju88 was shot down into Sea. 3 survivors.

Gerald adds:

> I learnt deflection shooting very quickly. Keep your speed or keep your height, one of the two. Sheep [Gilroy] and Morton were practical people, far more than say Bubbles or Rusty who were more academically minded. They weren't hands-on characters like a farmer would be, when he's got to do everything.

Ras Berry was the first to spot the enemy aircraft at 14.05, flying at an altitude of 9,000 feet on a southerly heading. Having identified it as a Ju88 the Spitfires closed for the kill but the German pilot took evasive action and sought cover in cloud. Carbury led his section down through the cloud to see if the German had gone below. Then, while he remained below the cloud bank, he ordered Green 2 and 3, Ras and Gerald, to position themselves above it in an attempt to catch sight of the fleeing German. The plan worked, the Ju88 reappeared over the cloud and Ras carried out a head-on attack, firing a two-second burst. Brian Carbury led Gerald in, each firing short bursts. Gerald experienced no return fire from the German gunners as he carried out his initial attack. The Ju88 pilot jettisoned the bomb-load (4 x 500kg bombs) and once again dived for the cloud. The Spitfires pursued with Carbury carrying out one of two No.1 attacks during which he closed from 250 to 50 feet. Ras carried out one further head-on attack and two No.1 attacks before running out of ammunition. Gerald fired approximately 215 rounds during a No.1 attack, opening fire at 300 feet, closing to 50. Since the raid on naval shipping in the Firth of Forth on 16 October 1939 when 16,000 rounds of ammunition were expended for one enemy aircraft shot down, the pilots had learnt the importance of getting in close to their prey before opening fire. The Ju88 was visibly damaged and

29

losing height, finally ditching in the sea. On following it down through the cloud and during a search of the area, Carbury noticed an oil patch on the surface of the sea and three of the crew with lifejackets in the water. A rubber dinghy was seen nearby. Having spotted a number of trawlers in the area, Carbury attempted to attract the fishermen to the crash site. Of the crew of four, three were reported as having survived when in fact there was only one. The aircraft had been on a weather reconnaissance from Aalborg when Green Section had shot it down into the sea at 14.40 hours. The regular sighting of these lone armed reconnaissance Luftwaffe aircraft prompted the nickname 'Weather Willie'.

Gerald learnt to keep the enemy in his sight when it was easy to lose visual contact beneath the nose of the Spitfire after opening fire. He took a great interest in deflection shooting and this was rewarded with success. He had been a good shot as a hunter, as had several other members of the Squadron. Indeed, most of the aces from the period had been good shots prior to becoming fighter pilots.

During the day Pilot Officer Philip Cardell arrived at B Flight from 263 Squadron. He was quickly given the nickname of 'Pip'. Three others who arrived with Cardell were sent to A Flight although Gerald also managed to get to know them: Pilot Officer 'Bill' Read and Sergeants Jack Stokoe and Alfred 'Joey' Sarre. Read became known as 'Tannoy' on account of his tendency to talk too much over the radio. Gerald kept in touch with the spirited Tannoy up until his death in 2000.

6 July saw yet more arrivals to increase the Squadron roll. Flying Officers Peter Pease and Colin Pinckney and Pilot Officer Richard Hillary. All were RAFVR pilots. Hillary and Pease were sent to B Flight where they were greeted by B Flight commander Fred Rushmer, whilst Pinckney went to A Flight at Dyce. Pease and Pinckney became known as 'Popper' and 'Pinker' (or 'Pinkers') respectively. Gerald describes Pinckney as: '. . . another tall chap and a very nice fella.' As with any new arrivals, these pilots went through a period of induction before being made operational. Gerald continues:

> Peter Pease was also a tall chap, six feet two, with light wavy hair. He was very good-looking. Hillary was a very nice chap; he was a year older than I was. He was very well dressed, very good-looking with a typical university hairdo – long hair! Not long as we know it today, with a pony-tail, but much longer than our hair, although ours wasn't too short, and combed into place with oil making it seem shorter than it actually was. But Hillary's was over his ears and over his collar, and we weren't allowed to have that! He was very well-spoken, was always very well-mannered and a very polite chap. The university had given him the finish that we didn't have and he had that air about him. We were a little more brash, I'd say. He'd been polished by the university. He seemed a lot older in manner and maturity than he really was.

Many of the 603 pilots were given nicknames. Over the years, these have become part of the legend of the Squadron and the Battle of Britain. Based on a surname or perhaps an aspect of the individual character that colleagues pick up on – 'Broody', 'Tannoy', 'Sheep' and probably the best example 'Uncle George' to name just a few – nicknames are an enduring part of British culture, from schooldays, through university, to adulthood when most are invariably left behind. However, with the armed forces nicknames do tend to continue to proliferate into adulthood. Many of the men of the Battle of Britain, be they staff, ground crew or pilots, were known by their nicknames and still are and despite the fact that the ferocity of the conflict brought men closer together for short friendships that have endured for a lifetime, some didn't even get to learn the first names of the colleagues they lost. Gerald would also acquire a nickname that would stick with him.

Members of the British armed forces read the *Daily Mirror* to keep up with the exploits of 'Jane'. Gerald shared the same interest in the cartoon but his nickname actually came from another strip-cartoon character, alongside 'Jane' and 'Blondie' in the *Daily Mirror*, called 'Just Jake'. In this cartoon there was a character called Captain A.R.P. Reilly-Foull* who wore a riding jacket, jodhpurs and boots of a huntsman and always had a broken cigarette in a holder clenched between his teeth. His character was unpleasant and lecherous and always chasing pretty young women, hence the play on words, 'Really Foul'. One of his expressions when he saw a good-looking young women was 'Stap-me, what a filly!' In 1994, during the first of many occasions spent in the company of Stapme and the first interview undertaken since his return from South Africa, he recounted:

> I used to cut out this cartoon every day and stick it on the wall of the dispersal hut at Montrose and that's how I got the nickname Stapme. Everybody in 603 called me that. As a result some of the squadron didn't even know my real name. Hillary didn't, for example. When he wrote *The Last Enemy* he called me 'Hugh' Stapleton which was incorrect and, to this day, writers that quote from his book, or use his book as a source for research, still make the mistake of calling me Hugh or think the nickname came from 'Popeye' or 'Blondie'! It wasn't until I left 603 that I lost the nickname. In a way the process started again.

Today, he prefers to be called Stapme by those who express an interest in his wartime experiences. When he took over command of 247 Squadron in August 1944, he ceased to be known as Stapme in favour of 'The Boss', a not unusual nickname for a CO.

It was during the months just prior to the Battle of Britain that a number of the younger pilots decided to grow a moustache. According to Stapme:

> It was a trend I believe came from the fact that a number of older, although not necessarily more experienced, pilots came to us from Army Co-operation squadrons after the battle for France. We simply decided to grow moustaches in order to look older. We were conscious of how much younger we looked than them. Those that tried to grow moustaches were successful, all that is

---

*Just Jake ran throughout the war and finally ended in 1952. Reilly-Foull was initially a secondary character to Jake but as his popularity grew he eventually took over the strip.

except for Cunningham. His hair was too short and curly, and there simply was not enough of it growing on his top lip, it looked awful and so he gave up.

What should also be considered is that, in addition to the very small number of army co-operation pilots who joined 603 Squadron, some of the auxiliary pilots themselves were much older and experienced, having been with 603 Squadron for some years prior to the war. There were also the regular and RAFVR pilots who were also sent to the unit at this time.

Although a little fluffy to begin with, Stapme's attempt to grow a moustache at the age of nineteen was eventually successful and he has kept it since that summer of 1940. The image of the Battle of Britain fighter pilot was stereotyped by the illustration of Flying Officer Kyte* in which he sports a fine handlebar moustache. To this day the name Stapme Stapleton and his splendid handlebar moustache are synonymous, thanks to a young pilot who had ambitions for a peacetime career in writing and who is about to enter the story.

Another interesting fashion trend from that period was the number of pipe smokers. For one or two of the youngsters this was also a means of appearing older. Stapme initially smoked cigarettes at a time when the dangers were unknown and it was particularly fashionable, whether or not you actually gained any pleasure from the habit. In 603 Squadron, Ian Ritchie, Ras Berry, Jim Morton, George Gilroy, Ken Macdonald, Count Stevens and George Denholm were pipe-smokers and, as contemporary photographs from the period show, the pipe was integral to the pose. Stapme gave up cigarettes for a pipe, a habit he maintains to this day.

When Pilot Officer Richard Hillary arrived at Montrose on 6 July one of the pilots present to greet him at B Flight dispersal was Stapme. Hillary later included a thumbnail sketch of him in his bestseller *The Last Enemy* and in doing so immortalised his name:

> Another from overseas was Hugh [sic] Stapleton, a South African. He hoped to return after the war and run an orange farm. He, too, was over six feet tall, thick-set, with a mass of blond hair which he never brushed. He was twenty and married, with a rough savoir-faire beyond his years, acquired from an early, unprotected acquaintance with life. He was always losing buttons off his uniform and had a pair of patched trousers which the rest of the squadron swore he slept in. He was completely slap-happy and known as 'Stapme' because of his predilection for Popeye in the *Daily Mirror*, his favourite literature.

---

*P/O Prune was the first character created by cartoonist Bill Hooper and writer Anthony Armstrong for *Air Clues*, the Journal of the Inspectorate of Flight Safety. *Air Clues* was based in Adastral House, MOD, but eventually went to a civilian publisher. The Inspectorate of Flight Safety was based at Kingsway, Holborn. The P/O Prune cartoon spawned a whole 'family' of Prunes including the rather dense AC2 Plonk and a number of attractive but empty headed WAAFs. Actor Humphrey Lestoq, who played John Gregson's flight commander in the WWII classic *Angels One Five* toured the variety halls playing F/O Kyte, whose catchphrase was 'Wizard Prang!' Bill Hooper died in 1996 aged eighty and his death prompted aviation historian/author, John Maynard, to record: '. . . his then unique contribution to the stern business of air safety was to save lives with laughter.'

Stapme comments: 'I didn't mind the thumbnail sketch of me he included in *The Last Enemy* but I never had any intention of becoming an orange farmer'.

Stapme joined 603 Squadron with 233 flying hours in his logbook. By 10 July 1940, the official date for the start of the Battle of Britain, he had added a further 140 hours flying Spitfires. He was fortunate to have had the opportunity to go into the battle with so many hours on type. Others were less fortunate.

With the fighting in the south ever-increasing in intensity, 17 July saw the Squadron suffer its first casualty of the Battle of Britain when Flying Officer Charles Peel failed to return from a sortie. He was reported 'missing'. John Young had earlier recommended Peel for further training but his advice went unheeded and Peel paid the ultimate price.

On the 20th Stapme was in action again. At 11.35 hours, Blue Section led by Flight Lieutenant Laurie Cunningham, with Flying Officer Waterston as Blue 2, and Stapme as Blue 3, took off from Montrose with orders to patrol the Peterhead area. At 12.05 Bubble and Stapme intercepted and shot down (shared) Dornier Do17P of 1(F)/120. The aircraft crashed in flames into the sea east of Aberdeen. Stapme had been close enough to identify the aircraft as A6+H (actually A6+HH). The crew of Leutnant Heur and two NCOs were reported 'missing'. The 603 ORB records the sortie:

20.7.40
Blue Section:
Time Up: 11.35 hours. Time Down: 12.45 hours.
1. F/L Cunningham
2. F/O Waterston
3. P/O Stapleton
Blue Section were ordered to patrol Peterhead and saw a Do17. Section attacked and e/a crashed in flames into the sea.

The composite combat report from HQ, 13 Group, to Fighter Command makes interesting reading:

F.C.C.R 190/1940.   FORM 'F' SECRET.

FIGHTER COMMAND COMBAT REPORT.

To: FIGHTER COMMAND.

From: No.13 Group, Intelligence

(A) Sector Serial No.   TN.156
(B) Serial No. of Order detailing Flight or Squadron to patrol   90
(C) Date: 20th July 1940
(D) Flight Blue Squadron   603 Sqdn.
(E) Number of Enemy Aircraft.   One.
(F) Type of Enemy Aircraft.   Do.17
(G) Time attack was delivered.   1205/1215
(H) Place attack was delivered. 30 miles East of Peterhead to 50 miles

North East of Peterhead.

(J)	Height of enemy	From 8,000 to 2,000 feet.
(K)	Enemy Casualties	One aircraft.
(L)	Our Casualties – Aircraft.	NIL
(M)	„ „ – Personnel	NIL
(N)	(i) Searchlights	N/A
	(ii) Anti-aircraft	N/A

(P) Range at which fire was opened in each attack on the enemy together with estimated length of burst.

Blue 1. One No.1 attack from astern opening at 600 yards closing to 200 yards firing one long burst of about 10 seconds. One beam attack to port opening at 400 closing to 100 yards firing remainder of ammunition in a burst of about 8 seconds. Total number of rounds fired: 2,800. No stoppages.

Blue 3. 8 bursts. No.1 attack at 300 yards closing to 150 yards firing a 3 second burst then another No.1 attack firing a 2 second burst then 3 beam attacks to starboard firing short bursts then No.1 attack from astern at 250 yards closing to 50 yards then last burst at 20 yards. No. of rounds fired: 2,800. No stoppages.

Blue 2. 5 bursts all from astern closing from 150 to 60 yards in each attack, the first burst being one long one of about 5 seconds the remainder being short bursts. No. of rounds fired: 2,640 (due to stoppage in No.1 port gun after 160 rounds fired).

(R) GENERAL REPORT. Weather. Banks of cumulus cloud between 400 and 9,000 feet of 6/10th. Visibility above 9,000 feet about 30 miles. Below 4,000 feet about 15 miles. Blue Section orbiting 30 miles East of Peterhead at 14,000 feet sighted Dornier 17 at about 8,000 feet against cloud bank about 15 miles away flying North. Section went into line astern and dived S.E. towards enemy aircraft. E/A fired first at Blue 1 (F/Lt L.J.G. Cunningham) from about 700 yards from upper rear gun position. As E/A was flying towards patches of cloud, Blue 1 therefore opened fire at 600 yards and followed him towards these patches. After Blue 1's first burst no further fire was seen or sustained from E/A. Blue 3 (P/O B.G. Stapleton) who was nearer enemy aircraft than Blue 2, owing to changed direction of flight, followed Blue 1 and delivered his first attack at about 5,000 feet following E/A in circular flight and noticing that guns below and above all seemed pointing at 80 degrees and not manned. E/A seemed to be endeavouring to point his front guns at him, hence circular flight. Blue 2 (F/O R.C.G Waterson [sic]) then came in and noticed wings of E/A seemed to be rocking but E/A seemed to have straightened out its course and he could see no signs of damage to aircraft. Blue 1 followed in again and noticed after his second attack E/A was flying very slowly and only about 100 m.p.h., at 3,000 feet. Succeeded by Blue 2 who noticed slight black smoke coming from port side of fuselage. Then Blue 3 who confirms black smoke in question. Then again Blue 2, followed by Blue 3. Then Blue 2 delivered his last attack at 2,500 feet and Blue 3 firing his seventh burst at 50 yards and his eighth at 300 yards when E/A was about 2,000 feet, making a note of lettering on its fuselage (black crosses on white background then A6 H all in black). Blue 2, followed down to 50 feet and saw E/A crash into sea at a shallow angle pointing E.S.E. in a sheet of flame and a terrific splash. Blue 2 saw 2 survivors swimming and waving. One seemed to be splashed with blood. Near them was a white object like a parachute but no rubber dinghy was visible. Blue 2 made a note of the bearing, time and airspeed of his return to Peterhead, this permitting arrangements being made with Coastal Command for an Anson to be sent to locate swimmers for speed boat which was immediately sent out from Aberdeen to endeavour to rescue them. Camouflage of this Do.17 was silver green all over except broken marks on wings.

Laurie Cunningham was too far away from the Dornier during his initial attack (600 yards) and it is highly unlikely that he hit anything. Generally, the pilots were learning to get in close before firing. Brian Carbury was already becoming an exponent of this. Stapme's recollections differ from the official report:

Montrose was a very exciting time for us because we had German aircraft to intercept. The 20th July was the first time I fired my guns in anger. We had a lot of German aircraft over on reconnaissance missions and that was when I shared a Dornier Do17 with Bubbles. There were three of us; Cunningham was leading with Bubbles as his No.2 and me as his No.3. Cunningham approached the bomber, but for some reason he didn't fire at it. Later, after we had landed, he told us that he had gone up to the aircraft to identify it, which was bloody nonsense! So Bubbles went in and opened fire and I followed behind and did the same. For some reason Bubbles refrained from carrying out another attack but when I closed in I could see the dorsal gun pointing straight up, instead of at me, which indicated that the rear gunner had been hit. I then flew in close formation alongside the aircraft and was able to make a note of its squadron letters and numbers before it landed in the sea. I got on the radio to tell them where it was so they could get a fix on me and get the Air Sea Rescue crew out to pick up the surviving crew members. When I returned to base they told me that they hadn't sent anybody out to rescue the crew because the weather was too rough, but it certainly was not. I had to land at Dyce after that patrol because, much to my amazement, my oil pressure gauge showed nought, but the temperature wasn't going up. So I realised I couldn't have lost my oil because my temperature gauge was OK. I remember once when Uncle George was A Flight commander at Dyce, he landed and he had what I remember as being a glycol leak, but the engine was still going, it hadn't seized. The manufacturer's engine identification plates fixed to the side of the engine, saying 'Rolls-Royce' etc., had melted and were buckled, but the engine was still running. That gives you some idea of the quality of the Rolls-Royce engine.

All 603 pilots had accumulated a great many hours flying time in recent months and although the intense air fighting had yet to start, some were already tired. Off duty, the pilots and staff tended to socialise in their respective messes, one or two of the local pubs or just remained on base, relaxed, read or caught up on their letter writing. A refreshing alternative came when on 31 July, in response to an invitation from the Earl of Dalhousie (Lord Simon Ramsay, the 16th Earl of Dalhousie), a number of B Flight 603 pilots took leave and went to stay at his fourteen bedroom hunting lodge at Invermark, Glen Esk. For three weeks during August 1940, a number of pilots spent their time at Invermark, fishing or swimming in Loch Lee and shooting. Lord Dalhousie provided all the equipment including fishing tackle, .22 full-bore rifles and a rowing boat. Stapme remembered that when they expressed the wish to go hunting Lord Dalhousie issued them with a full-bore rifle, but only a .22 calibre: '. . . he wasn't daft enough to give us anything bigger!' Brian Carbury, who eventually became 603's highest scoring pilot in the Battle of Britain, was in the first group to take up the offer and in a letter to his family back home in New Zealand dated 8 August, he wrote:

> We have a lodge near here, way up in the hills and we usually go up there for one or two days and have lots of good fishing and shooting grouse, hare, rabbits and now stag. Last week I got a young stag, 24 rabbits and four trout. It is marvellous getting up there away from it all and not having to worry about dress or anything.

Stapme and Bubble were also in the first group to visit Invermark and travelled up in Bubble's MG sports car which he was always tinkering with. On arriving at the lodge they were met by a tall, lean, elegant figure who had strolled out onto the gravel to greet them. Stapme unloaded their baggage and handed them to the man, assuming him to be a servant of some kind, and enquired: 'Where's the Earl then?' To which the stranger replied: 'You're looking at him.' After which he turned and walked into the lodge, carrying two large bags with the two young pilots in tow and Stapme feeling somewhat embarrassed.

Initially keen to take part, both fished on the loch and trekked many miles up into the hills in search of stag. During their first experience Bubble found the hill walking hard-going, perhaps as a consequence of being a little less fit than he used to be, so he borrowed a tractor and he and his colleagues clambered aboard and headed off for the high ground without getting tired-out before the hunt had even begun. Nevertheless, it wasn't long before Stapme and Bubble lost interest in hunting and on their way back to the airfield one sunny, summer's afternoon they came upon the Loch Lee Games which were taking place just down the road from Invermark at the tiny hamlet of Tarfside. Bubble stopped the car and the two young men watched what was akin to a mini Highland Games, involving the local children, their parents, evacuees (from nearby Brechin), some of whom were also staying in the lodge, and holiday-makers. As the families enjoyed a picnic on the grass watching the games, the two RAF pilots were intrigued and strolled over to see what was going on. Stapme was quickly encouraged to take part in the events, in particular 'tossing the caber'. Bubble also joined in. The youngsters took to their new friends immediately and by the end of the afternoon both children and adults waved them off in their car pleading with them to come again. Stapme has retained vivid memories:

I can't remember the exact number of times we went there but it was a quite extraordinary experience. Bubbles and I took Richard Hillary there on two different occasions. We never met the children one by one, there was always at least eight to ten of them. I first of all remember meeting a crowd and then the kids were fascinated by us I suppose. We were wearing our uniforms then and the kids sort of gravitated towards us. I think the parents were quite pleased to have them off their hands! They were full of questions. I remember flying over there which we were not supposed to do, but there were a lot of things that we were not supposed to do, and we still did them. We even chased some stags down from summer grazing to winter grazing for Lord Dalhousie, from high up, gently, by flying on one side of them, not too close. They moved down into the lower valleys. He had no ghillies to drive them down.

When Bubble and Stapme returned they brought a number of their colleagues with them who had been intrigued by the stories their fellow pilots had told them. As well as Stapme and Bubble, other pilots who visited the glen that summer included: Bolster Boulter, Ras Berry, Richard Hillary and Laurie Cunningham, who was less enthusiastic about taking part in the various games and became known as 'old frizzle-guts' as a result. He did however, take a shine to Rhoda Davie's sixteen-year-old daughter, also named Rhoda, and they were often seen in each other's company as a close friendship developed. In *The Last Enemy*, Richard Hillary recalled his displeasure at having shot a stag and vowed never to do so again. Stapme recalls his time with Hillary and of one of the flying exercises which took him over Glen Esk:

Hillary did not shoot a stag at any time we were there. The effort that would have been required – you would have had to walk for miles and been assisted by those who were skilled. I don't know where he got the idea from but it was wishful thinking and as far as the book is concerned, literary licence. Once, while he was with me, I shot a rabbit with my .22 rifle and the bullet went right through its throat. It was just sitting up looking at me. Unfortunately, I didn't kill the rabbit, I only paralysed it. I got hold of its back legs and hit its head against a rock, and Hillary was violently sick! If the incident did occur, then that rifle was the one which I was later to use at the Loch when I fired close to Dick Hillary when he was in the Luftwaffe dinghy.

We used to fly training exercises along the route of Glen Esk, in pairs, not in threes, as has been wrongly suggested. Had we been on patrol we would have invariably been in threes. During the training flights we underwent certain exercises. We carried camera guns and would, in turn, each act as hunter and hunted. It was great fun and valuable experience. We each tried to get on the other's tail, before swapping over. On one occasion I shook off my pursuer by going into a 20-30 degree dive and at 800-1,000 feet I did a sharp roll and broke away. He thought I would not be able to pull out of it, but I did, and managed to shake him off my tail, as the evidence on the camera gun film was to show.

Together the pilots took the children on picnics in Glen Esk or nearby Glen Mark. They also played games and swam in the loch. Rhoda Davie's ten-year-old daughter, Betty, has retained a host of happy memories from the summer of 1940:

> We used to play games at Migvie, where we were staying. The games consisted of kick-the-can, hide and seek and rounders. We used the painted white stones from the roadside as bases. We were playing one day when Bubbles and Stapme drove past particularly slowly. They were clearly keen to join in and it was Billy who wandered over and invited them. At that time Billy and Rhoda were both old enough to work, and were only with us at the weekends. When the afternoon was over the two pilots asked if they could come again and as they drove off I remember them waving and shouting, 'We'll be back!' The next time they brought Dick. He got on really well with our mother.
>
> We enjoyed so many picnics in the area. So much so that the daily delivery of bread by our local baker, Joe Guthrie, each morning became more important than ever. Our mother used to prepare a very large number of sandwiches in order to feed everyone, and we loaded them into a large wicker tomato basket.
>
> On one occasion we went on a picnic to Glen Mark. We all clambered into several cars and made our way over there. Over the river in the glen was a bridge made of two ropes suspended from mountings on either bank. One cable was for standing on, the other was for holding onto with your hands. Stapme made his way over to the other side. I remember what a tall, broad man he was. But then Bubbles and Dick tried to persuade me to go over. I said no. I was very timid. But Bubbles and Dick said they would go across with me, one either side, and urged me to 'Come on!' So I said that, with their assistance, it would be alright. As we made our way across, they bounced on the lower cable to make me feel even more insecure than I already was. Unfortunately, as we neared the other side, the bridge collapsed and we fell. Bubbles and I fell on the shingle, narrowly missing the water, but Dick fell straight in and he was soaked. He stripped off his wet clothes and we wrapped him in a blanket. For some reason Dick always wore his flying boots, and these took about three days to dry out.
>
> By evening time our adventures in Glen Esk would be curtailed by the swarms of mosquitoes and we retreated to the hayloft at Migvie where the pilots told us stories. The hayloft door was positioned to enable the sheaves to be unloaded from the back of the wagon, but the youngsters discovered that it was just the right height to use as a jumping platform. This time of story-telling in the hayloft was the perfect opportunity for me to get as close as I could to Dick. I really was very fond of him.

During this storytelling Stapme and the others were outdone by Hillary:

... he was an excellent raconteur. One story he told to the children was about Sredni Vashtar [Sredni Vashtar being a mythical polecat in the short story by Saki – a.k.a. Hector Monro]. Until recently, I had always remembered the story being about a red-eyed rat; an unpleasant character that he characterised as being a German. When the rat spoke, Dick would speak his lines in German and then translate for the kids. It had a marvellous effect.

Hillary called his Spitfire 'Sredni Vashtar'. While many pilots named their aircraft and had their ground crew paint the wording on the cowling, Stapme chose not to.

Sixteen year-old Sheila Robertson was also one of the children along with her younger sister. She considered Bubble and Stapme to be her favourites, with Richard Hillary a close third.

On one occasion the pilots arrived from Montrose with a rubber dinghy captured from a Luftwaffe Heinkel He111 which had been shot down off the north-east coast of Scotland by 603 Squadron. The pilots and children fooled around with the dinghy on the loch. Sometime during the day Richard stepped off the shore into the boat and proceeded to lie down and relax in the dinghy. Stapme had a .22 rifle which the Earl had given them to go hunting and raising the weapon to his shoulder he fired a number of shots into the water around the rubber boat and into the skin which formed the base of the dinghy. Seventeen-year-old Billy Davie panicked and told Stapme to stop before he hit Richard. A photo taken at the time by Bubble shows Richard was anything but scared. With a broad grin on his face he is attempting to retreat to the back of the boat, apparently worried that the punctures appearing in the base of the dinghy were getting too close to his crutch. The dinghy was left in the boathouse for future visits but was removed during their last day out in the glen and taken back to Montrose. Whilst Stapme does not remember the incident with the rifle he says: 'I had been a crack shot with a .303 rifle and if I had wanted to puncture the dinghy without hitting Dick then I would have, but I don't remember having done so.' Lord Dalhousie's concern at letting the pilots loose with anything bigger than a .22 rifle was understandable but they would soon be in charge of eight Browning .303 machine guns!

At Montrose, whilst on practice flights from the aerodrome the same pilots would take the opportunity to search out the children as they played in the glen and, having located them, they put on an impromptu flying display in their Spitfires. Back on the ground, the pilots enjoyed themselves in the company of those who became known as 'the children of Tarfside' following the publication in 1942 of Richard Hillary's best-seller, *The Last Enemy* in which he recounts his time in Glen Esk. He wrote:

Bubble and Stapme would both come up to Invermark but neither of them shot. How they employed their few hours of freedom will, I think, come as a surprise to a number of people, for they must have seemed from the outside as typical a pair of easy-going pilots as one could expect to meet anywhere. Stapme, with his talk of beer, blokes and carburettors, and Bubble with his absorption in things mechanical, might have been expected to spend their leaves, respectively, in a too-fast car with a too-loud blonde, and in getting together with the chaps in the local pub. In point of fact, they played hide-and-seek with children.

Tarfside was a tiny hamlet a few miles down the road from Invermark, and to it this summer had come a dozen or so Scots children, evacuated from the more vulnerable towns in the district. They went to school in Brechin, a few miles from Montrose, but for the holidays they came to the mountains, under the care of Mrs Davie, the admirable and unexacting mother of two of them. Their ages ranged from six to sixteen.

How Stapme and Bubble had first come upon them I never discovered, but from the moment that I saw those children I, too, was under their spell. That they really came from Brechin, that thin-blooded Wigan of the north, I was not prepared to admit; kilted and tanned by the sun, they were so essentially right against the background of heather, burns and pine. They were in no way precocious, but rather completely natural and unselfconscious. In the general confusion of introductions, one little fellow, the smallest, was left out. He approached me slowly with a grave face.

'I'm Rat Face,' he said.

'How are you, Rat Face?' I asked.

'Quite well, thank you. You can pick me up if you like.'

I gave him a pick-a-back, and all day we played rounders, hide-and-seek, or picnicked, and as evening drew on we climbed up into the old hayloft and told stories. Stapme, Bubble and I striving to outdo one another.

. . . It was with regret that we drove back to the aerodrome, and with the latent fear that we should not get back to Tarfside.

Certainly, the stunning scenery in Glen Esk was the perfect place for the pilots to relax and was in stark contrast to the aerodrome at Montrose. Years later the 'children' looked back at a wonderfully evocative period of their lives with great pride and admiration of the young pilots who enthralled them before flying off to fight in one of the greatest air battles, if not *the* greatest air battle, in history.

In 1996, Stapme returned to Glen Esk at the invitation of Angus Davidson, the only one of the children of Tarfside still living in the glen. The press were there to report on the occasion. During the Battle of Britain, the local folk followed the exploits of the Edinburgh Squadron and shared in the grief of the families who lost sons. Angus's mother even wrote to the mother of Bubble Waterston on hearing news of his death.

Stapme was the favourite of a number of the children, including Angus:

He seemed to have a foreign intonation and a very loud laugh. He was very tall. Stapme was great fun and always enjoyed himself to the full. Bubbles was probably the best-looking after Richard and, like Stapme, always let himself go. He was also great fun . . . On one occasion I was hiding and I dislodged something that made enough noise to give away my position. Stapme gave chase as I panicked and left my hiding place, but we crossed the yard and Stapme ran into a very large, very wet, pile of dung. He went in up to his knees and he stank. When he later went into the farmhouse, my mother asked me where that dreadful stench was coming from and turned, only to be confronted by the bulk of Stapme towering over her, which gave her a start! There used to be a large bough from a fir tree that hung over the road, on the other side of the road from the farmhouse, and Stapme used to climb onto it, put a leg either side, and pretend to be flying his Spitfire. The bough has been cut off now but you can still see the tree and from where it was removed.

For many years after the war Angus was unaware that Stapme had survived, but on discovering he had, promptly invited Stapme and his wife, Audrey, to stay. It was an emotional reunion and Stapme and Angus stayed up until the early hours during which time they consumed a considerable amount of single malt. During the visit, Angus also arranged for Stapme to re-visit Invermark Lodge and the current Lord Ramsay was there to greet him. The lodge hadn't changed in 56 years and Stapme enthralled his guests with his recollections of his time in Glen Esk and of his adventures in the remainder of the war. Yet more single malt was imbibed. Angus informed the commanding officer of RAF Leuchars of Stapme's impending visit and he was subsequently invited to the RAF Station for a guided tour. Sadly, it was an extraordinary coincidence that on 16 July 1999, the day of Stapme's arrival for his second visit to the Glen since 1940, the Earl of Dalhousie, Lord Simon Ramsay, passed away aged 86. Stapme has remained in touch with Angus.

Meantime, both A and B Flights, 603 Squadron, had been involved in a number of interceptions of enemy aircraft. At 11.47 hours on 29 July, Red Section at Dyce, consisting of P/O Bill Read and Sergeants Caister and Stokoe, intercepted two Heinkel He111s 12 miles inland of Aberdeen. Caister, who was leading the section, attacked one of the bombers prompting both aircraft to jettison their bombs and head for home. Both aircraft were lost in the cloud with no apparent damage having been inflicted. Neither Read nor Stokoe had managed to get close enough to open fire.

The following day dawned overcast and wet and conditions at Montrose and Dyce were poor. During the day KG26 carried out a number of bombing raids against Scottish cities from their base in Norway. At 11.45 Rusty Rushmer led Ras Berry and Peter Pease of Red Section on a patrol which led to the destruction of a Heinkel He111, 40 miles south-east of the airfield at Montrose. Rushmer, Berry and Pease were credited with a third of the kill. There were no survivors.

On 1 August 1940, the RAF Fighter Command Order of Battle showed that 603 Squadron had eleven Spitfires ready for combat and four more unserviceable. A total of twenty pilots were on-state. Squadron Leader 'Uncle' George Denholm had yet to be confirmed as commanding officer. On 15 August the Germans launched *Adler Tag* (Eagle Day) and on Saturday the 17th, 603 Squadron received orders to prepare for a move to RAF Hornchurch, Essex, No.11 Group, Fighter Command. They would be moving to the front-line. On 21 August Bill Caister was commissioned as a pilot officer and on the

23rd both A and B Flights were recalled from Dyce and Montrose in readiness. Richard Hillary later wrote:

> Broody was hopping up and down like a madman. 'Now we'll show the bastards! Jesus, will we show 'em!' Stapme was capering about shaking everyone by the hand, and Raspberry's moustache looked like it would fall off with the excitement. 'Eh, now they'll cop it and no mistake', he chortled. 'I've had just about enough of bulling about up here!' Even Boulter was out of bed, his ears twitching uncontrollably. Our relief squadron was already coming in, plane after plane engining down over the boundary. Rusty quickly allocated us to sections, and B Flight roared twelve strong across the aerodrome, dipped once over the mess and headed south.

Between 17th and 23rd August there had been time for a final visit to Tarfside but the pilots were too busy. With the Spitfires of 603 Squadron back at Turnhouse, the children of Tarfside were left wondering when the pilots, their friends, would next appear, eventually realising they had gone off to fight the Germans and would not be returning. Throughout the Battle of Britain the older kids scanned the newspapers for news of their heroes.

Having arrived at Turnhouse the pilots had to 'kick their heels' for a few more days before the order to move finally came. The weather prior to the move south was overcast and wet and a few of them accepted an offer by the Officer Commanding RAF Turnhouse, Lord 'Geordie' Douglas-Hamilton, to spend a couple of days grouse-shooting on his estate. The hospitality on offer made up for the poor weather but in the early hours of 27th August the call came in the form of an urgent telegram for them to return to Turnhouse. They were to be collected at eight that same morning. By ten they were back at Turnhouse and preparing to fly south.

By that time those who had been with the Squadron since they had been re-equipped with the Spitfire I had amassed well over 200 hours on type whilst Stapme had flown approximately 160. They had carried out many practice flights in order to hone their skills including: formation flying, navigation, night flying, formation attacks and, at George Denholm's insistence, dog-fighting.

The early production Spitfires carried no armour protection for the pilot and as a consequence of the early experiences of RAF fighter pilots, including the Advanced Striking Force (ASF) in France, the 603 ground crew personnel carried out a number of official modifications on the Spitfires before the pilots headed south. A 3mm alloy cover was fitted over the upper fuel tank to deflect rounds striking from a shallow angle, a 2″ thick chunk of laminated glass was bolted to the front windshield to provide protection from rounds fired from head-on, and 73lbs of armour plating was fitted to the cockpit behind the pilot's seat (including a $1/_4$″ thick piece of stainless steel behind the pilot's head) to provide protection from rounds fired from behind.* All this additional

---

*Any additional weight was crucial to the performance of the Spitfire and even the thickness of the back-armour was tapered.

protection was only effective against rifle calibre rounds and not the withering fire from 20mm cannon. By this time rear-view mirrors had also been fitted. Stapme and his colleagues were naturally apprehensive at what lay ahead but what they felt most was the determination to acquit themselves well in battle, to do their jobs to the best of their ability and to fight off the threat from the Germans. Their goal was clear and unequivocal and, having heard how tough the fighting in the south had been, some had confided in their loved ones that they would not be coming back.

CHAPTER FOUR

'NIGHT AND DAY, YOU ARE THE ONE'

'I talked with pilots as they came back . . . They stripped off their light jackets, glanced at a few bullet holes in wings or fuselage, and as the ground crews swarmed over the aircraft, refuelling motors and [reloading] guns, we sat on the ground and talked. I can tell you what those boys told me. They were the cream of the youth of Britain. As we sat there, they were waiting to take off again. They talked of their own work; discussed the German air force with the casualness of Sunday morning halfbacks discussing yesterday's football. There were no nerves, no profanity, and no heroics. There was no swagger about those boys in wrinkled and stained uniforms. The movies do that sort of thing much more dramatically than it is in real life.'

Ed Murrow
CBS Radio News

At 11.00 hours on Tuesday 27th August, all but four Spitfires of 603 Squadron took off from Turnhouse and headed south. Stapme was one of them. They stopped off on the way, first at Linton-on-Ouse and then Church Fenton to refuel, ensuring they reached Hornchurch with plenty of fuel still in their tanks. Shortly after they left Scotland, a Bristol Bombay took off with ground crew onboard under the command of Sergeants Andy Gillies and John Mackenzie. The rest of the ground personnel did not follow for another two weeks. The weather was poor with low cloud and drizzle. They were to relieve 65 Squadron which had only five pilots and 11 aircraft left and were being moved out of the front-line to rest and re-train. Richard Hillary, Colin Pinckney, Noel Benson and Pip Cardell followed the others at 16.00 in aircraft that had previously been unserviceable. By then the skies had cleared and the sun was shining.

On landing at Hornchurch the initial group was met by the station commander, Group Captain C.A. Bouchier DFC, who at his welcoming address informed the pilots they would be placed on readiness at 12.00 the following day. The pilots were then shown the Intelligence Room and given area maps and codes before being instructed to report back at 11.00 the next morning to finish the briefing. Compared to the very relaxed atmosphere of Dyce and Montrose, the situation at Hornchurch was very different. Having had just one section from each flight at readiness in Scotland, Hornchurch had three squadrons. Off duty, the atmosphere in the mess was tense. Stapme:

One of my most outstanding early memories of Hornchurch occurred not long after we had arrived. I watched a Spitfire land

and as the pilot walked across from his aircraft I could see that he was wounded and there was blood trickling down his face from his forehead. He was alright, it was just a scratch, but that was my first introduction to what was to come.

This event actually occurred on 30 September when Flying Officer Tony Lovell of 41 Squadron carried out a wheels-up landing on the airfield after his Spitfire had been hit in the starboard wing by a cannon shell. He had either been struck by a splinter or had struck his head as he touched down. The incident went unrecorded in the 41 Squadron ORB. By the end of the war Lovell had achieved the rank of wing commander and had 16 enemy aircraft destroyed to his credit, with six shared destroyed, two probably destroyed, nine damaged and four shared damaged, and one destroyed on the ground. He served in the Battle of Britain, the defence of Malta and various operations throughout the Mediterranean. He was tragically killed in an accident at Old Sarum in August 1945 when his Spitfire Mk.XII crashed as he pulled out of the second of two slow rolls just after take-off. He had flown throughout the war, undertaking one of the largest number of operational tours of any pilot in the RAF (70% of his wartime career was on ops), but is unfortunately not as frequently remembered as so many other aces. He was awarded two DFCs, two DSOs, and one DFC (United States), a quite rare collection. Tony Lovell is described by his son as: 'A low profile pilot, a diffident young man, withdrawn, intensely religious, introspective and the very antithesis of the Brylcreem set.' Had it not been for the war he would have been a Roman Catholic priest.

A number of the wives of the 603 pilots also travelled south to be near their husbands. Nancy Berry and Joan Stapleton moved into a house in Romford from where their husbands travelled to Hornchurch although that wasn't always possible, particularly during the height of the battle. Both Nancy and Joan were expecting at that time.

By now Stapme was an experienced pilot who knew he had a job to do, but his toughest learning experience was about to begin. He had seen colleagues in the Squadron perish in flying accidents, of which there had been many since his arrival, and another was posted 'missing', but in only a matter of hours some of his closest friends in the Squadron were reported missing or killed in action.

The Squadron was dispersed to the south-east side of the aerodrome, the opposite side to the hangars and administration block with the mess further away on the same side. The men kept together, even in the mess, and hardly ever saw the pilots from the other squadrons.

Conditions at dispersal were as basic for the pilots and ground crews as they had been at Dyce and Montrose but not as cold and muddy. If they lived in the mess, half a dozen pilots would climb out of bed at 04.30 hours, having been awoken by their batmen with a welcoming mug of tea, and make their way to dispersal in readiness for any surprise attacks. By 05.00 the aircraft had been warmed-up and the first patrol took place around breakfast time. In the meantime Stapme and Ras had made their way from their accommodation in Romford.

Eggs and bacon was sent over to the pilots from the mess. Some didn't live to see breakfast. When the battle was at its most intense, the pilots ate whenever they could. For the ground crew and pilots alike, the NAAFI wagon with its tea and 'wads' was a blessing and much appreciated, particularly when they too had to run the gauntlet with the threat of attack from the Luftwaffe.

The squadrons were ordered to scramble via the aerodrome PA system and many of the 603 pilots forever retained fond memories of the calm delivery of the voice of Ronnie Adam, the controller who was a veteran WWI RFC pilot with 73 Squadron and who had been shot down by the Red Baron and taken prisoner. Post-war he starred in many films and his life story makes fascinating reading. Although Stapme doesn't remember Adam, he does remembers his voice:

> We had a wonderful controller, I don't remember his name. He used to say: '603 Squadron, please get into the air as soon as possible, please get going chaps.' He spoke in such a mellifluous way. There was no urgency in his voice, no panic, nothing. It was a great influence.

The last patrol of the day at Hornchurch was sometimes as late as 20.00 hours.

On 28 August, the day after their arrival, the Squadron was immediately in action. By evening, Don Macdonald, Laurie Cunningham and Noel Benson were lost. It was a withering baptism, but the attitude of the other pilots was that there was a battle to be won and they just got on with their jobs. Whilst Don Macdonald only had around 20 hours on Spitfires in his logbook, Benson had considerably more than that and Cunningham had over 200. What they all lacked was combat experience against the Luftwaffe fighters and all three had been bounced from a superior altitude and probably never even saw what hit them.

Stapme was not included in the first patrol from Hornchurch which took off at 12.27 on 28 August. There were no casualties on this one and George Denholm claimed a Me109 probable. At 15.55 with Stapme again not included, the Squadron took off. Jim Morton and George Gilroy each claimed a 109 destroyed. Winston Churchill witnessed Sheep Gilroy's 'kill' from Dover, which was seen going down in flames. Ras Berry claimed a 109 probable but also saw Don Macdonald and Laurie Cunningham, his section's leader and No.3, shot down in flames. Both were reported 'missing'. Brian Carbury claimed a 109 damaged. Ian Ritchie's Spitfire was badly damaged by cannon and machine-gun fire from 109s. One armour-piercing round entered the rear of the fuselage, passed along the inside of the aircraft before penetrating the lower and thickest part of the armour behind the pilot's seat and hitting him in the back. He managed to fly his aircraft back to Hornchurch before being taken to hospital.

Stapme was given his chance during the last patrol of the day which took off at 18.36 hours:

> Uncle George used to cheat when we were scrambled. He would jump into his aircraft and, having started it, he would taxi out. He didn't do his belt up because he knew he had to wait for us. As everybody got into position, before we were airborne, he'd fasten his straps and say over the radio: '603 Squadron airborne!'

In effect, Stapme was filling 'dead men's shoes' in a patrol of 11 Spitfires, his aircraft being XT-R, L1024. Colin Pinckney, Noel Benson, Joey Sarre and Richard Hillary also flew from Hornchurch for the first time on this patrol. Hillary flew with Stapme on a number of occasions between 28 August and 3 September, the date on which Hillary's part in the Battle of Britain came to an end when he was shot down. Of the last patrol on the 28th, Hillary later recalled in his book *The Last Enemy*:

> During the climb Uncle George was in constant touch with the ground. We were to intercept about twenty enemy fighters at 25,000 feet. I glanced across at Stapme and saw his mouth moving. That meant he was singing again. He would sometimes do this with his radio set on 'send,' with the result that, mingled with our instructions from the ground, we would hear a raucous rendering of 'Night and Day.'

When his book, *The Last Enemy*, was published in 1942, Richard Hillary was aware that in bringing his experiences, and that of his friends and colleagues, to the attention of the public, he had also perpetuated the memory of those whom he had known who had made the ultimate sacrifice. This had been his intention and in doing so he consigned the names of, amongst others, 603 Squadron's Brian Carbury, Ras Berry, Uncle George, Peter Pease, Colin Pinckney, Peter Howes, Ken and Don Macdonald, Black Morton, Broody Benson, Sheep Gilroy, Bolster Boulter, Joey Sarre, and Stapme Stapleton to the realms of legend.

The image of a Battle of Britain fighter pilot flying into battle whilst singing is an evocative one, and could be construed as an act of bravado in the face of fear, but in Stapme's case he was enjoying himself and his work as a fighter pilot. Youthful reckless abandon (he was only 20) and an apparent lackadaisical attitude towards what was a deadly serious situation masked his real determination to do his duty well and stave off the threat that Germany and the Luftwaffe posed. It was this exuberance which allowed such young men to carry out tasks in the face of such adversity because the longer they survived, the more they experienced and suffered extreme fear and perhaps terror, first-hand. The wear and tear of battle started to take its toll, causing trauma as well as tiredness and fatigue. Whilst many pilots from the period remember the extreme nervous tension whilst waiting for the order to scramble and the great sadness at losing friends and colleagues, others talk of being too busy to think of the losses and the threat to their own lives and simply got on with learning the required skills as best and as quickly as they could in what was an extremely hectic period. In truth, for so many of the pilots involved in the great air battle over Britain in the summer of 1940, it was a period of intense excitement and comradeship that was never to be equalled over the years since. As is typical of veterans of war, years after the intense conflict which deeply affected them, for better or for worse, they are only able to find true comradeship back in the company of those with whom they served, believing it is only they who can truly comprehend and appreciate what they went through. A number of veterans of the Battle of Britain remember the period as '. . . the best years of my life' and '. . . I had a great time,' but they are quick to appreciate that they survived and recall the friends who were lost. Some do not find solace and simply refrain from discussing their experiences as if it is a forbidden subject.

Stapme tells why his radio didn't provide much variety of music to sing along to:

> The TR.9B-D (single channel, H.F.) radios in the Spitfire Mk1a were terrible but the later models (the TR.1133 for example) were as good as using the telephone. Once we were in the south the only station we could pick up with the TR.9B was Radio Luxemburg.

Thus the legend of Stapme singing as he flew into battle was born. Although he admitted to having a few 'butterflies' in his stomach at dispersal, he didn't sing to release nervous tension. Once airborne, the nerves disappeared with the thrill of flying and he concentrated on the job. He still thoroughly enjoys singing when the opportunity arises!

In comparison to Stapme's experiences, Joey Sarre was someone who suffered deeply. He was shot down a total of four times in quick succession during the battle. After the second time his family were notified he was 'missing' even though he was in hospital. Nobody had informed Uncle George he was safe. On returning to Hornchurch, his colleagues reacted as though they'd seen a ghost and he found that his personal effects had been packed and were ready to be sent home. Yet he was subsequently shot down on two more occasions. It was following his second escape that his friends noticed a significant change in his personality from which he never recovered. He was eventually taken off operations and became an instructor.

During the tea-time patrol on 28 August George Denholm claimed a 109 destroyed with Bubble claiming a probable. Stapme made no claims for this sortie and, sadly, Pilot Officer Noel 'Broody' Benson was shot down and killed. Ten of the 11 Spitfires which had taken off on patrol returned to base at 20.12 hours.

With the Squadron having lost Don Macdonald (22), Laurie Cunningham (23) and Noel Benson (21), with Ian Ritchie badly injured, a number of the pilots believed that if the current rate of attrition continued, they too would also doubtless be killed, a feeling reflected in their letters home.

In 1999, Stapme met Jean, the younger sister of Flying Officer Robin 'Bubble' Waterston, on the first of two visits. Jean recalled that Bubble talked of his friends in the Squadron and on occasion a few of his closest friends came to tea. Jean has fond memories of the period and cherishes the memories of her older brother who died doing what he believed in. Robin had told her he wouldn't be coming back, but was still committed to the cause. Jean was so happy to have met Stapme after so many years – the Battle of Britain pilot who had become very good friends with her brother and had himself become famous. For Stapme, Jean was the sister of one of his good friends who had died young whilst he had survived to enjoy a full life. So many years on, with the both of them now in their eighties, there was an immediate and tangible bond.

For 29 August 1940, the 603 ORB reads:

> At 15.15 hours nine aircraft of 603 Squadron took off to patrol Rochford at about 24,000 feet. When in position they were ordered to Deal, they saw eight Me109's coming down on them, also a further six Me109's in line astern. These six did not make any attempt to attack. A dogfight ensued and it was found that the Me109's operated in pairs. When attacked, it [No.1] dived [and] No.2 dived as well.

Having been bounced by the 109s, the pilots found themselves fighting for their lives. Boulter destroyed a 109 and Richard Hillary, Tannoy Read and Stapme each claimed a probable. On landing, the pilots recorded the combat as having occurred at 16.00 hours. Stapme wrote:

> When on patrol with 603 Squadron we sighted enemy fighters just south of Deal. P/O Read and myself broke away from the Squadron to engage two Me109s who were circling above us. P/O Read engaged the first and myself the second. After firing short deflection bursts the Me109 which I attacked went straight down out of my sight with smoke issuing from the engine. I then broke away and climbed into the sun.

Stapme opened fire from 150 yards and fired two, two-second bursts with no more than 30 degrees deflection, firing a total of 480 rounds. When attacking a Me109, Stapme recalled how the German fighter had a distinct advantage over the Spitfire in that it had fuel injection. When approached from behind, the pilot of a 109 could push the stick forward and, with the throttles wide open, dive straight down under power in an attempt to avoid being hit. This was referred to as a 'bunt' and the tell-tale sign was a puff of smoke from the 109's exhaust ports. It is likely that an inexperienced RAF pilot may have witnessed this puff of smoke when attacking, incorrectly believing he had hit the 109. By comparison, the Spitfire's Merlin engine had a gravity-fed carburettor and if a pilot attempted to carry out the same manoeuvre whilst pursuing a 109 it would lead to a momentary but significant loss of power due to fuel starvation, leaving the pilot unable effectively to pursue the enemy fighter but also vulnerable to attack himself. The Spitfire pilot, therefore, had to roll away and dive at the same time, ensuring downward pressure from gravity was maintained on the carb to provide a continuous flow of fuel.

Both Rushmer and Boulter sustained slight injuries in the dogfight with Rusty force-landing at Bossingham while 'Bolster' returned to base safely. Both pilots were subsequently rested. Bill Read made no claim as he was unable to observe the effects of his fire as his aircraft went into a spin.

At 18.10 ten Spitfires took off again on patrol from Rochford with Stapme flying XT-R, L1040. At 27,000 feet over Manston they spotted some 24 Me109s flying above them. They made no attempt to take advantage of their superior height so Uncle George led a climbing attack. In the ensuing dogfights Colin Pinckney, Richard Hillary and Brian Carbury claimed 109s destroyed but 'Pinkers' was shot down and was burned prior to baling out of what was Black Morton's regular aircraft, R6753 'Tigger', at an altitude of only 1,000 feet. Having failed in his attempt to reach Hornchurch and Lympne, Hillary crash-landed L1021 'Sredni Vashtar' in a field short of Lympne aerodrome. The burns to Pinckney's face and, more particularly, his hands, were severe enough to require hospitalisation and weeks of sick leave. Sergeant Jack Stokoe and Stapme each claimed a 109 probable over Manston. Stapme wrote:

> When enemy fighters attacked our Squadron I was separated from the rest. I climbed into the sun to 30,000 feet, and sighted one Me109 just going into a loop, catching him with a full deflection shot of 5 seconds. He continued upwards and did a bunt, going downwards beyond the vertical.

Stapme opened fire at 200 yards, closing to 50, firing 550 rounds in his one burst. Landing back at base at 19.30 Stapme recalled how any irregularities in the fighter pilot's vision could give grave cause for concern:

> Was that just a spot in your vision or was it an enemy fighter? As you glanced around the sky, spots in your vision invariably move more slowly than the speed of your eye movement giving the impression that it could be an enemy fighter. Coupled with marks on your canopy you had to be extremely alert. I found the enemy aircraft easy to spot against the blue sky. It was our anti-aircraft fire that quite often indicated to us the whereabouts of the incoming enemy fighters.

The Spitfire Mk.IIs had yet to reach the Squadron:

> The Mark II Spits with the more powerful Merlin XII engines incorporating the Coffman cartridge starter and a pressurised glycol/water cooling system, had an increased 18lbs of boost which we used in the climb. Unfortunately, this initially knackered the gudgeon pin on the pistons until an improvement was made.

At 10.35 on Friday 30 August just six Spitfires took off on patrol from Hornchurch. Black Morton claimed a 109 probable over Deal. Joey Sarre landed back at base with severe damage to the tail of his Spitfire and Uncle George baled out of Spitfire XT-D, L1067 'Blue Peter'. Both aircraft had been damaged by return fire from Me110s. Stapme was not involved with this patrol or the next.

The Squadron was again scrambled at 15.55 hours to intercept what turned out to be the heaviest raid of the day. Bubble Waterston shot down a 109 at 16.40 north of Canterbury but his own aircraft was hit during the combat, returning to base with a punctured oil tank. Brian Carbury celebrated his recent award of the DFC by shooting down another Me109 over London at 16.45 hours. Joey Sarre claimed a 109 probable five minutes after Carbury's kill, but then had the tail of his Spitfire shot off and he was forced to bale out.

The Squadron had been at Hornchurch for just three days. Stapme had flown three patrols. He muses on why some Luftwaffe fighter pilots became so successful:

> I remember two reasons why the German victories were so high, apart from skill. The first was that they never went on rest. They had leave, but they were never rested from their particular

squadron, ie: sent away as instructors. Consequently, they were far more skilled with flying in the same squadron, in the same aircraft, or the same upgraded version of the same aircraft, be it the 109E, F or G variant of the Messerschmitt. I was eventually taken off my favourite aircraft and flew Hurricanes and Typhoons up to the time I was made a POW. The second reason was that so many of the pilots had gained experience in the Spanish Civil War.

During their time off, the pilots drank together in the mess. A number of traditions developed over the years since 603 Squadron was formed which were intended to perpetuate the Scottish heritage of the unit. One example being that during dining-in nights and other formal functions the officers and guests entered the dining room of the officers mess to the accompaniment of a piper. Stapme reflects on the occasions at Turnhouse with amusement: 'It was too small a room to have bagpipes played in. The noise was deafening, we couldn't hear a bloody thing!' Another tradition was maintained by Uncle George after they had moved to Hornchurch. After dinner each evening, to remind his men they were in a Scottish squadron and to provide the Scots themselves with a little taste of home, he insisted his men toasted the unit with a glass of Drambuie. This tradition has now slipped into the realms of legend and at the time Stapme was not unhappy that it was maintained, without the piper.

On one occasion a group of 603 pilots, including Stapme, drove into London for a night out. It was after-hours and they had been looking for somewhere to continue a particularly lengthy drinking session and managed to force their way past a reluctant doorman into a fairly exclusive club in the West End. Stapme could drink beer all night without a problem and never touched anything else. In the early hours the management tried to turf them out as it was closing time, but the pilots refused to leave. The manager then threatened to call the Provost. It was George Denholm who informed the manager that the Provost Marshal was a squadron leader and so was he; anyway the Provost was away on leave! The party continued until daybreak with the manager of the club being tied-up and locked in his office!

Saturday 31 August 1940 was the Squadron's most successful day of the battle '. . . when, of the 63 enemy aircraft destroyed that day, they accounted for 14 – the highest individual bag that day.' Fighter Command lost 39 aircraft and most of the important sector airfields were bombed. Hornchurch was bombed at 13.15 and 18.00 killing a total of four 603 ground crew personnel: LAC W.J. Baldie, LAC J.E. Dickson and AC1 J. Worthington were killed in the lunchtime raid and AC1 Dickinson was killed in the tea-time attack. A total of 11 others were injured including AC1s Forest, Adams and Ritchie, and Sergeants Andy Gillies and John Mackenzie. Both sergeants had been at Montrose with Stapme and made a full recovery. The Squadron flew four patrols, the first took off between 08.30 and 08.55. The ORB records:

> 12 aircraft took off from Hornchurch. When over Canterbury at 32,000 ft, they saw below them 12 Me109's in line astern, weaving. The Squadron went into line astern and dived to attack

out of the sun. A dogfight ensued and 1 Me109 exploded in mid-
air for no apparent reason.

Stapme flew XT-L, L1020. Three 109s were destroyed with one each going to
Carbury and Gilroy, the third, whilst shot down by a 603 pilot, was not allotted
in the ORB. The pilots landed again at 09.35. The second patrol of the day took
place between 10.25 and 11.30 but went unrecorded in the Squadron ORB.

The third patrol of the 31st took off at 12.35 with Stapme flying XT-R,
X4264, with instructions to patrol the airspace over Biggin Hill. Large
formations of enemy bombers with fighter escort were detected crossing the
coast at Dungeness where the main formation split into two groups with
different targets. En-route to their designated patrol area Sheep Gilroy, with his
exceptional eyesight, spotted a formation of enemy aircraft high above.
Unfortunately, as the Spits climbed to intercept, these were lost. Ordered to
patrol the airspace over their own airfield they came across a formation of some
14 Dorniers with an escort of Me109s and what was reported to be the fictitious
Heinkel 113. With a height advantage the 603 pilots dived to attack. Ras Berry
and Brian Carbury each claimed two 109s destroyed, and Carbury claimed to
have destroyed two of the 'He113s' which were in fact 109s. Richard Hillary
and Ken Macdonald each claimed a 109 destroyed and Black Morton a Dornier
Do17 destroyed. At 13.15 Hornchurch was bombed. Fortunately the Squadron
was airborne at the time and the returning Spitfires were diverted to Rochford
at 13.56 where they were refuelled and re-armed. Stapme remembers hearing
about the bombing of his station and the lucky escape by members of 54
Squadron:

> I remember Al Deere [later Air Commodore Alan Deere OBE,
> DFC*, DSO, Croix de Guerre (France), DFC (US)] at
> Hornchurch. He was a lucky fella. As the Dorniers approached, he
> was attempting to take off with the two other aircraft in his section
> when the bombs caught up with him! There were about twelve
> Dorniers on their run-in to bomb the aerodrome and these three
> Spitfires were just gathering speed. Of course they weren't going
> faster than the Dorniers were flying, so the pattern of the Dorniers
> was faster than the Spitfires and whilst the bombs initially fell
> behind, they then overtook, straddling the Spitfires, sending Al
> Deere's aircraft corkscrewing into the air. Another chap was flung
> into a sewerage farm nearby while the remaining pilot clambered
> from his wrecked aircraft, which had done a cartwheel, wing-tip
> over wing-tip, and helped free Deere from hanging upside down
> in his cockpit, unable to get out and with fuel pouring around the
> top of his head from the ruptured fuel lines. In twenty-four hours
> the airfield was serviceable again. They hit the airfield and not the
> hangars. It was a grass aerodrome with no actual runways. If they
> had hit the hangars, some damage would have been inflicted.
>
> 'Daddy' Bouchier was the CO and he got everybody onto the
> airfield filling in the bomb craters. He was a little fella who was
> always willing to assist in any duties in order to keep everyone
> working as a team. He helped position the little yellow marker
> boxes on the airfield after the raid on the 31st in order to indicate

to the returning pilots a safe strip to land on. The pilots returning from combat remember seeing this little figure scurrying about, hastily positioning these markers to help guide them in. There was one strip left untouched by bombs at the southern edge of the aerodrome, which we could still land on when we returned at the end of the day. I remember Hornchurch being shaped rather like an Easter egg with the southern end as the fattest part and the remaining strip across that part.

I think it was the next day, we were all sitting in the mess, the weather was poor with low cloud and we were on our day off. We suddenly heard the ack-ack firing, which didn't have a chance of hitting the target, as an enemy Ju88 appeared at the last moment from the cloud over the airfield. The enemy pilot must have been as surprised as anybody to suddenly emerge from the cloud to find he was right over an aerodrome. He was also very close to the barrage balloons. Two aircraft managed to take off after him but there was too much cloud about to have any hope of finding him. But he planted his bombs right on that untouched strip.

At 17.51, 603 was scrambled for the fourth time with orders to patrol the airspace over Hornchurch at a height of 12,000 feet. Stapme flew XT-L, L1020, which was by that time an old, worn-out aircraft and, despite excellent work by the ground crews, it would have been difficult for it to keep up with the newer aircraft. Fifteen minutes after they took off the airfield was bombed again, albeit ineffectively with little damage inflicted on the airfield or station buildings. Sadly, a fourth member of 603's dedicated ground crew personnel was killed and a number of others injured. At 8,000 feet the pilots spotted a large formation of 109s and continually monitored them as they climbed to 30,000 feet where they encountered, what turned out to be, formidable opponents in 12 109s of I/JG3 over what was by then the Woolwich area. Brian Carbury shot down two over Southend before his own aircraft, XT-W, R6835, was hit by cannon fire, knocking out the compressed air system and causing severe damage. Although wounded in the foot, Carbury managed to land back at Hornchurch. The most successful pilot/aircraft partnership in the Battle of Britain had come to an end. Carbury had shot down eight Me109s in R6835 between 29th and 31st August with five kills achieved in three patrols on the 31st. The Hornchurch ORB records:

> Our squadrons, which had a very heavy day, accounted for no less than nineteen of the enemy and a further seven probably destroyed. 603 Squadron alone were responsible for the destruction of 14 enemy aircraft. Although we lost a total of 9 aircraft, either in combat or on the ground, only one pilot was lost.

Sadly, that pilot was the brightest character and Stapme's close friend Bubble Waterston. At 18.30 hours he was shot down by Me109s of I/JG3 and was either dead or unconscious when his aircraft dived onto Repository Road, Woolwich. None of his colleagues saw him go down but there were many eyewitnesses on the ground. From a vertical dive from high altitude, his Spitfire XT-K, X4273 was seen to make an apparent recovery, in that the aircraft levelled out momentarily, before once again resuming a near vertical dive into the ground. There was little left of Flying Officer Robin McGregor Waterston but what was found at the site was returned to Edinburgh where there was a memorial service at Warriston Crematorium attended by his family, friends and girlfriend, Patricia. He was 23.

When the mother of Angus Davidson, one of the children of Tarfside whom Stapme and Bubble had impressed enormously, wrote to Bubble's mother, Mabel, she received the following reply:

> My husband and I send our warm thanks for your kind letter of sympathy. Robin was so happy playing with the children in those all too few carefree 'leaves' they had at Invermark. He was the second youngest of a family of eight and they were all happy together. It is hard to bear, but these kind letters all help.

The letter still remains in the Davidson family as does a small wooden boat carved by hand by Bubble, who was an excellent model maker, for the children.

In the same initial attack which claimed the life of Waterston, Sheep Gilroy managed to shoot down a 109 but was then himself downed at 18.20, but managed to bale out. On landing, Gilroy was mistaken for a German by an angry mob and it was thanks to a bus conductress who recognised his accent that further injury was not inflicted. He was nevertheless hospitalised with burns he'd received in combat as well as the injuries received after he'd landed.

Ras Berry and Jack Stokoe each destroyed a 109 with Jack claiming another 'damaged'. Stapme claimed a 109 probable and completed the following combat report:

> When patrolling in line astern with the rest of the squadron I sighted bomber formation below us on the port. With two other aircraft I climbed into the sun for a favourable position, to make an attack on the bombers out of the sun, when five Me109's engaged us.
>
> These Me109's came out of the bomber formations climbing into the sun. Flying Officer Carbury engaged three Me109's and I engaged the other two. These two were flying in tight line astern. After giving the rear one a deflection burst of three seconds he pulled vertically upwards with white streams pouring from his engine.

Stapme attacked the 109s at 18.25 at an altitude of 25,000 feet north of Southend. This probable was in fact the aircraft which crashed and burned near Whalebone Lane gun-site, Chadwell Heath at 18.50 hours. The pilot of Messerschmitt Bf109E-4 (5339) of 3/JG3 was Oberleutnant Johann Loidolt who managed to bale out of the stricken fighter. It is possible he also had been attacked by Sergeant F.W. 'Taffy' Higginson of 56 Squadron.

As Jack Stokoe brought his Spitfire in to land at Hornchurch for the first time following the bombing of the airfield, he recalled seeing the yellow marker boxes laid out by the Station commander and members of his staff. Despite the need to put the loss of colleagues out of their minds and get on with the job, the death of Bubble Waterston on 31 August was a devastating blow to the pilots of 603.

In the edition of the Edinburgh *Sunday Post* newspaper, published on 8 December 1940, Stapme's photo featured prominently with a headline praising the Squadron's achievements of 31 August: 'Edinburgh Boys Bump Off 13 Jerries In One Day.' In addition to the very young-looking Stapme in flying helmet, the photograph included: Ras Berry, Brian Macnamara, Ludwik Martel, John Boulter and David Scott-Malden. Martel and Scott-Malden had yet to join the Squadron. Interestingly, the actual score was 14 with the loss of Waterston and two Spitfires.

On 1 September, Pilot Officer Dudley Stewart-Clark returned from leave. His passenger in his Bentley for the journey south from Scotland was the experienced and recently commissioned Pilot Officer Bill Caister who, aware of the heavy fighting his colleagues were involved in, had found the temptation to return early from leave irresistible.

After seeing the basic facilities at 603 dispersal, Stewart-Clark privately expressed consternation to Uncle George who accepted his offer to improve conditions. Stewart-Clark took advantage of his wealthy family connections, made a number of phone calls to Harrods and a short while later, a van arrived with a delivery of easy chairs, rugs and curtains to make their time at dispersal more comfortable.

At 07.28 on the morning of Monday 2 September, Stapme was in action this time patrolling Hawkinge. The 12 pilots scrambled had been at dispersal since 04.30. Stapme flew Spitfire XT-P, X4274. As he lifted away from the airfield he changed hands on the control column, selected undercarriage up, throttled back to climbing power, pitch back to 2,850 revs and as he approached to intercept the enemy he went through what had become his tried and tested routine: gun-sight on, gun button to 'fire', airscrew pitch to 2,650 revs for better performance, emergency boost override button pressed, seat height and Sutton harness OK and feet in upper stirrups of rudder bar. (With his feet in upper stirrups there were straps to secure them for combat. Additionally, with the legs more elevated the pilot was a little more resistant to the forces of gravity.) From their position just north of Hawkinge at 26,000 feet the pilots dived to attack a number of 109s flying in formation at 08.15.* Richard Hillary claimed a 109 destroyed but was shot down (the following morning) before he had time to complete a combat report. Jack Stokoe lost contact with his colleagues in the dive but came across a number of Me110s and Dorniers and attacked a 110 which he later claimed as a probable. Flying Officer Jack Haig and Ras Berry each claimed to have destroyed a 109. Following interaction between the two pilots it was decided they had attacked the same aircraft with Berry being the first to have opened fire. Three other 109s were shot down by either 603 or 54 Squadron but it was not possible to confirm who shot down which aircraft. It was one of the many occasions to which Stapme refers when more than one aircraft was responsible for bringing down the same German aircraft. In such cases, a high altitude attack may have inflicted slight damage but whilst diving to evade further attack, the German might then be attacked

---

*At this time, Uncle George implemented a major change in tactics. In an attempt to counteract the frequency with which his pilots were being bounced by enemy fighters from a superior altitude, after take-off he led the Squadron on a reciprocal heading to that given by the controller. On reaching an altitude of 15,000 feet the pilots turned onto a reciprocal course, the original heading given, but with less chance of being caught at a disadvantage while still climbing.

again and then again by other RAF fighters. Each RAF pilot did not necessarily see another attacking what he perhaps believed to be his prey. Thus the confusion begins. The Spitfires landed back at Hornchurch at 08.30. The action for the day had only just begun.

Around midday, a force of 50 Dorniers with their escort of approximately 250 fighters, was detected heading for Dover. At 12.08, as part of Fighter Command's response, nine Spitfires of 603 were scrambled and ordered to patrol Chatham. Stapme was flying XT-P, X4274, and five miles east of Sheppey he and his colleagues spotted a force of Me109s with the bombers still further below the fighters. The Spitfires dived to attack. Rusty claimed a Do17 destroyed whilst Hillary and Morton each claimed a 109 destroyed. Uncle George claimed to have damaged a 109. Eight Spitfires landed at Hornchurch at 13.35; Haig followed a short while after and force-landed with undercarriage still retracted due to damage caused by return fire from a Dornier.

With Stapme rested, at 16.04 11 603 Spitfires were ordered into the air to intercept another incoming force of bombers and fighters. Diving to attack, the pilots were soon embroiled in dogfights. At 17.10, Hillary and Stewart-Clark claimed a 109 probable and Brian Carbury claimed a 109 destroyed at 18.00 hours. Jack Stokoe was shot down by Me110 fighters at 17.25. He baled out of his burning aircraft but had been burned about the face and hands. He was admitted to hospital on landing. The remainder of the pilots landed at Hornchurch at 18.20.

At 09.15 on 3 September, in response to a large incoming force of German bombers and fighter escort, eight 603 Spitfires were ordered to patrol over Manston, where, at 22,000 feet, they spotted a small formation of Dorniers and their escort of 24 109s. The pilots dived to attack the fighters and Bill Caister and Peter Pease claimed 109s destroyed at 09.45. Meanwhile, according to the 603 ORB: 'P/O Stapleton took off with 54 Squadron and when south of Harwich, dived on to a Do17 and shot it down.' Despite this record and his own combat report stating he took off on patrol with 54 Squadron, 60 years later Stapme denies that was what happened. He correctly recollects the patrol as the one during which Hillary went down, having taken off as Brian Carbury's No.2, who was leading his section, with Hillary as No.3. He also recalls the tail of his aircraft, R6626, being hit during combat and, with the skies clear again and the other 603 Spitfires returning to base, Brian Carbury escorted him back to Rochford where he landed. In fact, the whole Squadron returned to Rochford where they were refuelled prior to flying the short distance back to Hornchurch. This went unrecorded in the ORB but at that time and out of necessity because of the relentless action the usual level of detail was missing from the diary. Richard Hillary also recalls Stapme's version of events in his book: 'I was flying No.3 in Brian's section, with Stapme Stapleton on the right. The third section consisted of only two machines.' To confuse matters further, the ORB, which is also unreliable, states that Brian Carbury is not listed as having flown that patrol. Stapme's combat report states:

> When patrolling with 54 Squadron, I sighted a formation of 15 Do17's, accompanied by 20 Me110's. The enemy aircraft were flying in line astern and weaving about in 'S' turns. As we had some 8,000 feet on this formation, the squadron went into line astern and attacked the Do17's. I fired at a Do17 which had one

engine stopped. I attacked on the starboard side, stopping the other engine with a deflection burst of four seconds.

Stapme attacked the Dornier 15 miles south-west of Harwich. His report shows that he delivered his attack at 09.45 at an altitude of 20,000 feet. If he *was* late in taking off with the other pilots of 603, and subsequently went on patrol with 54, and evidence in the 603 ORB as well as his own combat report states he did, he would have had to have been very late as 54 took off on their first patrol at 10.15. He shot down his Dornier at 09.45!

On landing at Hornchurch it was discovered that two of their number were missing. Richard Hillary and Dudley Stewart-Clark had both been shot down at 10.04 and 10.08 respectively, by Hauptmann Erich Bode of II/JG26. Hillary had shot at, and hit, a 109 but had risked continued pursuit of his prey when he should have broken off his attack. In doing so, he too was shot down. He managed to escape his burning aircraft but had been badly burned. Stewart-Clark had also baled out of his aircraft and was admitted to hospital with a bullet wound in his leg. Word soon reached the Squadron of Stewart-Clark's predicament but Hillary remained 'missing' for a while longer until news reached them that he was in hospital.* Stapme comments on the patrol:

> I flew No.2 to Brian Carbury and Hillary flew No.3. I have no idea why it was recorded that I flew with 54 Squadron that day, because I didn't. We didn't know he [Hillary] had been shot down. I was very concerned by the fact that my aircraft had been badly hit and was handling very badly. I hadn't seen the enemy aircraft that hit me. All I had experienced was the noise of the sudden clatter of strikes on my aircraft. All you hear is the takka, takka, tak! as the bullets hit your aircraft. I asked Carbury: 'What does my tail look like?' I knew that it had to have been hit by the lack of response from the controls; to which Carbury replied 'It looks like a bloody colander!' I landed at Rochford to find that both my tyres had also been punctured. Hillary's action that day has been well documented but that experience of mine has not been mentioned.

The composite combat report from 11 Group to HQ Fighter Command for this patrol is reproduced here:

```
To: S.A.S.O.
    A.M.L.O.
    P.L.O.
    H.F.L.O.
    D/A.Cdr.
    W/CDR. "I"

To:-   H.Q.F.C.
From:- 11 GROUP INTEL.              IG/242.          3/9/40
```

INITIAL COMBAT REPORT RECEIVED FROM HORNCHURCH:-

(A)   Canterbury area from 0915 hours to 1030 hours.

---

*The story of Hillary's recovery is legendary, thanks to his bestseller *The Last Enemy*. Stewart-Clark made a full recovery and returned to operational flying but was shot down and killed in France on 19 September 1941 as a flight lieutenant with 72 Squadron.

(B)   8 aircraft 603 Squadron left Hornchurch at 0915 hours.
             1 aircraft 603 Squadron left Hornchurch at 0915 hours,
             operating with 54 Squadron.

(C)   7 aircraft returned to Rochford to refuel.
             7 aircraft returned to Hornchurch at 1030 hours.

HORNCHURCH.

(D)   P/O Hillary missing. P/O Stewart Clark wounded.
             2 aircraft Cat.3.

(E)   1 Do.17 and 2 ME.109 destroyed.

T.O.R. 1321 hours. 3/9/40.

Later that day, Stapme claimed a Me109 destroyed and another probable over Biggin Hill. His tactic of getting in close before firing and then recovering lost height was paying off but '. . . getting in close scared the shit out of me!' He later talked about the loss of Richard Hillary:

> We didn't have much to do with Hillary after he had been shot down. Like the other casualties, we missed him, he was a very nice fellow. He couldn't have been a very easy man to get on with after he had been injured. That transformation from being a very good-looking young man with a big ego to a man with such injuries must have been terribly difficult. I don't know how he managed to cope with it. He didn't wear his goggles so the burns occurred from the forehead down to his nose. It is possible that his top lip may have been burnt when he took his oxygen mask off, which would have been as stupid as not wearing goggles, but what is more likely is that the flames that seared his lip were drawn in and fed on the flow of the flammable oxygen that continued to flow to his mask during his attempts to free himself from the inferno of the cockpit. He makes no mention of removing his mask. Nobody warned us of the dangers of the flammability of our oxygen supply in such situations. I was in situations when my aircraft had been hit and the engine was streaming glycol and smoke. I couldn't see a thing looking straight ahead. I was lucky in that my Spitfire never caught fire. But I can appreciate that it would have been like a blow-torch right in your face.

Hillary wasn't the only 603 pilot to be burned. Colin Pinckney, Jim Morton and Jack Stokoe all received minor burns when fire reached the cockpit of their Spitfires after they had been hit.

At 12.45, 12 Spitfires took off from Hornchurch with orders to patrol Gravesend and then Manston. Ken Macdonald and Sarre became separated from the rest and spotted six 109s 4,000 feet below. Diving to attack, Macdonald opened fire on one from astern which promptly rolled over and dived vertically. Sarre also opened fire on another 109 without result. He then force-landed when his engine failed. Meanwhile Bill Caister shot down a 109 off Dunkirk at 10.40.

The One That Didn't Get Away!

At 09.34 hours on 5 September 12 Spitfires of 603 Squadron took off from their forward base at Rochford with Stapme in N3196. At 29,000 feet they spotted 15-20 Dorniers 4,000 feet below with three more lower still, just south of Hornchurch. Stapme engaged two of the fighter escort, possibly of II/JG26, over Biggin Hill at 10.00 hours and managed to hit one. He later reported seeing glycol leaking from the radiator. As he attempted to finish off the 109 he was fired on by another and took evasive action.

Following this combat, Fred 'Rusty' Rushmer failed to return. His Spitfire, X4261, was seen to dive vertically away from the fray by Bill Read sometime between 09.34 and 10.34. Stapme says that Rusty just seemed to disappear. His aircraft dived at terminal velocity into the ground at Buckmans Green Farm. Etched on a wooden beam in a nearby barn is the inscription 'Spitfire 5.9.1940'. Following the crash local land workers rushed to the site and, realising that it had been an RAF fighter, took it upon themselves to undertake the macabre task of collecting the fragmentary remains of what had been Rusty Rushmer and placed them in a sack. A surface clearance team arrived and took charge. Rusty's remains were later interred in the churchyard at All Saints, Staplehurst, but due to so little of the pilot and aircraft being found the authorities were unable to confirm the identity of the pilot. The headstone over Rusty's grave therefore stated 'unknown'. In 1970 an aviation archaeology dig unearthed personal possessions of Rusty, including the half-hunter watch presented to him by his father on his 21st birthday.

The 5th of September has since become a day of mixed emotions for Stapme. The loss of Rusty left its mark and during July 1997 he paid a visit to Rushmer's grave in Staplehurst for the first time. It was an emotional time but he was relieved that he had finally managed to visit the grave of his colleague and utter a few moving words.

Eventually, after a long campaign, the MOD relented and the headstone was changed. Fred Rushmer at last had a known grave and on Sunday 6 September 1998, Stapme and members of the 603 Association (who travelled all the way from Edinburgh) attended a dedication service at All Saints. This was the first occasion on which he had met any of his former ground crew personnel since the war and he undertook many interviews for TV and newspapers that day, recounting his many fond memories of his flight commander. After the Battle of Britain, Rusty was given a posthumous Mention In Despatches for his cool-headed leadership.

Pilot Officer 'Robin' Rafter was also shot down with Rusty that morning on his first patrol with 603. Rusty was the Squadron's only fatality that day.

During the same combat in which Rafter had been shot down, Stapme brought down Messerschmitt Bf109E -4, <-, (1481). The 603 ORB records that Stapme:

> . . . dived to attack bombers but was engaged by 109's. Attacked a lone 109 which force-landed, pilot got out and tried to fire his aircraft by setting light to his jacket but was stopped by the LDV.

The 109 was flown by the now infamous Oberleutnant Franz von Werra of No.2 *Gruppe* – Group – Third Fighter *Geschwader* – Squadron (Stab/II./JG3).

Von Werra*, an arrogant, disingenuous character, added the title of 'Baron' to his name because he liked people to believe he was an aristocrat. He could perhaps be described as somewhere between a 'line shooter' of the worst kind and a compulsive liar; an egoist who would consider any means in order to achieve glory and fame. He later became the only German POW to escape successfully from captivity and complete a 'home run' during WWII when he escaped from a prisoner of war camp in Canada.** On 5 September, II/JG3, Udet, was led by its Kommandeur, Hauptmann Erich von Selle. Immediately behind him, to the left and right were his two staff officers, Leutnant Heinrich Sanneman, technical officer, and von Werra, adjutant. They were on a diversionary fighter sweep over Kent. Five minutes after turning for home over Croydon they were attacked from above by Spitfires of 41 Squadron between Ashford and Maidstone. As the Spitfires dived down the II/JG3 'Guard' yelled over the R/T: 'Achtung! Auchtung! Four to six Tommies above and behind, coming in to attack!' Von Selle called out his instructions: 'Stella Leader to everybody. Keep formation! Wait!' (Stella being the radio call-sign of the Gruppe for the patrol) As he spoke, three of the (41 Squadron) Spitfires dived almost vertically past and in front, through the fighter cover and towards the bomber formation below. Once they were past, von Selle spoke again: 'Stella Leader to Fifth and Sixth Staffeln. Stay put and watch out! Fourth – attack!' As von Selle dived to port, the others followed in turn but as they did so the 109 of von Werra was hit by a burst of gun-fire. Instead of going for the bombers, a section of three Spitfires had used their height advantage to dive out of the sun, attack the German fighters, thus covering their colleagues and catching the 109s by surprise. Nevertheless, it was only three Spitfires attacking a force of 30 109s.

The instant von Werra's aircraft shuddered under the impact of the rounds, he instinctively rolled his aircraft to starboard, the opposite direction to his colleagues, and dived almost vertically to avoid further attack. As he lost height he pulled out of the dive but continued his descent by carrying out spiral defensive turns. Believing he had shaken off the Spitfire he levelled out and glanced behind only to discover he was still being pursued. Von Werra believed he was still under attack from the same Spitfire which had carried out the initial attack at altitude when in fact Stapme had now pounced at low level. Von Werra put his aircraft into another dive, pulling out at low-level. He had run out of height, and proceeded to head for home by following the contours of the countryside.

Stapme sat on the tail of von Werra's 109, firing short bursts. In response the German went into a tight defensive turn, hoping to shake off the fighter by out-turning it and perhaps eventually getting the Spitfire into the Revi gun-site of his own aircraft. However, by now von Werra realised his engine was not running as it should be. He had lost coolant and knew it would soon seize. Frantically trying to keep the Spitfire in view, he carefully opened the throttle hoping to coax more power from the Daimler-Benz engine. The response was poor, the engine sounded sluggish and was labouring. Glancing at his instrument panel, he realised it was overheating.

---

*See Appendix for biography. **His exploits were made famous in the book by James Leasor and Kendal Burt entitled *The One That Got Away* published in 1956. It was subsequently made into a film starring the German actor Hardy Kruger as von Werra.

It spluttered, picked up and spluttered again and the 109 inevitably gradually lost height and Stapme succeeded in forcing it down. Von Werra carried out a wheels-up landing at Love's Farm, Winchet Hill, Marden at 10.10 hours.

It is possible that von Werra's aircraft was initially engaged and damaged by either Flight Lieutenant J.T. Webster or Pilot Officer George 'Ben' Bennions of 41 Squadron which had been sent up from Hornchurch 17 minutes before 603 took off from Rochford. Both squadrons were involved in the engagement over North Kent between 09.50 and 10.10 hours with 603 joining the fray shortly after 41 had bounced the fighter escort. The 41 Squadron ORB records Bennions as having seen the 109 he attacked streaming glycol and: '. . . going down eight miles south of Maidstone', the correct area for Stapme to have latched onto it after Ben had broken off his attack. Webster claimed to have damaged two 109s but did not see them crash, before attacking a third which was seen to invert before crashing near Maidstone. Whilst one of the first two 109s attacked by Webster may have been flown by von Werra, the third clearly did not carry out a controlled landing.

When researching *The One That Got Away*, James Leasor and Kendal Burt soon became aware of von Werra's propensity for embellishment and lying and so relied heavily on official documentation from the period. They also included an eyewitness account of von Werra's arrival in England which provides us with a fascinating flavour of the atmosphere at that time. Just after 10.00 hours on the morning of 5 September, local schoolmaster, Donald Fairman, was pottering in the garden of his cottage at Curtisden Green, in the heart of the Kent orchard and hop-growing country, when he witnessed Stapme shoot down von Werra. The sound of air battle was something Fairman had grown used to during the preceding weeks and the nearby anti-aircraft battery added to the cocophony of sound. Leasor and Burt wrote:

> Suddenly, above the pulsating drone of the engines came the rising howl of diving fighters, followed by bursts of cannon and machine-gun fire. Confused dog-fights developed all over Mr Fairman's personal patch of sky. As the formation passed overhead he saw two fast machines spiralling down, the leading one clearly in trouble. Its engine spluttered and banged, now and again leaving a puff of black smoke behind. When the following aircraft fired a short burst, the other waggled its wings violently. They came lower and lower and then passed out of view behind the trees. A plane suddenly skimmed over the trees round the garden, the engine making a series of bangs. In the split second it was overhead, Mr Fairman clearly saw a black and white cross on the fuselage and a swastika on the fin. As it disappeared he heard a long burst of machine-gun fire, which he identified as coming from a searchlight battery just down the road on Mannington's Farm. A moment later there was a loud bump, followed by a tearing sound, and Mr Fairman knew that the plane had crashed only a few hundred yards away, probably on one of the big fields on the east side of Winchet Hill. He hurried into the house and changed into his Home Guard uniform.
> His car was parked outside the cottage, but petrol was rationed

and scarce. He had a nice sense of values. He slung his rifle over his shoulder and set off on his bicycle. However, by the time he arrived at the scene of the crash, the pilot, Oberleutnant Franz von Werra, who was uninjured, had already been taken prisoner by members of the searchlight battery.

The stories told by von Werra himself of how he was shot down varied widely, and all of them differed from the foregoing account based on official records and the testimony of eye-witnesses. Sometimes he is quoted as claiming to have shot down three British planes that morning (*The Times* 27.1.41) before 'colliding with another Messerschmitt and being forced down' (*New York Herald Tribune*, 25.1.41). To the New York correspondent of the *Daily Express* he claimed to have destroyed only the fighter that attacked him. But he was consistent on some points; he always maintained that his Messerschmitt caught fire when it crashed, and was burned out, he himself being miraculously thrown clear of the wreckage and knocked unconscious.

He also told various tales about the manner of his arrest after crashing, without, apparently, ever remembering the right one. He usually said that members of the Home Guard with old-fashioned shotguns advanced upon him in the field from several directions. Some would creep forward cautiously while others knelt down and drew a bead on him. Then those kneeling down would get up and advance a few paces while the others covered him. Finally, he said, they all rushed at him. The German aviation magazine *Der Adler*, in an article dealing with von Werra's exploits illustrated by 'artist's impressions', shows him being led away from the burning Messerschmitt by two sour-looking Tommies in full battle order, including steel helmets and fixed bayonets.

In fact, the truth about von Werra's crash-landing and capture are in stark contrast to the versions he had passed on during interview. As photographs show, his aircraft was untouched by fire and, according to his biographers and supported by official documents, he was actually detained by: '. . . the hatless, collarless, shirt-sleeved and unarmed cook of the searchlight battery, who dashed out of the cookhouse as soon as the plane crashed and was first on the scene!' They also wrote:

The actual crash was witnessed by several men loading boxes of fruit on to a lorry in the yard of Love's Farm. They had been startled out of their work-day unconcern by a long burst of Lewis-gun fire from the nearby searchlight battery. Then a plane just cleared the trees on Winchet Hill and swooped over the farm buildings in a right-hand turn. It disappeared momentarily behind the orchard a little higher up on the other side of the road, and came into view again just as it was about to land, its wheels retracted, in a field a quarter of a mile away. It bounced off the ground a few feet, then ploughed up the stubble for thirty yards or so before coming to rest in a cloud of dust.

For a few tense seconds nothing happened. Then the hinged

hood of the cockpit opened and the head and shoulders of the pilot appeared. He pulled off his leather helmet and looked around him slowly, then hoisted himself out of the cockpit and jumped off a wing on to the ground.

He stood looking at the aircraft. Meanwhile soldiers coming from the searchlight battery were hurrying across the long fields in ones and twos.

As soon as he noticed the soldiers entering the field, the pilot seemed to pull himself together, and looked quickly in every direction, as though he were about to run away. If that was his idea, he thought the better of it. Instead, he took some papers from the breast pockets of his uniform jacket, replaced something or other [which he clearly didn't want to destroy], then squatted down. The men by the lorry saw a flicker of flame and a wisp of smoke on the ground in front of him. The leading soldier evidently thought the German was trying to set fire to the aircraft, for he shouted and started running. The pilot glanced up and unfolded the papers to make them burn more quickly. They were effectively destroyed.

The first to reach him was the unarmed cook. Hard on his heels came several of his fellow gunners, carrying rifles. Von Werra was thoroughly searched. Everything found in his pockets, together with his identity disc and wrist watch, was placed in his helmet and carried by one of the soldiers. Two men were detailed to guard the aircraft, and the remainder of the party set off across the field in the direction of the searchlight battery. The prisoner walked a few paces ahead, covered by the soldiers' rifles. He walked slowly, with studied nonchalance, one hand in his trouser pocket. No attempt was made to hurry him.

They passed from the field on to a path through an orchard. At the first low bough he came to, the prisoner shot up one hand and grabbed an apple. He took a great bite out of it without a backward glance. The soldiers looked at one another but said nothing. Von Werra was about to reach up at the next low bough, but this time the muzzle of a rifle was jabbed in the small of his back. 'Keep moving!' He moved slowly, munching thoughtfully.

High above, he could hear the Heinkels, Dorniers and Junkers flying home with their Me. escorts. In little more than half an hour the pilots would be pulling off their helmets, lighting cigarettes, and strolling towards the huts and tents on the advanced airfields in the Pas de Calais. While he, Franz von Werra, was being led along a cinder track towards the huts of a British searchlight battery. It was absurd.

The searchlight men were very pleased with themselves for they thought that it was their Lewis gun that had shot down the Messerschmitt [a claim which perpetuated for some time after]. They were even more gratified when they saw the thirteen notches painted below the swastika on the fin of the plane, for they obviously represented victories claimed by the pilot.

There were free rounds in the Woolsack Inn at the top of Winchet Hill that night, and the next issues of local papers gave the searchlight men credit for having brought down 'a leading Nazi fighter ace.' In both respects the papers were quite wrong.

Leasor and Burt also record details of who they believed had shot down von Werra:

> In contrast to von Werra's stories, the combat report of the Spitfire pilot who shot him down was brief and to the point. He simply said he attacked a formation of enemy fighters and fired a good burst from 48 degrees astern into one Messerschmitt, which then rolled over and crashed near Maidstone. He was Flight Lieutenant John Terrence Webster, of No.41 Squadron, based at Hornchurch. He had just been awarded the DFC . . . . After shooting down von Werra on the morning of 5 September, Flight Lieutenant Webster went into action again in the afternoon and was killed.*

Von Werra was initially taken under armed guard by army vehicle to Headquarters, Kent County Constabulary, Maidstone before being interrogated at No.8 Kensington Palace Gardens, the London District POW Cage. Towards the end of September he was eventually sent to POW Camp 1, Grizedale Hall, Lancashire, the only camp in the country at that time for captured German officers. On 7 October von Werra escaped from an exercise party on a route march but was caught six days later and sent to POW (Officer's) Transit Camp 13 at The Hayes near the village of Swanwick, between Alfreton and Ripley, in the Nottingham, Derby area. He managed to tunnel out of that camp and was once again on the run. He attempted to steal a Hurricane at RAF Hucknall, home of 16 SFTS, but was eventually apprehended. He was sent to a POW camp in Canada but escaped from a train and returned to Germany, via the United States and Mexico, a hero with the Nazi propaganda machine making full use of the story. He returned to operational flying but was forbidden to fly over Britain in case he was captured again. On 25 October 1941, he led a patrol away from the airfield at Katwijk and dipped his aircraft over his cottage as a parting wave to his wife. Twenty miles out to sea his engine developed a fault and his aircraft was seen to tip forward (bunt) and dive into the sea like a stone. Only days earlier General Ernst Udet had killed himself (von Werra's unit had been named after the WWI ace and national hero) and Colonel Werner Mölders, the brilliant Luftwaffe fighter ace and leader, was reported killed in an accident, so news of von Werra's death was kept from the press for a month. Perhaps the announcement of the death of a third ace and national figure was too severe a blow for German morale. When they did announce his death they stated that von Werra had met an end befitting a hero, in action while leading his *Gruppe* in repeated attacks against the Russians. Later, in total contrast, the Court of Enquiry set up by the German Air Safety Branch to investigate the loss of von Werra's aircraft ruled that the accident was as a result of engine failure and the pilot's carelessness.

---

*Webster was killed when, at 15.25 hours during combat over the Thames Estuary with Do17s and 109s, his Spitfire collided with that of Squadron Leader H.R.L. 'Robin' Hood, also of 41 Squadron. Webster managed to bale out but fell dead, while Hood was posted 'missing'.

The 603 ORB for 5 September 1940 records the patrol in which von Werra was shot down as being between 09.34 and 10.34 hours and: 'P/O Stapleton 1 ME.109 Destroyed [von Werra] and 1 ME.109 Probable (Emitting white smoke and ME109 broke away waggling its wings). P/O Morton 1 ME.109 Damaged. F/Lt Rushmer – Missing. P/O Rafter – Missing.' In his combat report Stapme wrote:

> I was diving to attack them (the bombers) when I was engaged by two Me109's [the 'Rotte', the typical Luftwaffe tactical formation consisting of leader and wingman]. When I fired at the first one I noticed glycol coming from his radiator. I did a No.2 attack and as I fired I was hit by bullets from another Me109. I broke off downwards and continued my dive. At 6,000 feet I saw a single-engined machine diving vertically with no tail unit. I looked up and saw a parachutist coming down circled by an Me109. I attacked him (the Me109) from the low quarter, he dived vertically towards the ground and flattened out at ground level. I then did a series of beam attacks from both sides, and the enemy aircraft turned into my attacks. He finally forced-landed. He tried to set his radio on fire by taking off his jacket and setting fire to it and putting it into the cockpit. He was prevented by the LDV.

Stapme's view of von Werra's antics in trying to destroy certain items from his pockets was from the cockpit of his Spitfire as he flew over the site and was therefore brief and limited. He was also reliant on limited intelligence passed to him once he was back at Hornchurch. Hence the confusion.

In his combat report Stapme doesn't mention any flying characteristics which would indicate that the aircraft had been damaged, or whether it had been streaming glycol when he attacked it.

The parachutist being circled by the 109 was Robin Rafter of 603 Squadron. Rumours of the Germans murdering pilots as they hung defenceless in their parachute harnesses existed at that time. Stapme believes it is possible that he attacked the same 109 which Bennions or Webster had engaged earlier even though it was no longer streaming glycol. He reflects on his pursuit of the German fighter:

> I noticed that its airspeed had dropped dramatically and I pressed home an attack, followed by another before allowing the pilot to carry out a forced landing. I remember seeing my tracer strike the 109 and was concerned that I was flying at low-level, with a village in my apparent line of fire.
>
> Contrary to the myth that has developed over the years, I have no doubt that the pilot was making no attempt to open fire on Rafter as he hung seriously injured (as I later discovered) in his parachute harness. He was merely concentrating on self-preservation and happened to be circling in the vicinity of Rafter. The 109 was clearly disabled with the pilot looking to evade further attack and get his aircraft down. Why risk murdering the parachutist knowing that his aircraft was damaged and a forced landing, on enemy territory, was imminent?

It is entirely possible that whilst von Werra had the opportunity to open fire on Rafter, he may have had no intention of doing so and was simply too preoccupied with his own plight to even consider shooting at Rafter before Stapme attacked. In a letter to his mother, Rafter confirms that von Werra *had* been in a position to open fire before being driven off by a Spitfire.

Initially, on landing, Stapme had thought the pilot was waving his jacket in salute to his victorious attacker and so he waggled his wings in response. Later, as reports came in, he believed the wave was a deception by von Werra who had actually been in the process of setting light to certain papers in his pockets. Stapme was not aware of the full facts before writing his combat report, and later was very interested to learn the identity of who he had shot down:

> It was sometime between the end of the war and when I moved to South Africa that I was told the name of the pilot I had shot down on 5 September. Later, when the film came out, I learned of his reputation as 'the one that got away'. I was in South Africa when it came out and didn't see it until many years later, but I knew of its significance.

The Composite Combat Report issued by 11 Group Intelligence to Headquarters Fighter Command, confirming Stapme's success, reads:

> S.A.S.O.
> A.M.L.O.
> P.L.O.
> H.F.L.O.
> D. A. Cdr.
> W/CDR. "I".
>
> H.Q.F.C. INTEL.
> From:- 11 Group, Intel.
>
> COMPOSITE COMBAT REPORT 603 SQUADRON – RECEIVED FROM HORNCHURCH.
>
> 12 Spitfires 603 Squadron left Rochford at 09.32 hours. Whilst at 29,000 feet between Canterbury and Maidstone they sighted 15/20 Do.215 in tight vic formation with three stragglers below and behind at 19-21,000 feet. Several Squadrons of ME.109 and at least one Squadron of HE.113 were stepped up to 25,000 feet and weaving about the bombers. Our fighters dived down on the formation, some engaging the bombers and some the fighters. Although six bombers were engaged no results were observed as the enemy escort fighters attacked. One ME.109 shot down by 603 Squadron was seen to force land in a field south of the Ashfield (sic) Redhill Railway line. Enemy pilot was setting fire to this aircraft when a LDV was seen to approach. Another ME.109 not claimed by 603 Squadron was seen smoking on top of a haystack.
>
> Enemy Casualties:- 1 ME.109 destroyed (Force landed south of Ashfield/Redhill Railway line).
>
> 1 ME.109 probable (Spiral dive with glycol smoke).
> 1 ME.109 damaged (pieces off).

Own Casualties:- F/Lt. Rushmer and P/O Rafter and 2 a/c. missing.
F/Lt. Rushmer seen to bale out but no news yet received.
Further aircraft Cat 1.
Ten aircraft landed Rochford 1034 hours.

R. 1538.   5.9.40

Note the reference to the 109 'smoking on top of a haystack'! The 603 pilots had yet to learn of the fate of Robin Rafter and Fred Rushmer. The parachutist seen to bale out was actually Rafter and not Rushmer.

The Spitfire Stapme saw 'diving vertically with no tail unit' was that of Robin Rafter (X4264) which had probably been shot down by 109s of II/JG26 over Marden. He was wounded in the leg during the combat but, more seriously, had received severe head injuries when, as his aircraft plunged tailless and out of control, he had been thrown with terrific force through the canopy. He was hospitalised and out of action until November. He subsequently recorded his experiences from 5 September in a letter home to his mother:

> I very nearly shot a Spitfire down by mistake, but then saw on my starboard side, underneath me, an Me109. I got all fixed and started my dive on to the 109 and was nearing it when I saw in my rear view mirror a couple of 109s on my tail. I took what evasive action I could, but found two a bit of a problem. I started to get away from them when my tail must have been damaged and all movement on the control column was to no avail, thus putting my machine out of control so far as I was concerned. Well, by this time I had a little piece of shrapnel in my leg, and probably owe my life to the fact that my machine was out of control as the Jerries evidently found difficulty in getting their sights on me as my machine was going all over the place. Luckily I was very high up and it then occurred to me to bale out. My oxygen tube had already became detached, but I had great difficulty in undoing the pin of my harness to loosen myself out of my seat. I eventually got the pin out, but could not get out of the aircraft. By this time the Jerries had ceased firing at me but I had no idea where I was over. The next part of my experience was rather a miracle. The machine's nose dropped violently thus having the effect of throwing me forward, the force so great that I went through the canopy thus injuring my head. You can't imagine my surprise. I was then at about 15,000 feet and floating about in the air rather like a cork. You will understand why when I explain that instead of diving at 400 mph, I had rapidly slowed down to about 180 mph, as the human body never falls faster, that being the 'terminal velocity' [actually 120 mph].' I then felt so light that I had to look and ensure that I was wearing a parachute. Luckily I had given it a slight inspection that morning. I pulled the cord and the chute opened up and I breathed once more. Then the most terrifying experience happened. I floated right down through the aerial battle that was taking place. I came through it without a scratch, but noticed a 109 coming towards me, and you've no idea what a

damned fool you feel suspended in mid-air with an enemy fighter buzzing around you. Well, he never fired at me as a Spitfire came and drove him off. Whether he would have done cannot be said.

Although Rafter's mother will have been relieved when she was eventually informed her youngest son was injured but safe, it was hardly a letter to comfort an extremely anxious mind.

On 6 September, following the patrol of 12.45-14.02, the Squadron lost Pilot Officer Bill Caister, who was shot down in combat over the Channel and carried out a wheels-up landing near Guines, France. He was captured and remained in German captivity for the remainder of the war. Eager to return to the fray, mid-way through his honeymoon, he had only been married for a week. Stapme flew Spitfire N3196 and the only claim by 603 was for a 109 'probable' by Ken Macdonald.

The stress and strain of battle flying quickly took its toll on the 603 pilots. Being bounced by enemy fighters was an ever-present danger and many more pilots had been lost as a consequence of attacks from altitude, out of the sun, as opposed to being shot down in dogfights. Tactically, the Germans were more likely to avoid dogfights. Stapme has particularly clear memories of one incident which occurred during the battle:

> Boulter and I were riding together in a section of two during an 11 ship patrol when suddenly green tracer began to appear silently between my aircraft and that of Boulter, who was on my port side, and drop away into the distance. In an instant we instinctively broke away in opposite directions, me to starboard, Boulter to port – and dived steeply away to avoid being hit. I recall spent green tracer dropping away in front of my aircraft as I dived. I have retained a clear picture in my mind of the oil-streaked underside of Boulter's Spitfire as he broke, a split-second before I did the same.

The experience of Boulter, by that time a flight lieutenant, and Stapme, saved them but even battle-hardened pilots were vulnerable, particularly when tired. Tiredness was a killer in itself simply because the fighter pilot could not afford a momentary lack of concentration. The British air defences were being pushed to the limit and whilst demands for replacement aircraft were being met, thanks to Lord Beaverbrook and the many people working in the aircraft industry, replacement pilots were another matter. Churchill later commented:

> This period (24 August – 6 September) seriously drained the strength of Fighter Command as a whole. The Command lost in this fortnight 103 pilots killed and 128 seriously wounded, while 466 Spitfires and Hurricanes had been destroyed or seriously damaged. Out of a total pilot strength of about 1,000, nearly a quarter had been lost. Their planes could only be filled by 260 new, ardent but inexperienced pilots drawn from training units, in many cases before their full courses were complete.

Bullets, Tea and Beer!
On Saturday 7 September the Luftwaffe made a significant change in tactics. Instead of targeting the RAF, with its destruction a vital prelude to invasion, and believing Fighter Command to be on its last legs, the Luftwaffe began full-scale attacks on London. The plan was to draw up the RAF fighters in large numbers to defend the capital, where the German fighters would be waiting to finish them off (the belief also existed that by bombing London, the threat to civilians may yet force capitulation). The RAF was in fact far stronger than the Luftwaffe aircrews were led to believe, resulting in a shattering effect on their morale when they were confronted by a still formidable foe. On the basis of information that had filtered back to Fighter Command HQ a timely change of tactics was implemented. The RAF fighter pilots were authorised to fly in pairs, with the 'wingman' protecting the tail of his leader who would carry out the attack. This was the tried and tested method adopted by the Legion Condor during the Spanish Civil War.

The morning of 7 September dawned fine at Hornchurch. It remained unusually quiet before the first contacts appeared on the screens at the Dover and Pevensey RDF stations at 11.55 when a force of Me109s kept at a tantalising distance just off the English coastline in an attempt to provoke Fighter Command into sending up fighters before the main force of bombers and fighters arrived. Any RAF fighters sent up specifically to intercept risked being caught on the ground refuelling as the armada made its way towards its intended targets. 66 Squadron were already on patrol and given orders to intercept the 109s.

At 15.40 the radar stations at Foreness, Dover and Rye confirmed the approach of a significant force of what was approximately 300 Heinkel 111s and Dornier Do17s and 600 fighters. At 16.20 the squadrons responsible for providing protection of the capital – 1, 303, 501 and 504 – were sent up. As in previous raids the German formation caused consternation at Fighter Command HQ, when it split into separate groups and did not appear to be approaching the assumed targets of the RAF airfields of 11 and 12 Groups. In fact they were going for strategic targets in London itself as part of the continuing prelude to invasion.* The Blitz now began in earnest.

Fighter Command sent up 23 squadrons to repel the incoming raid which was by then spread over 800 square miles of sky. Against such an overwhelming force the RAF fighters did their very best to get to the bombers and hinder their progress against vastly superior numbers of escorting German fighters, and 603 Squadron had a successful day.

At 16.44 hours, 12 603 Spitfires left Hornchurch with instructions to patrol the airspace above their own airfield and intercept an incoming force of German bombers with fighter escort. Former Army Co-operation pilot, Pilot Officer Brian Macnamara, claimed a He111 destroyed which was later

---

*This change of tactics was confusing to Fighter Command. If an invasion of Britain was to be successful, the significant military establishments, including the airfields of 11 and 12 Group, the RDF installations – the early warning system – and the aircraft factories, had to be put out of action. They were in fact still operating normally. Even the German Naval Staff failed to understand the change in tactics. The lack of activity by day also added to the confusion when the Luftwaffe bomber forces waited for nightfall before returning to bomb London.

confirmed and Brian Carbury destroyed two Me109s and claimed another probable. At that time the 603 pilots, like many others in Fighter Command, mistook what were actually 109s for the He113, the existence of the 113 being a fairly successful deception by the Luftwaffe as such an aircraft did not exist. Carbury's claims, therefore, were all 109s. Black Morton claimed one 109 damaged and one probable. Joey Sarre continued to suffer when he was shot down; his slight injuries required hospital treatment. Uncle George and Peter Pease both had to carry out forced-landings after their aircraft were hit in combat.

Memories of 7 September remain vivid in Stapme's mind, even after 60 years. His Spitfire, N3196, code XT-L, was hit when the Squadron was bounced yet again and he eventually made a forced-landing at Sutton Valence. He was unhurt.* Stapme's aircraft had been badly damaged by cannon and machine-gun fire and soon after being hit he discovered he no longer had aileron and flap control. The radiator had also been punctured. Watching all the time for the threat of further attack, he steered his aircraft back over the Channel towards the English coast. With careful use of the throttle he eventually made landfall and looked for a convenient place to crash-land but held off putting the Spitfire down until loss of forward speed and altitude enabled him to carry out a successful wheels-up landing. Visibility from his cockpit had been practically zero as the coolant (glycol) tank and/or the hoses had also been damaged:

> I didn't see or hear anything apart from the loud and shocking takatakatak! as the bullets and cannon shell hit my aircraft. The first thing I did was open the hood. Glycol came whipping into the cockpit. My aileron cables had been severed by a cannon shell and I could only fly straight and level. When I came to my senses, I found my hands undoing my straps. I regained my composure, re-fastened them and headed inland. I glided, using intermittent bursts of the engine, for about twenty miles. I had the radiator flaps fully open to delay overheating for as long as possible. When I used the engine, the glycol vapour seriously inhibited my forward visibility.

Having successful belly-landed his aircraft in a hop garden at Forsham Farm, Sutton Valence, without injury to himself, he climbed out, partially closed the canopy, stepped off the wing, walked round his Spitfire surveying the battle damage and removed his flying helmet, goggles and oxygen mask as he went. One cannon shell had exploded between the two central machine guns in the starboard wing, completely flattening the two guns. The .303 ammunition belts hung from the gaping holes in the aircraft's damaged wing surfaces. Stapme glanced up to see an RAF pilot descending by parachute. He landed in an orchard close-by. He met up with him and discovered he was from a Hurricane squadron. The pilot was Sergeant Alan Deller of 43 Squadron. Having destroyed a Me109 he himself was shot down following combat over Ashford.

---

*It is likely that Uncle George, Peter Pease and Stapme were shot down by Oberleutnant Heinz Ebeling or Hauptmann Joachim Müncheberg. Ebeling was the commanding officer of the 9th Staffel and Muncheberg the commanding officer of the 7th Staffel of JG26. Between them they had amassed 35 'kills'.

He baled out and his aircraft, V7309, crashed and burnt out at Babylon Farm, Sutton Valence. Deller had delayed opening his parachute until he was clear of the combat area. He had heard the rumours of enemy fighters opening fire on British and Allied pilots as they hung in their parachute harnesses and he wasn't taking any chances. As he neared the ground he pulled on one or other of the risers, as he had been told to do, in an attempt to steer clear of the trees of an orchard which lurked menacingly below. All he succeeded in doing was inadvertently spilling some of the air from the canopy which promptly increased his rate of descent and he crashed through the branches of the trees at a far greater speed than if he had simply done nothing. He damaged his back in the heavy landing, an injury which caused him problems for the rest of his life. Although the time recorded for Deller's combat was 15.30 hours, this has to be wrong as he was the only pilot and aircraft to come down in this area on this day apart from Stapme.

Earlier, a couple had been driving by in their car, a four-cylinder Austin Ruby saloon, looking for a good spot for a picnic. They pulled up at a suitable access point to a field at Forsham Farm and laid out their meal on a table cloth. As they relaxed, watching the action overhead, they witnessed Stapme's landing. Both Stapme and Deller now made their way towards the picnickers and the gate out of the field. Stapme recalled: 'All that was going on above them – dogfights and rat-a-tat-tat – and there they were having a picnic!' As they approached, the couple invited the two pilots to join them for a cup of tea, after which Stapme asked if they would drive him and his companion to the nearest pub, which they did. The pilots huddled on the back seat, one clutching his unopened parachute, the other a hastily rolled up bundle of silk, along with their other sundry flying equipment. A few moments after leaving the crash site sixteen-year-old George Underdown, who had seen the disabled Spitfire as it flew low over his home at Spring Cottages, dashed into the field at Forsham Farm hoping to catch a glimpse of the pilot, but he was just too late. Disappointed, it would be 57 years before he finally met the 'gallant fighter ace' of the Spitfire marked 'XT-L'.

After a number of pints at the pub (the King's Head at Sutton Valence), Stapme telephoned his brother Deryck who was then working at the Air Ministry. He asked him if he would arrange a suitably impressive car to drive to Kent to pick them up and return to Hornchurch. His brother duly obliged and sent a large camouflaged 'limo' in the form of a Humber Super Snipe station wagon, which was apparently a familiar sight in the RAF at that time. Being chauffeur-driven through the gates at Hornchurch in such a vehicle gave Stapme a great deal of amusement. The onlookers believed there was someone of far greater standing in the back than a 20-year-old pilot officer.

In 1996, Stapme returned to Kent and the scenes of his experiences in the summer of 1940. During a lunchtime session in the King's Head, he retold his adventures to a number of fascinated locals. However, the story truly came full-circle in 1997, when Stapme returned for a second time. George Underdown had been tracked down and finally met his hero in the field where XT-L, N3196 had crashed, 57 years ago to the day. A Spitfire flypast was laid on following which there was a surprise appearance by the Duxford-based B17 Flying Fortress, the Sally B. The crew had been contacted and informed of the occasion and kindly added an impromptu flypast as part of the day's display programme at the Biggin Hill air show. Even more recent was the discovery that a local lad, worried that he might be committing a grave offence, surreptitiously photographed Stapme's Spitfire from a field adjacent to that in which it stood at Forsham Farm, after Stapme and Alan Deller had cadged a lift to the King's Head.

Following the combat on 7 September Black Morton wrote in his diary:

> At 15,000' saw large Balbo approaching from SE with much AA all round it. V. [Very] powerful escort of 109 and 110. Squadron attempted a beam attack on the bombers; but we were in a poor position, being slightly below if anything, and had to wrangle to protect ourselves from the escort.
>
> . . . Five of us managed to join up over base at about 21,000'. Ken leading, Pease, Stapme and I think Brown ['Brown Job' – Boulter] and Tannoy [Read] though I'm not sure of them. Stapme was doing guard above. The rest of us were in vic climbing hard to get above a Balbo coming in from the same direction as the first one at about 21,000'. I suddenly saw a 109 sitting about 30 degrees behind Pease shooting like anything for a moment, meanwhile he half-rolled and pushed off. Pease was streaming glycol and went down in a gentle turn. He force-landed on the aerodrome OK. Stapme didn't see the Hun till too late . . . .
>
> When I landed, there was Pease and his A/C still strong. George with a hole in his port wing you could stand up and turn round in . . . Stapme force-landed. Sarre missing (he turned up later).

The following day Black Morton added the poignant line: 'There are now too many battles and I am too tired to write accounts of them all.'

Having been shot down, Stapme didn't ponder on his fortuitous escape of 7th September, and what might have been, unlike some. He also recalls never feeling tired, unlike some others. By the 11th he was once again in action and yet another brush with death had no lasting effect. For many, the experience of being shot down was terrifying and left the individual traumatised and unable to continue as combat pilots to any great effect. In those days the only way to get over such an experience seemed to be by flying again as soon as possible and carrying on with the job. While the fighter pilots were aware they could be shot down, some never really believed it could happen to them. The surprise and shock of it happening caused great anxiety because subconsciously they had realised for the first time that they could lose their life. Consequently, each time a pilot recalled a near-miss or is reminded of it, he is unnerved, perhaps to the point where he believed he had lost his nerve and could no longer carry out the duty of a fighter pilot. The choice was to give up or return and take on what was a very personal and lonely fight. Psychiatric help was not an option in those days and recovery was in the hands of the individual. Some perceived themselves as cowards but they were no longer boys playing with fast cars and aeroplanes but grown men who had suddenly realised their particular dream involved risking death. Physically, the men were in fine health with a natural love of life. However, with their mind in a state of upheaval, with its physical manifestations, they would be unlikely to pass a pilot's medical examination due to their mental state. Once they took to the skies again they would inevitably suffer an attack of nerves, possibly as bad if not greater than before, but having proved to themselves they could still do the job, confidence and a return of control may have been forthcoming. Stapme escaped a number of near misses. On one occasion a German 7.92mm bullet punched through one side of his canopy and out the other, narrowly missing his head. Stapme experienced nothing more than relief that he hadn't been hit. Others were not so lucky and suffered debilitating breakdowns, elements of which remained for the rest of their lives.

On 9 September the Squadron was again in action when some 200 bombers targeted London. Harried all the way by fighters from 11 and 12 Groups, in the face of such stern opposition many were forced to ditch their bomb-loads in the suburbs of the capital before turning for home. 28 failed to return. Stapme didn't fly on the 9th. He recalls a number of occasions when, with time off, he and his colleagues drove into London for what usually turned out to be drinking sessions:

> On one occasion there were three of us driving into town in my car which I bought from Max Aitken for £12 [Flight Lieutenant J.W. Max Aitken DFC, CO of No.601 Squadron. Later, Group Captain J.W.M. Aitken DFC, DSO, MC (Czech), AE]. An air raid started and we came upon a building which had just been hit and was on fire. I stopped the car and we all leapt out to help out as best we could.
>
> Usually, if we drank into the early hours we stayed at the accommodation in Jermyn Street (Turkish baths); it was cheap. We could also acquire cheap booze from a place called Hoey's Wine Club. Elsewhere it was expensive. We then dashed back to Hornchurch for the morning action.

The weather on 10 September was overcast with heavy rain foiling the Luftwaffe attempts to continue its bombing operations over Britain.* Hitler was forced to review his plans to invade, postponing making a decision on the invasion until 14 September. In reality, if the Germans were planning to invade, conditions were hardly suitable. Air superiority had not been achieved because, as was so obvious to the German bomber crews, Fighter Command had not been defeated.

Air Vice-Marshal Keith Park assessed the change in tactics by the Luftwaffe – from two or three separate large bombing raids, to two waves in quick succession approximately 15 minutes apart, with a total force of 3-400 aircraft – and ordered his controllers not to send up too many squadrons to engage the initial wave but to hold others ready to send up to intercept the second wave which usually proved to be the larger of the two. As usual the Spitfire squadrons were directed to intercept the fighters whilst the Hurricanes attempted to attack the bombers. On 11 September, the heavy cloud of the previous day disappeared

---

*Contrary to popular belief the summer of 1940 did not consist of endless fine weather and clear blue skies. Had that been the case the outcome of the Battle of Britain may have been different When the weather conditions were unsuitable for flying, little or no combat took place, with minimum risk to the pilots. Meanwhile, aircraft production continued apace.

overnight and the morning light revealed fine weather in most areas. It was ominously quiet, as had been the case for the previous four days but at 14.45 the RDF stations along the south-east coast detected a build-up of enemy formations from Calais to Ostende. Details were passed to 11 Group HQ and various units were subsequently brought to readiness, including elements of the Duxford Wing.

At 15.15 hours, two large formations of approximately 300 aircraft crossed the Channel, made landfall between Deal and Foreness and headed inland. As the bomber force approached the Thames estuary they turned towards London and as they did so, the leading bombers were intercepted by fighters of 12 Group. A number of dogfights broke out at high altitude, between Herne Bay and Shoeburyness, and Gravesend and Tilbury.

At 15.16 hours, 12 aircraft of 603 Squadron took off from Rochford with Stapme in X4348. They climbed to an altitude of 28,000 feet over Hornchurch where they joined forces with 41 Squadron. Instructed to patrol Maidstone, they sighted a large formation at 20,000 feet, just south of London heading north, consisting of He111s and Me109s, just above the main formation. 41 Squadron dived to attack with the fighters of 603 following behind in line astern. Interestingly, the escort of 109s did not come down from their superior altitude to protect the bombers although the Spitfires were engaged by the close escort of 110s.* Stapme claimed a Me110 probable and a Me109 damaged over south London. The ORB reads: 'P/O Stapleton 1 ME.110 Probable (both engines dead).' He also recorded:

> When patrolling with the squadron I saw a large 'Balbo' of enemy aircraft approaching from the east. At that moment my oxygen gave out and I dived to 18,000 feet. Then I sighted a Me110 at 20,000 feet heading south-west.
>
> I did two beam attacks and damaged both engines. By this time I was over the coast at 15,000 feet. Glycol was streaming from both engines of the e/a but he was not losing much speed.
>
> After that engagement I came down to 4,000 feet over Dungeness. I sighted a Me109 at 2,000 feet heading for France. When he saw me he dived to 100 feet approximately and continued on a steady course. I caught up after five minutes of flying and gave it two long bursts from dead astern at 250 yards. Glycol issued from his radiator. By this time I could see the coast of France quite plainly, so I turned back.

Stapme noted the time of his attack as being 16.25 hours, initially south of London at an altitude of 20,000 feet. The Balbo consisted of 100 Me109s, 110s and He111s. He reflected:

> Closing to a range of 50 yards was not a problem if the enemy aircraft was a fighter, but closing to within 50 yards of a bomber was daunting. The enemy aircraft seemed massive. If you opened

---

*Newly arrived from an Army Co-operation squadron, Jim MacPhail claimed a He111 destroyed which was seen to crash. Brian Carbury DFC, claimed another Heinkel probable which was observed with the starboard engine dead and undercarriage down, Ras Berry and Tannoy Read each claimed a Me110 damaged and Bolster Boulter, Brian Macnamara and Pip Cardell each claimed a He111 damaged.

fire and hit the bomber there was the risk of damage to your own aircraft from the large amount of debris that flew back at you. Conversely, when we carried out head-on attacks, debris didn't pose a problem but it was vital you judged correctly the speed you approached the enemy bomber. With a closing speed in excess of 550 mph there was the very real risk of flying straight into the enemy aircraft.*

The weather deteriorated on 12 and 13 September which brought about a reduction in enemy activity and, importantly, a much needed break for the British defences from the regular large-scale raids. During daylight hours the Luftwaffe continued to carry out reconnaissance missions and nuisance raids employing single aircraft.

On 14 September a number of small-scale raids took place during the afternoon, consisting of Do17s, He111s and Ju88s escorted by Me109Es. They crossed the Kent coast between Deal and Folkestone, and also flew eastwards along the Thames estuary.

At 15.20 hours, 12 Spitfires of 603 Squadron took off with Stapme flying X4348, and joined 222 Squadron, their stablemates at Hornchurch, over Rochford. At 24,000 feet south of Hornchurch they spotted a large number of Me109s at superior altitude but although they went into line astern they did not dive down on the RAF fighters. With the 603 pilots believing they would be bounced and unsure as to what tactics to adopt, they later reported that they formed defensive circles and climbed towards the enemy. As they neared the German fighter formation, occasionally Spitfires broke away to attack individual 109s. Carbury, Macnamara and Boulter each claimed a 109 destroyed.

Losses inflicted on Fighter Command on this day were greater than those of the Luftwaffe; one of the rare occasions that this occurred.

The 15 September is now celebrated as Battle of Britain Day. On that day in 1940, the Luftwaffe were confronted by over 250 aircraft, tenaciously flown by the pilots of Fighter Command. The 11 Group Intelligence Bulletin summarised the day's events:

> The first major attack of the day, during the period 11.00-12.35, crossed the coast between Dungeness and North Foreland and headed for London. The attack split into two parts, one going for the Thames Dock area, the other for West London. Observer Corps reports suggested that bombers formed a high proportion of the enemy raids. About 120 E/A were employed. To meet this attack the following squadrons were detailed to intercept raids:- 72, 92, 501, 253, 222, 603, 229, 303, 257, 504, 46, 249, 66, 41, 605,1 (Canadian) and all these engaged in combat except 222 Squadron. In addition 73 Squadron intercepted an enemy raid. During the period 14.00-

---

*Flight Lieutenant Gerald Edge (later Group Captain G. Edge OBE, DFC) flew with 605 and 253 during the Battle of Britain and recalled head-on attacks: 'If you left it until your last hundred yards to break away from a head-on attack, you were in trouble. With practice, you got to judge when to break. But once you knew how, a head-on attack was a piece of cake. When you opened fire, you'd kill or badly wound the pilot and the second pilot. Then you'd rake the line of them as you broke away. There was a lot of crashing among the bombers when we attacked head-on.'

15.30 hours a second large attack developed involving 230-250 E/A. The raids crossed the coast between Hastings and Dover and the I.A.Z. To meet this attack the following squadrons were detailed to intercept the raids:- 73, 603, 222, 501, 605, 72, 66, 92, 41, 253, 46, 1 (Canadian), 303, 229, 17, 257, 213, 249, 504 and 607. All these squadrons intercepted, and in addition 602 Squadron and one A/C of Station Defence Flight, Northolt intercepted enemy raiders.

Between 17.45 and 18.30 hours a tip and run raid on Southampton was made by 30-40 E/A. No.607 Squadron were detailed to intercept a raid and were successful in doing so.

An outstanding feature of the results of air combats today is that the destroyed enemy bombers are in a proportion of two to one to the destroyed enemy fighters.

603 Squadron was scrambled at 11.20 with Stapme flying X4348. Uncle George, Jim MacPhail and Ras Berry each claimed 109s destroyed and Tannoy Read damaged a Dornier Do17.

At 13.00 hours the RDF stations once again began to detect the movement of another raid. Half an hour later confirmation of a huge build-up of aircraft came and Air Vice-Marshal Keith Park placed the fighter squadrons of 11 and 12 Group at readiness. The second wave of German bombers with their fighter escort formed-up and were over the Channel heading towards England in less time than the first, giving Park less time to get his aircraft airborne and appropriately positioned whilst other squadrons were on the ground being refuelled and re-armed after the first interception.

At 14.14, 13 603 Spitfires were scrambled again and ordered to join 222 Squadron but did not see them. 10 miles east of Chatham they made contact with the enemy. The Composite Patrol Report from 11 Group Intelligence to HQ Fighter Command reads:

603 Squadron. 15/9/40 1415-1530 hours.

. . . sighted about 200 Me110's and Me109's at 21,000 feet. Underneath there were about 15-20 He111's in vics of 3 at 20,000 feet. One pilot saw two formations of about 20 Do17's without escort, and states that the leader of the second formation had white under surfaces and white on the fuselage. It was also noticed that one He111 had three red or orange bars on the upper wing surface in addition to the black crosses.

603 was one of the first squadrons to intercept the raid. Sergeant George Bailey, recently arrived from 234 Squadron at Leconfield, destroyed a 109 which crashed south of Sheerness. Pilot Officer Keith Lawrence had also come from 234 Squadron with Bailey, both filling 'dead men's shoes'. Lawrence destroyed a 109 over Maidstone and claimed two more damaged. Ras claimed a Do17 destroyed (with 222 Squadron) and a 109 probable and Brian Macnamara claimed a Do17 damaged which was seen with black smoke coming from the starboard engine and the 'starboard rudder shot about.' Uncle George damaged two Do17s which he pounced on as they lagged behind the rest of the formation. During his attack his own aircraft was hit by return fire which shattered his instrument panel. Flames began to appear in the leg-well and he was forced to bale out. He had a fortunate escape.

Stapme destroyed Dornier Do17Z (3405), U5+FT, of 9/KG2 which crashed into the sea five miles north-east of Herne Bay at 15.15 hours. The aircraft had been on a sortie to bomb St. Katherines Docks in London when it was attacked by Pilot Officer Pattullo (46 Squadron) and Stapme. During his attack its starboard engine had been severely damaged and the crew ditched their bomb load before crashing into the sea. The pilot, Obergefreiter Karl-Oskar Staib and wireless operator, Unteroffizier Hans Hoppe, baled out of the stricken Dornier but were killed. The body of Hoppe was washed ashore on the Isle of Sheppey three days later and the body of Staib came up on 30 September at Graveney marshes. The other crew members, Gefreiters A. Hoffmann and J. Zierer, were rescued from the sea by the Royal Navy. Stapme was flying Spitfire X4348 and later reported:

> When patrolling with my squadron, I sighted 25 He111's and 50 Me109's. While diving to attack, I found myself going too fast to pull out on the enemy, so I continued my dive. About ten minutes later, I sighted two Me109's in light vic. I fired two deflection bursts at one and glycol streams came from his radiator. They dived into the cloud. Later I saw one Do17 over the Thames estuary heading for the clouds. I did several beam attacks and he dived to 100 feet. He flew very low indeed and pancaked on the sea five miles NW of Ramsgate. I experienced no return fire.

Stapme recorded the time of the attack as 14.50 hours, ten miles south of Chatham at an altitude of 20,000 feet. During the engagement he fired 2,800 rounds. He also claimed to have damaged a Me109 (streaming glycol) over the Channel five miles north-east of Ramsgate. On his return to base he noticed another Do17 that had 'pancaked' on the sea in the Thames estuary. The crew were in the process of escaping from their aircraft before it sank. Stapme saw a British convoy about five miles away, entering the estuary, and attempted to gain their attention to make them aware of the plight of the German airmen. As he got closer the convoy opened fire on him, to which he responded by returning to base, taking the matter no further!

Sadly, Flying Officer Peter Pease was killed on this patrol when he was shot down by Me109s as he attacked a formation of Heinkels. His flaming Spitfire was seen to dive vertically from altitude and eventually crashed at Kingwood, near Chartway at 15.07. Peter had seen a great deal of fighting since moving down from Turnhouse. The effect of his death on friend and colleague Richard Hillary was profound.

By the end of the day the pilots of 603 had accounted for five Me109s destroyed, one probable and two damaged, and two Dornier Do17s destroyed with three more damaged. They had lost one pilot and two Spitfires. The German losses for the day were substantial (although not nearly as high as claimed at the time). However, the effect on the morale of the Luftwaffe aircrews was significant. Despite all the losses the German propaganda machine stated had been inflicted, in addition to the damage to Fighter Command airfields, the RAF was *still* a force to be reckoned with.

The 'Big Wing' was called to assist 11 Group on two occasions on 15 September. The Wing consisted of 19, 242, 302, 310 and 610 Squadrons and was led by Squadron Leader Douglas Bader, OC 242 Squadron at Duxford. It had been ordered to patrol the Canterbury area but had been called into action too late. Climbing hard to attain the all-important tactical advantage of altitude, the pilots had only reached 14,000 feet when they spotted formations of enemy aircraft 4,000 feet above. Bader maintained the climb towards the hostile aircraft in an attempt to intercept the raiders but his squadron was bounced from above and behind between Kenley and Maidstone by the escorting Me109s. Bader ordered the Spitfire squadrons to continue on course and attack the bombers while the Hurricanes attempted to take on the escorting fighters, thus reversing the strategic role of the Spitfires and Hurricanes. Whilst the Big Wing failed to inflict large-scale losses on the Luftwaffe bombers the presence of such a large force of fighters did keep several of the free-hunting patrols occupied and made it easier for other RAF squadrons to penetrate the escort cover and get through to the bombers.

During the ensuing dogfights, the eight Spitfires of 611 Squadron, led by Squadron Leader James McComb, engaged a formation of Dornier Do17s. McComb ordered his pilots into right echelon and dived to attack the bombers. He opened fire on one of the aircraft, inflicting serious damage. Meanwhile, Pilot Officer Peter Brown (Yellow 2, A Flight) followed up the attack by his CO but was forced to break-off due to oil from the damaged enemy aircraft covering the windscreen of his Spitfire. He later completed a combat report:

> After evading enemy fighters, I attacked formation. One burst at Do215 after Red 1 had put engine out of action. Oil or Glycol from E/A covered up my windscreen and I had to break away.
>
> Then attacked one E/A which broke away from enemy formation and turned; I used deflection and then E/A went into steep spiral dive. I attempted to follow, but dive was too steep. I noticed that the escape hatch above the pilot's seat was hanging open due either to my fire or crew escaping. I did not see any crew bale out as a large formation of Me110's appeared – I escaped into cloud. No damage to our aircraft.

Peter later recorded that the enemy force consisted of 30 E/A and noted the time of his combat as being 14.45 hours at 15,000 feet 'approximately over Tunbridge Wells'. The enemy aircraft he was credited with having destroyed was a Heinkel He111. He fired a 1-2 second burst at 250 closing to 100 yards followed by 3-5 second bursts from 250 closing to 100 yards.

Although the Big Wing had been caught at a disadvantage, claims by its pilots following this action amounted to 26 enemy aircraft destroyed, eight more probably destroyed and one damaged. An extreme case of over-claiming. The losses of the Wing that afternoon were: two pilots killed, two wounded with three aircraft written-off and two more damaged. By the end of the day the Luftwaffe had lost 58 aircraft – 32 bombers and 26 fighters – with the aircrews being killed, wounded or captured; none would return to the fray.

With inaccurate or ineffective bombing and having suffered heavy casualties the Luftwaffe failed to achieve the goals set. Ultimately, it was the failure to achieve air supremacy by destroying the RAF on the ground and in the skies over southern England that finally persuaded Hitler that invasion (Operation Sealöwe – Sealion) was no longer an option.

Fifty-seven years later, during the summer of 1997, Peter Brown and Stapme met for the first time at the annual Battle of Britain Exhibition at the Military Heritage Centre, Purfleet. Since then they have become friends, meeting on numerous occasions, including the Battle of Britain Fighter Association reunions at RAF Lakenheath when the topic of conversation invariably leads to a discussion on tactics and the personalities with whom they had served.

On 16 September, Uncle George recalled that, since the Squadron had moved south, it had been: '. . . the most crowded three weeks of our lives.' For the 603 pilots, it seemed they'd been at Hornchurch for an age when in fact they had only been there for three weeks. Many lost count of the number of patrols they'd flown, were suffering from fatigue and, with the reckless abandon of youth gone, were finding each aerial combat debilitating, both on body and mind. Years later many recalled the intensity of that period of their lives. In many cases they bonded quickly with colleagues, certainly quicker than in peacetime, and although some had only known particular characters for a few days, the circumstances of war, the threat of invasion, and a time of extreme excitement, created an environment in which friendships flourished, the memories of which have lasted a lifetime.

On 17 September, 603 took off from Rochford at 15.15, joined forces with 41 Squadron and engaged a large number of 109s at 25,000 feet over Chatham. Pilot Officer George 'Ben' Bennions led the twelve Spitfires of 41 Squadron as they climbed towards the enemy but during the climb they became embroiled in a dogfight ahead of 603 Squadron, who were also attacked by diving 109s.

Stapme claimed a Bf109E 'probable' south of Canterbury in X4348. As other 109s came in to attack he took evasive action and broke away. Bolster Boulter destroyed a 109 and Ras Berry and Pilot Officer John Soden* damaged a second and third.

Significantly, on 17 September, Hitler postponed Operation Sealion.

At 09.10 on 18 September, ten 603 Spitfires, including Stapme in X4348, took off from Rochford and sighted two formations of 109s over Maidstone, one formation above and one below. The 603 pilots dived to attack the lower formation and a dogfight ensued. Uncle George claimed a 109 damaged but the Squadron lost Pilot Officer Peter Howes, recently joined from 54 Squadron when he was shot down. His aircraft crashed near Ashford with the 21-year-old still in the cockpit. Sadly, he died having failed to destroy any enemy aircraft.

Putting the tragedy behind them, 11 Spitfires took off from Rochford again at 12.35, with Stapme again flying X4348. At 25,000 feet they intercepted six 109s. Ken Macdonald led the Squadron in place of Uncle George who, once again, had the painful task of composing a letter to next-of-kin. Macdonald struck first during the patrol when he destroyed a 109. Black Morton damaged another 109 as did Tannoy Read. Some of the pilots flew four patrols on the

*Soden had recently joined 603 Squadron from 266 at Wittering which had operated with 11 Group at Eastchurch and Hornchurch during August before once again returning to Wittering. During his time in the south with 266 John Soden had seen combat against Me109s and claimed a share of a 115 seaplane on 15 August. He was shot down by 109s the following day. He force-landed near Oare, Faversham, and was hospitalised with leg wounds. On returning to his squadron he was subsequently posted to 603 Squadron where he inevitably found himself filling dead-men's-shoes.

18th. Whilst some of the pilots were exhausted, Ras Berry proved an exception, showing no sign of fatigue and proving to be an excellent fighter pilot and role model to the less skillful.

On 23 September the Squadron was scrambled at 09.25 with Stapme flying N3244. Jim MacPhail's Spitfire was damaged in combat and he was forced to bale out. Bolster Boulter and Carbury each destroyed a 109 with Ken Macdonald claiming a probable. On the 24th Brian Carbury was awarded the DFC and Sheep Gilroy returned from sick leave. He had also recently been awarded the DFC and helped boost the level of experience in the Squadron.

On 27 September, Pip Cardell was killed. With Stapme rested for the first patrol, ten 603 Spitfires took off from Rochford at 11.46 and at 18,000 feet over Maidstone encountered four Me109s which they chased out over the Channel where they overhauled and attacked them. Between 12.00 and 12.15 Uncle George and Brian Macnamara each claimed a damaged 109. During the flight back to their airfield Dexter and Cardell spotted two more 109s which they pursued. In mid-Channel Dexter destroyed one while Cardell destroyed the other, but they were then bounced by five other 109s. After a short engagement the two RAF fighters made for home but Cardell appeared to be in some trouble. Unable to make land he baled out just offshore from Folkestone Pier and, at a height of only 4-500 feet, dropped into the sea. Dexter thought he saw movement from Cardell and, unable to gain the attention of anyone on the ground to the plight of his colleague, force-landed on the shingle beach, commandeered a rowing boat and some assistance, and rowed frantically to rescue Cardell. Sadly, he was already dead.

That afternoon, eight Spitfires of 603 Squadron took off at 15.10 with Stapme back in action in P9553. During his first day back on operations after being shot down and burned on 29 August, Colin Pinckney claimed a 109 probable. Ken Macdonald and Ras Berry each claimed to have destroyed 109s whilst Ras and Uncle George claimed another destroyed and a probable between them.

Whilst based at Rochford Stapme remembers the airfield being bombed:

> We watched these Dorniers coming in towards the airfield at about 12,000 feet. The sky was bright and sunny. As we watched we could almost anticipate when they were about to drop their bombs. Someone shouted: 'They're gonna drop their bombs now,' and we dived for the nearest shelter. As the bombs exploded the ground seemed to rise up like being in a boat on a choppy sea. A hand suddenly appeared, grasping the door-frame. It had a gash across it and was covered in blood. The rest of the hand's owner struggled into view, very dazed, but was OK, apart from the cut on his hand. I had expected much worse.

At 09.40 on the morning of 28 September eight 603 Spitfires took off with Stapme in X4348. At 10.20 Flight Lieutenant Ken MacDonald, who was again leading 603, was shot down over Gillingham when the Squadron was again bounced by 109s of II/JG26. Unable to make it back to base he looked for a place to force-land. He ran out of time and in order to avoid loss of civilian life he steered his now flaming Spitfire over the site of Brompton Barracks, home to the Royal Engineers, and jumped clear. His body landed on the parade ground, his 'chute having failed to open at such a low altitude. He died instantly. The Squadron had lost an experienced pilot, an excellent and highly respected leader, and a very close friend of all the 603 'old hands'. He was 28 and the heroic act was witnessed by a number of soldiers. His close friend, Black Morton, claimed a 109 probable and later sought revenge for the death of his colleague. For some the battle became personal.

Following the morning's tragedy, Ken's colleagues were again in action when eight Spitfires took off from Hornchurch at 13.10 and joined 222 Squadron on the 'Maidstone patrol line' at 15,000 feet. Stapme refers to such sorties as 'cab-rank patrols' on account of the fact that they were invariably sent up to relieve another unit on patrol. Together the two squadrons climbed to 30,000 feet to investigate vapour trails but, having failed to locate any enemy aircraft, both squadrons returned to the Maidstone patrol line. 222 Squadron left to patrol at lower altitude due to lack of oxygen and 603 spotted a force of 109s at 23,000 feet and dived to attack. Sheep Gilroy destroyed a 109 which went down in flames. 'Old Gent' Jack Haig and Tannoy Read each claimed 109s damaged. Haig's deteriorating eyesight was causing some concern. George Denholm and other close colleagues were aware of the problem but kept it from higher authority. Suffice to say Old Gent never flew Guard!

While on patrol on 29 September, Uncle George was leading eleven 603 Spitfires when he spotted four 109s below. Stapme was in R6736. Ras was down sent to investigate and attacked a 109 on which he inflicted severe damage. He was then engaged by another 109. He managed to turn the tables on the German fighter and, latching onto its tail, saw pieces fly off as he opened fire. With smoke pouring from the engine cowling, the 109 dived for the cloud. Had Uncle George sent a less competent pilot down to investigate, his decision may have ended in tragedy.

At 13.06 on 30 September 11 Spitfires of 603 took off with Stapme in Spitfire P9553. The pilots were soon embroiled in combat and met with considerable success. Black Morton wrote in his diary:

> Squadron took off 11 A/C and climbed through 10/10 [cloud cover] from 6,000'-7,000' to 30,000' south of the river. I was leading Yellow [section] behind George. At 30,000' somewhere between Biggin and Maidstone saw about 40 bombers in tight vics at about 15,000' with many 109's up to our height flying towards London. . . About 20-30 109's appeared 1,000' below us . . . squadron went in line astern and attacked.

Frenzied dogfighting ensued and Morton damaged a 109 which he then pursued as it sought cloud cover:

> I started to turn in to attack again when two Spitfires suddenly dived down and the leading one gave the Hun a burst from dead astern. He immediately burst into flames and went down. I went down through the cloud and circled the fire with the other two to see who they were. They turned out to be Berry and Stapleton. Berry having shot him . . . it's probably a good thing Berry came along, though I don't think the Hun would even have made it home by the way he was going and the glycol he had lost . . .

It was one of the best shows the Squadron has had. I feel it makes up a little for losing Ken [Macdonald] quite a suitable revenge. We got six confirmed: Razz [most 603 pilots used this spelling as opposed to 'Ras'] 2 (one with some help from me), Bolster 1, Soden 1, Stapme 1, and self 1. Four probable: Old Gent [Haig], Dewey, Darling and self. Two damaged: Darling and self. All without a single bullet among us.

The following claims were recorded in the ORB:

P/O Berry 2 Me109's Destroyed – Both in flames.
F/O Boulter 1 Me109 Destroyed – In flames.
P/O Soden 1 Me109 Destroyed – Crashed into ground.
P/O Stapleton 1 Me109 Destroyed – Crashed into ground.
P/O Morton 1 Me109 Destroyed – Blew up.
   1 Me109 Probable – Stayed upside down, thick black smoke.
F/O Haig 1 Me109 Probable – Glycol stream.
F/O Dewey 1 Me109 Probable – Black smoke and glycol, slowed up.
Sgt. Darling 1 Me109 Probable – Uncontrolled spin.
   1 Me109 Damaged – Bits blew off.

By then, Boulter had been promoted to flight lieutenant.

At 16.00 the Squadron once again took off on patrol and Peter Dexter claimed another 109 damaged. Stapme was flying X4348. On this day 603 received a signal from 11 Group, HQ, complementing them on their achievements. It is not known if Uncle George showed it to his pilots, but if he did it would perhaps have been lambasted by some and met with cold silence from others:

Group Commander sends warm congratulations to 603 Squadron on their successful fighting without casualties to themselves, showing exceptional leadership and straight shooting.

Unfortunately, it would appear that Keith Park's intended message was misinterpreted during transcription. He would certainly have been familiar with the statistics; 603 had suffered terribly. The message was typed into the 603 ORB and the following comment has since been added: '9 killed, 9 wounded, 1 missing, 1 POW – In 30 days!' During September, Stapme and a number of his 603 Squadron colleagues each flew in excess of 50 hours. Although he had flown 35 hours in August and would add a further 40 hours in October, September proved to be by far his most intense period of aerial activity.

On 2 October, the Squadron took off at 09.20 and by the time they returned at 10.57 they had lost another experienced pilot when Peter Dexter was shot down by 109s. After an intense struggle to escape from the cockpit of his Spitfire, he finally managed to scramble clear but had received a severe wound to his leg, caused by a cannon shell splinter or bullet, which kept him in hospital for some time. Stapme was flying X4348.

Brian Carbury, Peter Dexter, Pilot Officer Peter Hartas, who had joined the Squadron on 24 September, Sergeant George Bailey who had been sent to 603 from 234 Squadron at Middle Wallop on 10 September, and Jack Haig were all credited with having destroyed Me109s. Boulter and Flying Officer Henry Matthews claimed probables and Ludwik 'The Pole' Martel claimed a 109 damaged. Matthews had been sent to 603 Squadron from 54 Squadron on 30 September. By that time 54 Squadron had been moved from Hornchurch to Catterick. Ludwik Martel had joined 603 on 28 September and, like Matthews, had also been sent from 54 Squadron. Both were pilots sent to make up the numbers following recent losses.

On 5 October Stapme was rested and did not fly but it was clear the strain was continuing to take its toll on the surviving experienced members of 603 when Black Morton was shot down and badly burned. They had been scrambled at 11.10 and climbed to 25,000 feet from where they spotted a number of Heinkel 111s and Me110s. As they dived to attack they were intercepted by the escorting 109s and dogfights ensued. Black managed to bale out but in the few seconds it had taken him to scramble clear the 100 octane-fed-flames blowing back in his face in a blast in excess of 300mph had burned his face and hands. On leaving the cockpit he passed out, possibly due to hypoxia, and fell from 21,000 feet to 4,000 feet before opening his parachute. His part in the Battle of Britain was over and the scars on his forehead remained for the rest of his life, until his untimely death in 1982.

On 7 October, 11 Spitfires of 603 were scrambled at 15.44. Stapme was flying X4248. Brian Carbury destroyed a Me109 but the Squadron lost Flying Officer Henry Matthews, who was shot down and killed. He was interred with his Spitfire when it plunged into the ground near Godmersham Park, Kent.

Sergeant John Strawson was also shot down and carried out a forced landing in the River Thames. He received a blow to the head on impact with the surface and when he tried to open the canopy, the water rushed in, momentarily pinning him to his seat. The head wound later required nine stitches. Nevertheless, he was fortunate to escape as his Spitfire had begun its descent to the riverbed and was partially inverted by the time he frantically scrambled clear. He was picked up by an MTB (Motor Torpedo Boat) and taken to the Royal Naval Hospital at Chatham. Having arrived at 603 Squadron on 3 October he had been shot down on his first patrol and had been lucky to survive. While he was in hospital a more serious condition developed when his body erupted in a mass of painful sores which was subsequently diagnosed as being due to the amount of sea water he had swallowed whilst trying to fight his way clear of the cockpit. This reaction took some time to bring under control. After sick leave he returned to 603 Squadron. His part in the Battle of Britain with 603 Squadron has previously gone unrecorded but at the time of writing his family had just received notification that John *will* be awarded the 'Clasp' and have his name added to the Master List of Battle of Britain aircrew.* Both Strawson and Matthews had been posted to 603 on 3 October to make up the numbers.

---

*John Strawson survived the Battle of Britain but was killed in North Africa in 1942 whilst commanding 260 Squadron when he stepped on a landmine as a member of a ground party surveying possible sites for advanced landing grounds. The reason why he had not been awarded the Clasp can perhaps be attributed to the lack of detail and a number of inaccuracies in the Squadron diary for this period. However, a 11 Group Composite Combat Report ultimately provided the necessary evidence.

Pilot Officer David Scott-Malden, a good friend of Black Morton from their days together at Winchester, flew his first patrol with the Squadron on this day. Scottie was to prove an outstanding fighter pilot and enjoyed a successful post-war RAF career.

On 8 October, the Squadron was scrambled at 11.35 and were engaged by Me109s. Ras Berry, by now a Flying Officer DFC, claimed a 109 probable. Stapme was flying X4348. From 10 October Stapme enjoyed a couple of days rest during which time he remained at home in Romford with Joan who was seven months pregnant. Although he relaxed, bathed and caught up on sleep and reading, thoughts of Squadron were never far away. At 09.42 on the morning of the 10th eleven Spitfires of 603 Squadron took off from Rochford and were engaged by Me109s 10 miles north-east of Cap Griz Nez. Owing to dense cloud only six aircraft landed back at Rochford with three landing at Coltishall and the other two landing at Martlesham Heath. Brian Carbury and P/O Soden were each credited with a 109 while Colin Pinckney claimed the damaged.

On the 12th Stapme was flying X4348 with ten other 603 Spitfires scrambled at 14.45 hours. Bolster Boulter, David Scott-Malden and John Soden each claimed a Me109 probable. The patrol between 12.30 and 13.15 on 14 October consisted of only two Spitfires flown by the experienced Flight Lieutenant Jack Haig and Brian Carbury sent up to intercept a Ju88, which Carbury claimed as damaged.

The next day the 603 Squadron Spitfires took off at 15.15 hours with Stapme flying X4348. The ORB records Stapme's success:

> Twelve aircraft took off from Hornchurch, climbed to 30,000 feet and patrolled the Dungeness area for about an hour. The Squadron saw smoke trails and various formations of Me109's in the distance, but were unable to get close enough to attack. P/O Stapleton who was slightly below the Squadron saw 5 Me109's in line astern 5,000 feet below going across the Squadron's bows. He could not get in touch with the rest of the Squadron, so he dived and attacked the rear Me109, destroying it. He saw 11 and 13 in large black letters on the fuselage on two of the Me109's, and something between the number and the cockpit, which he was unable to distinguish. P/O Read was also behind and above the Squadron and was chased by about 10 Me109's, the first one opened fire and P/O Read had to force-land owing to engine trouble.

Stapme had destroyed the 109 over Bethersden, 10-15 miles off Dungeness.

On Thursday 17 October 11 Spitfires took off from Hornchurch with Stapme flying P7324. The intelligence report reads:

> Taking off at 1315 hours the Squadron was ordered to join 41 Squadron over base and proceed to Maidstone patrol line, 41 Squadron leading. Returning over base they were ordered to climb independently to 30,000 feet and vectored 190 at approx. 1345 hours. When at 20,000 feet P/O B.G. Stapleton, No.2 rear guard, sighted about 40 Me109's stepped up in sections of 7 or 9 and in echelon to starboard from 18,000 to 25,000 feet,

going S.E. He informed the leader, F/Lt Boulter, who said 'lead on'. The Squadron was veering to the right; P/O Stapleton, who was 500 feet above, passed over to the left of the Squadron towards bandits and was lost sight to the remainder. He caught up and engaged five of lower section of the 109's who circled to the right, and was able to easily turn inside and position himself on the end E/A and put in a 5 second burst from 150 yards closing to 50 yards. The E/A wobbled and went into a dive emitting both black and white smoke. The leading E/A now began to fire, though out of range, so P/O Stapleton dived, after the damaged E/A, in doing so he easily outdistanced the 109's, he saw his late target in a terrific vertical dive, and last saw it at 10,000 feet going towards the sea off Dungeness. The Squadron in the meantime saw some unidentified aircraft ahead, then noticed some white trails immediately overhead, so climbed and discovered 41 Squadron at 27,000 feet.

Cloud 8/10 at 2,000 feet with haze below.
Clear above but for isolated patches.
The 10 aircraft landed at about 14.30 hours.
P/O Stapleton proceeding by a few minutes.
Enemy casualties: 1 Me109 probable (P/O Stapleton).

No.603 Squadron had been up against the 109s of Stab I./JG53. Later, 11 Spitfires took off from Hornchurch for what turned out to be a relatively short interception, landing at 17.40. In Francis Mason's *Battle Over Britain* the author records that Spitfires of 603 Squadron shot down Messerschmitt Bf109E-7 (4138) on 17 October. The 109 crashed into the Channel at 17.30 hours and the pilot, Hauptmann Hans Meyer, Gruppe Kommandeur, StabI./JG53, was killed. The victory was not credited to any specific pilot in 603.

At 12.55 on the 20th Stapme took off from Hornchurch in Spitfire P7324. He and his colleagues joined up with 41 Squadron and were ordered to patrol the Maidstone line. When in position they were then ordered to climb on a northerly heading. On reaching 30,000 feet they noticed anti-aircraft fire, an indication of enemy aircraft activity. 41 Squadron informed 603 of some 50 Me109s ahead of them and then proceeded to follow them in to attack. The ensuing dogfights seemed to spread across the sky with the two squadrons clashing with the Luftwaffe fighters and some were pursued from the Hornchurch area over the Kent countryside and over the coast at Dungeness and out to sea. Stapme and the six other 603 pilots were embroiled in combat over Canterbury. Colin Pinckney and Pilot Officer Robert Dewey, who had recently joined 603 Squadron from 611, claimed 109s destroyed with Dewey claiming another damaged. Stapme and Sergeant Andy Darling claimed 109s probably destroyed, and Uncle George claimed a sixth 109 damaged. Scotsman Andy Darling, from Auchterarder, Perthshire, had been posted to 603 Squadron from 611 at Digby.

On 21 October Stapme was promoted to Flying Officer. On the 27th he was rested when 12 Spitfires took off from Hornchurch at 12.50 hours. In the ensuing combat Robert Dewey was shot down and killed, Pilot Officer David Maxwell was shot down but survived the crash-landing without injury but Stapme's fellow South African, Flying Officer Claude Goldsmith, was shot down and seriously injured when he crash-landed. He was carefully removed from the wreckage but died of his injuries the following day. The Squadron's only success during this patrol was by Ras Berry who claimed a Me109 damaged.

On the 28th Stapme was again rested. The first of two patrols took place between 13.10 and 14.55 when eight 603 Spitfires engaged 109s in combat. Sheep Gilroy destroyed a 109 with Jack Haig and Tannoy Read claiming two more damaged. At 16.11 six 603 Spitfires took off again with Pilot Officer Archie Winskill (later Air Commodore Sir Archie Winskill KCVO, CBE, DFC*, RAF [Ret'd]) who had joined the Squadron from 72 Squadron at Leconfield on 17 October, and Sergeant Andy Darling each claimed a 109 probable. Darling also claimed another damaged.

Stapme and Archie Winskill were destined to meet on numerous occasions during the war years, and he is particularly indebted to Archie for assistance given in getting him removed from a delivery flight (No.2) and eventually sent to Central Gunnery School, Catfoss, where Archie was based at the time. He later referred to Stapme as: '. . . a damned good pilot.'

Officially, it was decided that the Battle of Britain was fought between 10 July and 31 October 1940, although the air battle continued into 1941, when many Luftwaffe pilots believed the battle actually ended. By 31 October the veterans of 603 had quite naturally noticed the decline in the Luftwaffe's aerial activity and there were fewer patrols flown. Stapme flew approximately 150 hours on Spitfires during the Battle of Britain, bringing his total of flying hours on Spitfires to 290 and his total of hours flown since the seemingly far-off days of White Waltham to 523. By the time the Squadron was relieved and sent back to Scotland they believed the battle had been won. An opinion Stapme maintains to this day.

Heavy losses were inflicted by both sides. The Luftwaffe lost 1,882 aircraft while Fighter Command lost 1,017, with approximately 2,662 and 537 Luftwaffe and Fighter Command aircrew killed respectively.*

Stapme's squadron also finished the battle as the top-scoring daytime fighter unit in Fighter Command. During the 32 days engaged in the battle they made 85.8 claims for victories with 57.5 confirmed (resulting in a 67% accuracy of claims made). Of the victories, 47 were Me109s, more than any other squadron. Significantly, the Squadron also lost 30 aircraft with 14 pilots killed, which was high.**

In comparison, 609 Squadron were the next highest achievers with 51.5 victories from 86 claimed (an accuracy of claim rate of 60%). Whilst both 603 and 609 Squadrons were Auxiliary units until embodiment occurred on 23 August 1939, throughout the Battle of Britain 603 Squadron consisted of Auxiliary, RAF Volunteer Reservists and Regulars. So, whilst the top-scoring squadron was an Auxiliary unit not all the victories were claimed by auxiliaries. More than half of the Squadron's victories were by Brian Carbury and Stapme (both Regulars), and Ras Berry (RAFVR) with the CO, George

---

*I chose to use the more recent figures from *Battle of Britain Then and Now* as opposed to the earlier assessments of Denis Richards (1953) and Wood and Dempster in *The Narrow Margin* (1969).
**Statistics from *Battle of Britain Top Guns* by John Alcorn.

Denholm, Jim Morton and George Gilroy representing the auxiliaries. It is not this author's intention to set one squadron's achievements against another but the success of 603 Squadron in the Battle of Britain is something that Stapme is very proud of, particularly as he too became what was unofficially known as an 'ace' during that period.

Having gained a great deal of experience in a very short time, Stapme was particularly aware that no matter how much he had learned and gleaned from those around him, luck had also played a significant part in his survival. From the peacefulness of Tarfside to the nervous exhaustion caused by frequent aerial combat, a battle was over but he knew that the war still had to be won. Over the next few years John Boulter, much liked and respected with great leadership potential; Colin Pinckney, tall, handsome and charismatic; Dudley Stewart-Clark, like Pinckney, from a wealthy background, and the 'very good-looking, well-spoken, well-mannered and very polite' Richard Hillary, were colleagues who shared the excitement and tragedy of the summer of 1940, but did not see the end of the conflict. Eventually, many of his fellow pilots in 603 Squadron were moved on to jobs where others benefited from their experience. Be it as instructors, or in positions of command.

Stapme was in action again on 5 November when ten Spitfires of 603 Squadron took off at 14.45 on a 'Defensive Patrol' with Stapme flying P7436. They patrolled the Maidstone patrol line before carrying out a sweep over Kent where they saw a number of Me109s. Archie Winskill managed to get close enough to open fire but without result and Sergeant Patrick Terry, an experienced pilot who had joined 603 from 72 Squadron earlier that month, was wounded and crashed on landing. He was admitted to Charlton Hospital near Canterbury. On this day an experienced new arrival joined from 611 at Digby. Sergeant Ron Plant's contribution to the history of 603 Squadron was to prove significant.

On 7 November, Stapme (flying Spitfire II, P7528) shared in the claim for a Me110 along with seven other members of the Squadron. All eight signed the original of the following report:

<u>Intelligence Patrol Report.</u>
<u>603 Squadron – 1355 – 1515 hours – 7/11/40.</u>

11 aircraft left Hornchurch 1355 hours and were sent on Easterly course to N. of Thames Estuary to intercept bandits reported near convoy 'Arena'.

F/Lt. Boulter led the Squadron. As no E/A were encountered until Squadron were past their supposed location Squadron turned and asked for news. Were told to continue on their new returning course and at 1425 hours, when at 9,000 to 10,000 feet about 10 miles N.E. of Rochford, they sighted a single Me.110 at about the same height.

F/Lt. Boulter gave its position to the squadron and put them into line astern. After identifying a/c as hostile squadron went in to attack.

As eight pilots fired, separate combat reports have not been made out but their stories are incorporated in this report, which is signed by each of them.

F/O Gilroy, who was flying Guard 1, was the first to attack. As there was about 5/10 cloud and he cut the corner and went into attack the E/A, which had turned through South to S.E. It was diving for cloud and he opened fire at long range, closing to about 50 yards. There was return fire from the enemy gunner but it was ineffective. E/A went into a turn to port, then broke away upwards to starboard, with port engine smoking (Fired 2,400 rounds).

P/O Berry, followed F/O Gilroy in, saw him break away and did a port quarter attack from astern. E/A pulled straight up vertically and he did a full deflection attack on it. E/A dived vertically towards sea and went in with port engine smoking. There was no signs of its crew (Fired 1,600 rounds). Meanwhile other Spitfires attacked the E/A.

Sgt. Stokoe, got in two bursts, beam converging to quarter, from about 200 yards, just after F/O. Gilroy broke away. E/A was on top of its turn and another Spitfire was attacking. Sgt. Stokoe saw E/A go into sea. (800 rounds).

P/O Stapleton [by then F/O], was Guard 2 and was underneath rest of 603 Squadron. He dived right down to 1,000 feet and saw E/A do a controlled stall turn and then dive slightly. P/O Stapleton met it head on and gave it a 3 second, 2 ring deflection burst (Fired 400 rounds).

F/Lt. Boulter, after putting Squadron into line astern, approached E/A and saw it start to climb. It then turned slightly to port and dived. It then straightened out and as F/Lt Boulter came into range he saw another Spitfire attack it. He waited till his Spitfire broke away and then attacked as it did a climbing turn. It then dived down into sea (fired 2,800 rounds).

Sgt. Darling, Blue 2, fired three bursts at E/A. The first was a deflection on the same level, the other two from above as E/A dived and he dived after it. (Fired 800 rounds).

P/O Winskill, was flying in Red 3 position. He went in with Sgt. Darling as E/A came out of steep turn to left. He got right behind it as it dived and later saw it go into sea. (Fired 525 rounds).

P/O Prowse, was flying 'Charlie' 2 as Squadron was put into line astern. He saw E/A ahead and got in a short deflection burst from about 300 yards as it turned. Later he saw it go into sea. (Fired 80 rounds).

No assistance from A.A.
Cloud 5/10 at 4,000 feet.
11 aircraft landed Hornchurch 1515 hours.

Our casualties: Nil.
Enemy casualties: 1 Me.110 destroyed (Shared by F/Lt Boulter, F/O Gilroy, P/O Winskill, P/O Prowse, P/O Berry, P/O Stapleton, Sgt. Stokoe, Sgt. Darling).

Sometime during this period Stapme flew a patrol during which he became separated from his colleagues. A not unusual occurrence but on this occasion he found himself well to the west. He eventually recognised a significant landmark which helped him navigate his way back to Hornchurch:

Having attended school in Totnes, Devon, I spotted the Torquay to Paddington railway line – having been attracted by the plume of smoke from a London-bound steam train in full flight. This also confirmed I was actually a considerable distance off-course. With a familiar landmark now in sight I followed the route taken by the railway.

From Paddington he broke away to the east and as he made his way across the capital he was able to confirm his whereabouts by recognising significant landmarks:

First, I spotted Nelson's Column in Trafalgar Square, then the highest point in London. From there I recognised Embankment and Northumberland Avenue. There were barrage balloons on barges sitting in the Thames. The wind was blowing the balloons southwards and I knew I had to fly along the north bank of the Thames in order to miss the steel hawsers which curved up from north to south. I eventually arrived at the River Ingrebourne, which runs close by the airfield at Hornchurch, turned left (north) at the creek, and after a one minute circuit I landed at Hornchurch in what was, by that time, very poor weather.

Stapme's final claim with 603 Squadron was on 11 November when he destroyed a Me109 20 miles north-east of Ramsgate. Interestingly, he explains his concerns regarding the number of claims made by some pilots during the battle:

I could never understand how some pilots got so many 'kills', bearing-in-mind the ratio of kills to probables to damaged, because I was only in the position to shoot at aircraft that weren't shooting at me on three occasions. These were: the Dornier [20 July], the 109 of von Werra [5 September] and a Messerschmitt 110 [11 September] which I had hit in the port engine just prior to running out of ammunition. He was flying over and to the right of Dover and I started shooting at him. I found the Ack Ack to be generally behind me because they don't allow for the speed of the aircraft they were firing at. The 110 might have got home, he might not. The pilot was in control of the aeroplane but he took no evasive action whatsoever. I just happened to be there and catch him going home.

On 8 November 12 Spitfires of 603 Squadron took off at 15.50 hours for a 'convoy protection patrol.' The pilots were all flying the recently delivered Spitfire Mark IIA with the extra 18lbs of boost. Stapme was in P7528 in a section led by Bolster Boulter with Flight Lieutenant Mark Kirkwood flying No.2. The ORB reads:

Squadron sighted many enemy aircraft and became split up. Sgt. Stokoe destroyed 1 ME109 and damaged 1 ME109. P/O Berry DFC damaged 1 HE113 [actually a Me109E]. Our casualties:- P/O [sic] Kirkwood missing and F/O Gilroy slightly wounded and aircraft undamaged.

Flight Lieutenant Mark Kirkwood had just arrived from 610 Squadron at Acklington, a move he made at his own request. It was later confirmed that he had been killed in action.

At 11.45 hours on 11 November 12 603 Spitfire IIAs took off on another 'convoy protection patrol' (protecting convoys in the Thames estuary) with Stapme flying P7528. During the patrol at an altitude of 20,000 feet they spotted a force of Ju87 Stukas with an escort of Me109s spread over a wide area, approaching the Squadron from the north-west. Splitting into two flights, the pilots dived to engage the German fighters which dived to evade interception. During the dive in pursuit of the 109s, the 603 pilots came across approximately 20 Ju87s flying in 'vics' of five. They subsequently attacked the fighters and Stapme, P/O Harry Prowse, recently arrived from 266 Squadron at Wittering on 20 October, and Uncle George Denholm each destroyed a 109. Colin Pinckney claimed a 109 probable and Peter Olver a Ju87 probable. This success was without loss and all but one aircraft landed back at Hornchurch at 12.50 hours. The final pilot followed after being forced to refuel and rearm at Manston.

On 13 November, George Denholm received official notification that Peter Pease, initially reported 'missing' on 15 September, had been killed. All hope of his having survived had long-since evaporated and therefore the news only served to confirm their worst fears. The following day Sheep Gilroy returned to the Squadron from the Station hospital as 'non-effective sick' following injuries received on 8 November.

On 15 November 1940, Stapme's award of the Distinguished Flying Cross (DFC) appeared in the *London Gazette*. The presentation of the award didn't come until some time later when he was back in Scotland. He recalls with pride:

> I travelled down from Drem with Razz Berry and we were presented with our awards by the King at Buckingham Palace. There was a queue of award recipients and the event was made more memorable when an Indian wearing a turban was presented to the King and saluted so briskly he struck himself in the head, lost his balance momentarily, tottering slightly as he regained his footing! After the ceremony we travelled back to Scotland almost immediately.

At 08.00 hours on 17 November Stapme took off from Hornchurch in P7315 with nine other Spitfire MkIIs of 603 Squadron on a defensive patrol. They joined forces with Spitfires of 41 Squadron at the north-east end of the Maidstone patrol line when they spotted about 30 Me109s which 603 Squadron dived to attack. Sergeant Jack Stokoe destroyed a 'He113' (actually a Me109). Ras Berry and Bolster Boulter each destroyed a 109 while Colin 'Pinkers' Pinckney claimed a 109 probable. They landed again at 09.40.

At 13.55 the Squadron was scrambled again and 11 Spitfires took to the air from Hornchurch. They encountered a Me110 and eight aircraft attacked and destroyed it. They were subsequently credited with a share of the kill. Stapme was flying P7528. All aircraft landed safely back at the airfield at 15.15.

There was no flying the following day due to bad weather. The 19th saw some operational flying but on the 20th the weather once again curtailed flying operations. For some of the newcomers these interludes were frustrating. They were keen to acquit themselves in battle before it was all over. But for the experienced pilots and ground crewmen who had been present throughout the battle, the weather provided a welcome respite. They were exhausted and looked forward to a bath, and perhaps to catch up on their letter writing to let their friends and family know how they were, and even a night out in the capital. The pace of the aerial battle had lessened, was less frenetic and the pilots took to the skies less frequently.

On 21 November 603 Squadron claimed what turned out to be their one hundredth confirmed enemy aircraft destroyed. At 11.55 hours five 603 Spitfires took off from Hornchurch. The leading section consisted of Sheep Gilroy leading Archie Winskill and Sergeant Ron Plant with Uncle George and David Maxwell making up a section of just two aircraft.

Sheep Gilroy spotted a lone He111 and led his section in to attack with Ron Plant following his two colleagues. Whether a misjudgement of his actual closing speed on the bomber or even a deliberate attempt to ensure the Heinkel would not make it home, Plant was seen to open fire but did not break away, flying straight into the aircraft. His body was later found in the wreckage of his Spitfire (a false report stated that he fell dead in his parachute). On returning to Hornchurch the 603 pilots told of Plant's sacrifice and his kill was confirmed when the Heinkel was reported to have crashed near Faversham. Plant was a Coventry lad who had heard the reports of the recent and terrible blitz on his home city. Although we shall never know for sure, in light of the effect such reports would have had on him, his family believe it is conceivable that he had deliberately sacrificed his life to down the German bomber. The manner of Plant's death had a profound effect on Stapme and over the years he has retold the story many times.*

At 11.40 hours on 23 November Stapme took off from Hornchurch in Spitfire P7528 with 11 other colleagues. When they were ten miles to the south-west of Dover they spotted 20 CR42s of the Italian Regia Aeronautica (Air Force) travelling west. The 603 pilots attacked the formation from astern but found they were past the slower Italian fighters before they could open fire to any great effect. In turning quickly in pursuit of their prey they tended to stall their aircraft. By the time they had recovered they had to mount a fresh attack. The Fiat CR42 was a bi-plane that was vastly outclassed by the Spitfire but whilst it lacked speed, in this instance its manoeuvrability prevented even greater losses. No 603 Spitfires were hit. Archie Winskill claimed two CR42s destroyed; Brian Macnamara and Ras Berry each claimed one CR42 destroyed with Ras claiming another probable; Sergeant Darling claimed two destroyed; Bolster Boulter claimed one CR42 probable and Pilot Officer 'Scottie' Scott Malden claimed two CR42s damaged. They all landed again at 13.30 hours.

On the 29th Stapme did not fly operationally. Meanwhile, at 09.50 hours nine Spitfires of 603 took off from Hornchurch. During their climb to altitude, Pilot Officer 'Robin' Rafter's aircraft was seen to dive out of

---

*In January of 1941 Uncle George wrote to Plant's parents in response to their request for information of how their son had died. In a poignant letter George was able to provide details of Plant's last flight and at the same time inform them that their son had brought down the Squadron's one hundredth kill which proved something of a comfort to the grieving parents.

formation. He was subsequently killed when his aircraft crashed into the ground at East Sutton, near Broomfield. This accident has been previously reported as having occurred during the return trip to Hornchurch. Rafter only returned to the Squadron on the 26th after being shot down on 5 September, the day Stapme shot down von Werra. As the incident was witnessed whilst the Squadron was climbing to altitude the most probable cause was due to the failure of Rafter's oxygen supply with the onset of unconsciousness due to hypoxia/anoxia (O_2 starvation). Although the records show the height at which he was seen to break away as being 13,000 feet, this was a rough estimation. Hypoxia and anoxia can occur at altitudes over 14,000 feet. The cause was recorded as 'unknown' although confirmed as not by enemy action. One other possible cause of a blackout, apart from lack of oxygen, may have been due to the residual effects of the severe head injury received on 5 September.

Immediately following Rafter's loss the rest of the Squadron came across a lone Messerschmitt Bf110 which was attacked and shot down.

The function arranged to celebrate 603 Squadron's one hundredth enemy aircraft destroyed, had been arranged for the evening of 29 November and despite the tragedy which had occurred that morning there was never any question of the function being cancelled. It was the will of the fighter pilots and would have been seen as an opportunity to salute dead comrades rather than not attend and mourn. Many colleagues had been lost during the preceding weeks. Stapme recalled the event:

> We all voted to have a party to celebrate the Squadron's one hundredth victory. And what a night it was! We chose to have the function at the Dorchester, and it was very formal. Daddy Bouchier was invited as the CO of the Station. Peter Olver and his sidekick (we called them the 'heavenly twins') and I went into London in my Ford V8 with the dicky seat being used for the third passenger in the back, as it was only a two-seater. After the dinner we slipped out from the speeches because we were getting a bit fed up, and had a night out on the town. We went to the Turkish baths in Jermyn Street, which I remember as having Russian and Turkish printed on vertical neon signs outside (which were not lit during the blackout). It was a Turkish bath that also provided accommodation. We went in and had our 'bath' and then lay on our bunks; it cost six shillings and sixpence a night, and we didn't have to book-in, unlike the hotels. It was either Olver or his sidekick, I can't remember exactly who, but as one of them lay naked on their bunk the other got the alcohol rub and poured it over the other bloke's balls! Of course, he took off, because it burnt like hell. It doesn't burn when it's rubbed on a chap's hands when he gave you a massage, but poured over the softer tissues it does. He took off down some wooden steps leading to the plunge pool, but the tiles were wet, and as he tried to get to the soothing water of the pool, he was going so fast he couldn't slow down, and he finished up on the floor against the lagged pipes that provided the heat for the steam rooms. Despite being lagged in asbestos

they were still as hot as hell. I got down there in time to see him trying desperately to get away from the heat of the pipes, but his hands and feet were just slipping on the wet tiles as he tried to get up and away. It was the funniest thing I've ever seen in my life!

Interestingly, the cost of the function was covered by a member of the Squadron who wished to remain anonymous and whose name has remained unknown until recently when Stapme revealed that the kind mysterious benefactor was actually the Reverend James Rossie Brown, the 603 Squadron Padre. Rossie Brown was devoted to his pilots and was a good friend to many who served in 603 and a popular figure at Turnhouse for many years before, during and after the war.

CHAPTER FIVE

AFTER THE BATTLE

On 3 December, 603 Squadron moved to what had been their advanced airfield during the battle, RAF Southend (Rochford). By now there was less operational flying and the seasonal weather brought about days of little or no activity in the skies over southern England. Stapme recounts an unpleasant memory of his time at Rochford:

> On one occasion we stayed overnight at a county mansion which, amongst many luxurious features, had sunken baths. On another occasion we spent an evening at the Plough and Sails [at Paglesham, a short drive north-east of the aerodrome at Rochford] near the River Roach. We had a hearty meal of oysters, brown bread and stout. Unfortunately, we all suffered from oyster poisoning and, having dashed for the nearest convenience, didn't know which end it would come out of first! We were very ill, to the extent that there was an enquiry which found that, what had been freshwater oysters, had been plucked from the riverbed under a sunken barge lying up-river which had a copper-bottomed hull, and the copper had contaminated the oysters.

In December Joan Stapleton gave birth to a son, Mike. While speaking with him about his father's life, he was quick to quote the exact wording on his birth certificate under 'Father' – 'Flying Officer B.G. Stapleton DFC.'

On 13 December 603 was officially moved from the frontline, back to Scotland and RAF Drem where Stapme had attended FTS twenty months before. On the 17th the pilots flew their Spitfires back to Scotland. Joan and baby Mike left the shared accommodation in Romford and moved the short distance to Chislehurst where they spent the remainder of the war living with her parents.

At Drem 603 Squadron received a fresh influx of pilots for integration into the unit and much of the flying was geared towards practice with George Denholm as keen as ever that his pilots should be as ready as possible for combat. It was also a time for the experienced, battle-weary pilots to attempt to unwind from the stress and strain suffered during the previous three and a half months. They had been at the front for a long time and had seen many of their colleagues injured and killed. The young men had grown up very quickly. Whilst many recall the period as exciting, others suffered grief at the loss of colleagues and of ultimately terrifying experiences. These would last for a lifetime, as would the grief to those families of 603 pilots who had lost their loved-ones. Uncle George Denholm was also one of those who suffered.

Whilst they were away from the frontline fighter versus fighter combat, the threat of death or serious injury still prevailed. Flying accidents on the slope at Drem were common and several of the pilots were lucky to walk away unhurt. As well as practice flights, the operational flying took the form of patrols to intercept enemy intruders and protect shipping off the coast and in the Forth estuary.

At 12.55 hours on Christmas Day 1940, Blue Section, 603 Squadron, Flying Officer Brian Carbury, DFC and Bar and Battle of Britain ace, led awestruck Sergeants Squire and Wilson to intercept what was reported to be a hostile aircraft. At 1,000 feet, 12 miles north-east of St Abbs Head they intercepted a Ju88 and Carbury carried out two attacks during which the undercarriage of the Junkers was seen to drop down and the starboard engine 'omitted black smoke and eventually stopped.' Blue 2, attacked twice with no visible results achieved. All three Spitfires landed at Drem at 13.50 hours. Brian Carbury was a popular man with officers and ground crews and easy to get on with. He had little time for those officers who treated the lower ranks with disdain. He was an excellent instructor and fine role model to those to whom he passed on the benefit of his experience. Whether he requested the move or others decided to put his talents to better use is not known but on 30 December Brian Carbury along with the newly-married Jack Haig went to 58 OTU at RAF Grangemouth for evaluation and training as full-time flying instructors. Neither saw operational flying again during the war, for very different reasons.

During early January 1941 the Squadron received an influx of seven sergeant pilots. All arrived straight from OTU and Stapme and the other experienced pilots set about passing on the benefit of their experience to the newcomers. Further flying training followed along the lines of the exercises they had undertaken as trainees at FTS but with Battle of Britain veterans as part of an operational fighter squadron. During this period the slope at Drem continued to claim victims. On 12 January Jack Stokoe and John Strawson, who had only recently returned to the Squadron following his exploits on 7 October, both crashed on landing. On the 14th Stapme and the other veterans of 603 said a fond goodbye to Ian 'Woolly Bear' Ritchie who had been posted to Cambridge University Air Squadron.

On 23 January Brian Carbury returned from Grangemouth to remove his belongings. On the 25th Jack Stokoe was commissioned as a pilot officer. In later life he believed this had been late in coming. On the 29th Brian Carbury said goodbye to his colleagues when he was sent to No.1 Personnel Deployment Centre (PDC), Uxbridge, before returning to take up his instructional duties with 58 OTU, Grangemouth.

On 12 February Stapme and the other Squadron veterans said goodbye to Jack Stokoe when he was posted to 54 Squadron which was at Catterick at that time. He had become bored with practice and limited operational flying and was keen for more action. On 23 February he got his wish when 54 Squadron moved back to Hornchurch where they had shared the airfield with 603 during the previous summer. Stapme and Jack didn't meet again until September 1997, during the annual Battle of Britain Exhibition at the Purfleet Military Heritage Centre.

Within a very short space of time there had been a number of accidents on

the slope of Drem aerodrome. Until 16 February George Gilroy had been the
only serious injury. However, on that cold day in February 1941, tragedy struck
when, according to the ORB: 'Boulter was seriously injured when his aircraft
was crashed into by a Hurricane at Drem while taking off.' This was not the
way Stapme saw it, as he made clear:

> I saw the accident that resulted in his death, in fact I was flying in
> his section. We had just landed at Drem and he was steering his
> Spitfire across the airfield towards the hangars when another
> Spitfire, which was in the process of taking off, hit his aircraft
> side-on, right on the cockpit. The other pilot had not seen him as
> the slope on the Drem airfield contributed to the lack of visibility.
> It was a very sad end to a very talented pilot.

Years later the 603 ground crew personnel recall:

> Boulter was in the process of taking off when he hit the other
> Spitfire as it taxied across the airfield, taking a short cut instead
> of carrying on after landing and using the 'perimeter track' [it was
> a grass airfield] area, thereby passing behind Boulter's Spitfire.

Those members of the ground crew who had served him so loyally during the
Battle of Britain were first on the scene. Having dashed across the airfield they
clambered onto the wing-roots and looked into the cockpit. The sight which
met their eyes was something they never forgot. The airscrew of the other
aircraft had hacked through the side of the fuselage, including the cockpit,
smashed the front of Boulter's face, a mass of torn flesh and smashed bone, and
practically severed his legs as it continued on its downward path. He was
carefully removed from the cockpit and taken by ambulance to the hospital at
East Fortune (today the Museum of Flight). Sadly, he died the following day
due to multiple injuries and shock. Having survived so many combats during
the Battle of Britain, Bolster had been killed in an avoidable and tragic
accident.

The interpretation of events by the ground crew conflicts with that of
Stapme, who could be considered the most reliable source as he was flying
with Boulter when the accident occurred. There were two other squadrons at
Drem, 43 Squadron, equipped with Hurricanes, which adds credibility to the
entry in the 603 ORB, and 600 Squadron which had a detachment of Spitfires
at the airfield when the accident occurred. Unfortunately, the accident record
card has not survived. Flight Lieutenant John C. Boulter was 28 and is buried
in Dirleton Cemetery, overlooking the old aerodrome at Drem. On 1 February,
Cuthbert Orde had sketched a portrait of Boulter during a visit to the
aerodrome. Today, the original hangs in the officers mess at 603 Squadron's
Town HQ in Edinburgh. Orde also produced sketches of George Denholm, Ras
Berry and Stapme during the same period but Stapme has not seen his portrait
since.

Before news reached the Squadron that Boulter had succumbed to his
injuries, Tannoy Read was posted to 59 OTU. Those original members of 603
Squadron from the Phoney War and Battle of Britain were getting fewer.

During February the weather took its toll on the flying and when they did
get airborne it was for practice flying. On 28 February Stapme and his

op left: John 'Jack' Rouse Stapleton at his desk in
dia. Portrait taken for his family in England.
gned: 'With love from Dad.'

op right: Myrtle Stapleton (née Borland), Stapme's
other. Taken in Paignton during one of her many
sits from India to see her children.

Bottom left: Portrait of Jack and Myrtle Stapleton's
children: Marjorie, Gerald and Deryck.

Bottom right: Pilot Officer B.G. Stapleton in mis-
match mess kit at 13 FTS, Drem.

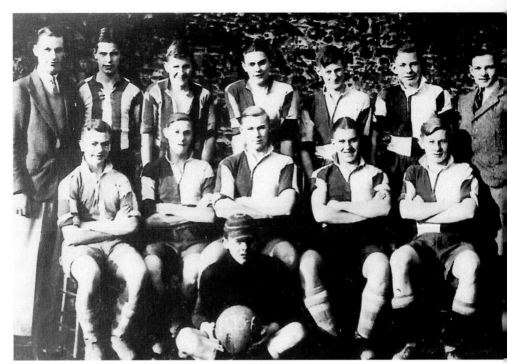

Top: King Edward VII School, football 1st XI, season 1935/36. Stapme is back row, third from left, Deryck is centre front and Captain. Note the difference between their shirts. Deryck had been awarded his colours (quarters), Stapme had yet to receive his and is still in stripes.

Bottom: A Flight, 603 (City of Edinburgh) Squadron RAF Turnhouse, 1939. From left to right: Bill Caister; Ken Macdonald; George Gilroy; Black Morton; Pat Gifford; George Denholm and Ian Ritchie.

Top: RAF Turnhouse at readiness, winter 1939. Flying Officer John 'Dobbin' Young (note name on Mae West), and Pilot Officer Ian 'Woolly Bear' Ritchie.

Bottom left: Pilot Officer Don Macdonald was shot down and killed during his first patrol from Hornchurch. This photo was taken in early 1940 at the family home in Murrayfield. Like Stapme, he grew a moustache in order to appear older

Bottom right: RAF Drem, 22 April 1940. Flight Lieutenant Fred 'Rusty' Rushmer, B Flight Commander. According to Stapme '...the nicest person I knew.'

Top: RAF Turnhouse, June 1940. B Flight at readiness. Pilot Officers Noel Benson and Ras Berry, Stapme, and Flying Officer Bubble Waterston working on his MG, SN5578. Like Bubble, Broody Benson was also a talented mechanic.

Bottom: RAF Turnhouse 1940. Flight Lieutenant Laurie Cunningham with Spitfire XT-M, L1021, 'Auld Reekie'. Later this aircraft passed to Pilot Officer Richard Hillary, who renamed it 'Sredni Vashtar'.

p: RAF Montrose, July 1940, B Flight. From left right, back row: Corporals Harry Barnes and antley; Flight Sergeant Mackie; Sergeants Andy lies and Sanderson; Corporal Murray. Front row: lot Officer Ras Berry; Flight Lieutenant Fred ushmer; Pilot Officer Noel Benson.

ottom left: '...and then there was one.' B Flight spersal, behind the gun-butts at Montrose, August 40. Flight Lieutenants Laurie Cunningham (centre left) and Rusty Rushmer (centre), and Pilot Officers Stapme Stapleton (ruffling his flight commander's hair), and Richard Hillary. Photo taken by Bubble Waterston.

Bottom right: 'Delectable Bubble'. Flying Officer Robin McGregor Waterston, taken at Turnhouse, 1940. Stapme's closest friend in 603 Squadron who was killed on 31 August '...a wonderful, happy-go-lucky person who lived life to the full.'

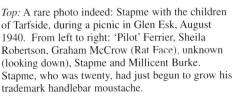

Top: A rare photo indeed: Stapme with the children of Tarfside, during a picnic in Glen Esk, August 1940. From left to right: 'Pilot' Ferrier, Sheila Robertson, Graham McCrow (Rat Face), unknown (looking down), Stapme and Millicent Burke. Stapme, who was twenty, had just begun to grow his trademark handlebar moustache.

Bottom left: No. 603 Squadron's top-scoring ace of the Battle of Britain, Pilot Officer Brian Carbury

(left) shown here whilst with 41 Squadron at Catterick, astride Hawker Fury K3879 which had crashed due to '...poor show-off flying' by Pilot Officer Derek French, a colleague of Brian's. On the right is Pilot Officer Arthur Slocombe.

Bottom right: Recklessness of youth! Loch Lee, Glen Esk, August 1940. Stapme fires a .22 rifle into the bottom of a captured Luftwaffe dinghy as Richard Hillary makes every effort to avoid being hit.

op inset: The only photo of Stapme in flying helmet. ...aken during the Battle of Britain, this photo formed ...art of a montage which headed a full page article ...n 603 Squadron in the *Sunday Post* (Edinburgh). ... was published on 8 December 1940 but features ...ction of 31 August.

op: Hauptmann Franz von Werra, Kommandeur, ...Gruppe I/JG53. Photo taken after his return to

Germany as a hero following his 'home run' from captivity in Canada. Note the Ritterkreuz. (*The Goss Rauchbach Collection*)

Bottom: Shot down by Stapme on Thursday 5 September 1940, Messerschmitt Bf109E-4, <+- (1480) of Stab II/JG3, flown by Oberleutnant Franz von Werra at Love's Farm, near Marden.

Top: A clever photographic reconstruction by Stapme's nephew, John, depicting 7 September 1940, when Stapme force-landed near Sutton Valence. Note the ammunition belts hanging out of the starboard wing of XT-L, and ahead lies the hop garden he just managed to avoid.

Bottom: Spitfire Mark Ia, XT-L, N3196. Photo taken surreptitiously following Stapme's force-landing at Forsham Farm, near Spark's Hall, Sutton Valence, Kent, on 7 September 1940, by R.B. Gardiner, hence the poor quality and distance between aircraft and photographer. N3196 was delivered to 603 Squadron on 3 September 1940 and was lost on 9 April 1943 when it dived into the ground at Shotley Bridge, Northumberland.

Top: Stapme with Great Dane on the wing of Hurricane IIA, Z2966, 257 (Burma) Squadron, RAF Honiley, taken between late January and April 1942. Stapme flew Z2966 on 18 February.

Bottom: Stapme on flying exercise with 257 (Burma) Squadron based at RAF Honiley. Taken between late January and April 1942 when the Hurricanes were replaced by Spitfires. Stapme removed his flying helmet and oxygen mask for the photo.

Top: Stapme, A Flight Commander, 257 Squadron, RAF Warmwell, photo taken between January and April 1943. Seen here lying on the nose of his Typhoon at A Flight Dispersal.

Bottom: Stapme (right), A Flight Commander, 257 (Burma) Squadron, in the crew room at RAF Warmwell. Photo taken between January and April 1943.

Top left: Group Captain Charles Green DFC, Commander 124 Wing, Eindhoven, November 1944.

Top right: A dramatic shot of Typhoons launching their 60lb rocket at a railway line. 'As soon as the target disappeared beneath the nose, you fired.' There were many instances of aircraft being hit during the attack and continuing their attacking dive, straight into the ground.

Bottom: 247 (China-British) Squadron, B.6 (Coulombs), August 1944. This group photo was taken shortly before the departure of Squadron Leader Robin McNair DFC, Officer Commanding 247 Squadron during the closing of the Falaise Pocket, and Stapme taking over as CO. McNair is centre front, with Stapme on his left. To McNair's right is Flight Lieutenant Jimmy Bryant who took over command of 247 after Stapme was shot down. Second left middle row is Flying Officer Fricky Wiersum; back row third from right is Warrant Officer T. Jones and back row far right is Warrant Officer Ray Stanley.

Top left: Flight Lieutenant Basil 'Tatters' Tatham, Eindhoven, November 1944.

Top right: Stapme climbing onboard his Typhoon IB, MP126, ZY-Y, 'Excreta Thermo'. Note artwork by Flying Officer 'Spy' McKay and plaster over Stapme's left eye, protecting the stitches received in his fall in Eindhoven. Stapme sent a copy of the photo to his mother with the note: 'This photo is of myself if you don't recognise me. I hope you like it. I don't know whether you have had my address but it is somewhere in Holland and to reach me it is: 247 Squadron, 124 Wing, RAF. All my love mother, Basil.'

Middle left: Wing Commander Kit North-Lewis, 124 Wing, with his own Typhoon 'KN-L'. Eindhoven, November 1944.

Bottom: Stapme in a somewhat informal pose in his personal jeep surrounded by members of 247 Squadron. Tatters Tatham is seated on the bonnet in service cap.

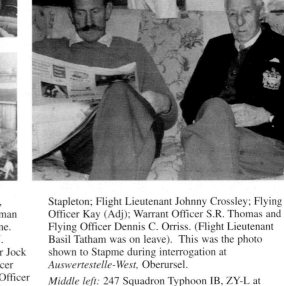

Top: 247 (China-British) Squadron, Eindhoven, November 1944. Note the captured MG42 German machine gun and Mauser rifle in front of Stapme. From left to right, back row: Warrant Officer N. Carter; Flying Officer J. Porter; Warrant Officer Jock Bull; Flying Officer C.G. Monk; Warrant Officer H. Brown; Warrant Officer T. Lewis; Flying Officer R. Jackson. Middle row: Warrant Officer R.G. McGregor; Warrant Officer Ray W. Stanley; Warrant Officer S.G. Jones; Flying Officer Fricky K. Siersum; Stewart; S. King (Eng. Off.); Flying Officer A. Pincombe; Flight Lieutenant E.A. McGee and Flying Officer 'Spy' McKay (IO). Front row: Warrant Officer Michael G. Croft; Warrant Officer S.L. Williams; Warrant Officer J.A.D. Meecham; Flight Lieutenant Dave Crawford; Squadron Leader B.G.

Stapleton; Flight Lieutenant Johnny Crossley; Flying Officer Kay (Adj); Warrant Officer S.R. Thomas and Flying Officer Dennis C. Orriss. (Flight Lieutenant Basil Tatham was on leave). This was the photo shown to Stapme during interrogation at *Auswertestelle-West,* Oberursel.

Middle left: 247 Squadron Typhoon IB, ZY-L at Eindhoven. Note the former Luftwaffe hangar in the background has been cleverly disguised as civilian housing.

Bottom left: Opened in October 1942, this cell-block provided solitary confinement for Stapme and more than 100 prisoners.

Bottom right: Thurlby Lodge, May 1962. Father and son, Jack and Stapme Stapleton.

Top: Brothers and sister together. Sarnia, Pinetown, South Africa in 1994. From left to right, back row: Marjorie (Stapme's sister), brother Deryck, Harvey's girlfriend. Front: Harvey (Stapme's son), Stapme and Audrey.

Bottom left: On the 50th anniversary of the Battle of Britain, Stapme and Audrey flew over from South Africa to attend the commemorative dinner at the Savoy Hotel, London. (*Sound Stills Ltd.*)

Bottom right: Formal portrait of Squadron Leader B.G. Stapleton taken in Pinetown, South Africa, 1994. Note the unusual medal arrangement. From left to right: Distinguished Flying Cross, 1939-45 Star with Battle of Britain Clasp, Atlantic Star, France/Germany Star, Defence Medal, War Medal and Distinguished Flying Cross (Dutch).

p left: Reunited with two of the children of Tarfside. om left to right: Stapme, Betty Davie (née Johnstone), ho shares fond memories of the 603 pilots, especially ichard Hillary, and Angus Davidson. Taken at Betty's me near Blairgowrie in 1998.

p right: During 2000, Stapme, as guest of the BBMF, AF Coningsby, climbed aboard former 603 Spitfire k.Ia, P7350, in the markings XT-D Blue Peter as flown S/L 'Uncle' George Denholm.

ottom left: Officers Club, RAF/USAF Lakenheath, ffolk, 1999. As guest of the 48th Tactical Fighter ing, USAF, the Battle of Britain Fighter Pilots

Reunion saw Stapme and Ben Bennions talking about their experiences in the Battle of Britain. Whilst Stapme was credited with shooting down von Werra, it will never be known for sure if the 109 Ben had attacked at high altitude was that flown by von Werra.

Bottom right: Stapme with grandson Cameron, guests at RIAT, RAF Cottesmore, 2000. Cameron is sitting in the Battle of Britain Memorial Flight's Spitfire Mark Ia, P7350 known as 'P7' which saw service with 603 during the Battle of Britain for a brief period.

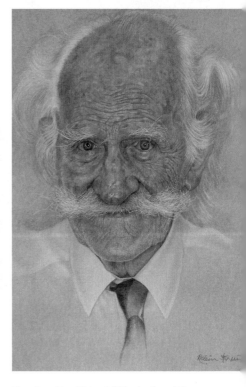

Top: Royal International Air Tattoo (RIAT) 2000, RAF Cottesmore. With former 603 Squadron Spitfire Mk.Ia, P77350, now BBMF, as backdrop. From left to right: former Luftwaffe Me109 fighter ace, Major Hans-Ekkehard Bob; Flight Lieutenant Ludwik Martel, colleague of Stapme's in 603 Squadron;

Dornier pilot, Heinz Möllenbrok and Stapme.

Bottom left: With son Mike, reunited in 2000.

Bottom right: Portrait of Stapme by Robin Elvin drawn in 2000.

colleagues moved back to their home base, RAF Turnhouse, where he had first reported for duty 14 months before.

Throughout March practice flying and operational flying continued. On the 24th the ORB records: 'Flying Officer Stapleton DFC, proceeded to HQ Fighter Command for interview.' This took place at Bentley Priory the following day and was probably regarding a posting to another unit. He returned to Scotland by train on the 26th.

Tour-expired, he was posted to 4 Aircraft Delivery Flight (ADF) at Grangemouth, on 27 March 1941. No.4 ADF was formed on 10 March 1941 as the Aircraft Delivery Flight, Grangemouth, but redesignated 4 ADF from 13 April 1941. The aircraft included: Airspeed Oxford Mk I & II, de Havilland Dominie I, Westland Lysander III, Bristol Beaufighter VIF, Miles Master III, North American Mustang I, Avro Anson I and Hawker Typhoon IB. To quote Stapme: 'We didn't do any aerobatics, we just flew straight and level to wherever we had to go, deliver the aircraft and fly back to Grangemouth, usually in a Dominie.'

This was a busy period for Stapme and not all trips went according to plan. Following the delivery of a number of aircraft to RAF Acklington, Stapme and his colleagues climbed aboard 4 ADF's twin-engine Dominie which had followed them down from Grangemouth for the return trip. During refuelling the aircraft's two 30 gallon tanks were inadvertently overfilled and as it accelerated across the airfield during take-off the tail section rose from the ground causing fuel to pour from one of the overflow pipes, straight onto the exhaust. The engine burst into flames and the pilot aborted take-off and brought the aircraft to a standstill just short of a hedge near the perimeter of the aerodrome. Seconds later the crew and passengers made their escape as a fire-tender arrived on the scene. According to Stapme: 'In extinguishing the flames a Blenheim which stood at dispersal behind the Dominie was also covered in white foam.' He remembers with amusement his 21st birthday:

> We delivered a number of aircraft to Inverness and promptly went
> off to celebrate my birthday in a hotel in town. One of the pilots
> was unable to drink and later flew us all home. The pot we used
> to pee in during the return trip was quickly filled but we had
> nowhere to empty it and yet more to be passed!

Of the 22 June 1941, Stapme responded to an Air Ministry circular asking for volunteers for the Merchant Ship Fighter Unit (MSFU): 'I was a bit fed up with flying all over the bloody place, so I volunteered.' He was attached to the Experimental Catapult Flight at RAE Farnborough on temporary duty on 27 June, where he flew Fairey Fulmars in preparation for service onboard a Fighter Catapult Ship (Camship) carrying out ship-based launches:

> It felt strange as the sides of the Fulmar were much lower than the
> Hurricane or Spitfire. I felt as if I would fall out. The Fulmar was
> a big aeroplane (over 40 feet long with a wingspan of over 50
> feet) powered only by a single Merlin I engine.

The aircraft was mounted on a rocket-powered bogey situated on old railway lines which had been erected on the airfield. Stapme climbed aboard the aircraft for his first flight and, in accordance with procedure:

I applied one-third flap, opened the throttle to full power, fastened the lever in position using the locking wheel (to prevent the throttle being forced closed by the 3.5 G-force, shutting down the engine) and, whilst holding the control column with my right hand, I tucked my elbow against my right hip, again to prevent the G-force from causing me to lose my grip on the column and send my hand against my chest. When ready I raised my left arm to signal I was ready.

The rockets were then fired and the aircraft was launched into the air. (Charles Crowfoot was in charge of the launch pad and was famous for wearing a bowler hat whilst carrying out his duties.) On completion of training Stapme was sent to MSFU, Speke*, Merseyside, where he carried out the same exercise but on Hurricanes. Stapme again:

The MSFU was formed to combat the menace of the Focke Wulf 200 Condor on our shipping convoys and in my experience involved a Hawker Hurricane being launched from a merchant ship by means of a ramp and a series of 13 solid-fuel rockets (not by means of a catapult which was the earlier method) fired in sequence. First nine, then two followed by another two. The inhabitants of Speke who lived closest to the base came to recognise the sound of rockets being test-fired. As each set of rockets fired the Hurricane flew down the ramp with the throttle open before the latches were released and the aircraft took off. The ship's mate was responsible for controlling the release and started the first rockets as the ship was in a downward roll. By the time the Hurricane reached the end of the ramp the roll would have reached its pinnacle and with the speed of the aircraft at about 80 miles per-hour the Hurricane was propelled into the air in an upward trajectory.

There were always two pilots detailed to each convoy. Once the mission was completed the unfortunate pilot had the choice of either baling out of his aircraft or 'pancaking' on the surface of the sea. He would then be picked up by his ship. The intention of the pilot was indicated to the convoy escorts by a left or right-hand circuit.

Stapme made a total of four crossings with convoys and although on one trip his colleague did take to the skies to intercept an intruder, Stapme was never actually required to do the same. On one occasion he recalls a signal reaching his ship that his colleague had been picked up by a destroyer and given rum. The message read: 'Pilot very wet outside, now very wet inside!' On another occasion, when the alarm sounded Stapme jumped to his feet but as he attempted to dash out on deck he was so intent on hurdling through the hatch he forgot to stoop and smashed his forehead on the top edge of the hatch, knocking himself out.

His first trip was onboard the *Empire Foam*, owned by the Evans, Thomas and Radcliff shipping company, which he described as a 'rust bucket'. The

---

*The MSFU was formed at Speke on 5 May 1941, and the aircraft used between 5 May 1941 and June 1943 included: Sea Hurricane IA, L1889 KE-E; Hurricane I, Z4936, KE-M; Hurricane I, W9313, LU-S; Hurricane I, V6756, NJ. Also used Spitfire I, N3051; VB, AD371; VC, JK514; Hurricane X, P5188; IIB, BW841; Tiger Moth II, R5077; Master III, DM195.

convoy took the shortest route across the Atlantic stopping off at Halifax, Nova Scotia. Shortly before docking at Halifax, Stapme climbed aboard the Hurricane and was launched from the ship and flew to the airfield near Enfield. He eventually rejoined his rust-bucket which continued to New York. Meanwhile, his aircraft was towed back to Halifax and through the streets back to the docks. When the *Empire Foam* docked at Halifax during the return leg of the trip the aircraft was once again loaded onboard the take-off ramp in readiness for convoy escort duty back across the 'Pond'.

Whilst in New York Stapme attended a lunch at the Towers Hotel, Brooklyn, following which there were a number of speeches from both American and British speakers. In particular, he remembers the speech made by Sir Tom Jones, British Minister for Shipping, which poked fun at the Allies. He told the Biblical story of Noah's Ark adrift in a great ocean and heavily weighed-down and near-sinking by all the animal faeces which had mounted up onboard from the many pairs of creatures which he had rescued prior to the impending great flood. Finally, Noah decided to ditch the whole lot over the side and into the sea: 'This he did and in 1492, Christopher Columbus discovered it!'

Prior to docking at Liverpool at the end of the return journey, Stapme was again fired-off from the ship and landed a short time later at Speke. The aircraft was then returned to the docks for the next crossing.

Promoted to Flight Lieutenant on 21 October 1941, for his service on the North Atlantic convoys Stapme was awarded the Atlantic Star. The MSFU at Speke was disbanded on 7 September 1943.

CHAPTER SIX

FLIGHT COMMANDER & GUNNERY INSTRUCTOR

On 14 January 1942 Stapme was posted to 257 (Burma) Squadron at Honiley on 'Supernumerary Flying Duties'. Equipped with Hurricane Mark IIA, B & Cs, the Squadron (code 'FM') was at that time non-operational with its pilots undergoing intensive flying training exercises as part of an on-going programme to hone their individual and collective flying ability and bring the newly qualified pilots in the Squadron up to scratch as quickly as possible prior to being made operational. The exercises included: air tests (aircraft and systems performance), night flying (take-off, instrument flying, navigation and landing during the hours of darkness), cloud and local flying (instrument flying in blind conditions, reconnaissance and familiarisation of local terrain), formation flying (with other squadron aircraft), camera gun practice and dog fighting (gunnery practice and post-flight assessment of results – particular favourites of Stapme), cross-country (practical navigation exercises), D/F (directional finding) and homings (using available navigation electronic equipment), Havoc co-operation flying exercises (practice flights in support of Douglas A20 Havoc bombers) and air to sea firing on seaside ranges. As a veteran of the Battle of Britain Stapme didn't follow the same strict training regime as the less experienced pilots in the Squadron but oversaw much of the work and flew the occasional training exercise. He soon settled in to his new squadron and became friends with a number of the pilots, in particular Flight Lieutenant R.S. 'Dusty' Miller. Stapme reflects on this period as busy but fairly uneventful.

Having spent his first few days at Honiley settling in and finding his way around, Stapme had to wait a while for his first flight with 257 as flying was cancelled between 18 and 23 January due to bad weather. Eventually, between 14.05 and 14.55 hours on the 25th, Stapme took off on a 'non operational sector recco' in Hurricane Mark IIA, Z2446, in order to familiarise himself with the local terrain. At 20.25 hours on 26 January the only operational patrol flown by 257 in January and February occurred when Flight Lieutenant Mason (Commander 'A' Flight) took off in Hurricane IIA, Z3025, on a 'N/F (night flying) Scramble' to intercept an intruder. He landed again at 21.30 without success. Between 17.10 and 17.50 hours on 28 January, Stapme flew a 'N/F test' in Hurricane IIA, Z2808, and between 18.10 and 18.40 hours he carried out 'dusk landings' in Hurricane IIC, BN 386. On 31 January he flew a 'Havoc co-operation' exercise in Hurricane IIB, Z3669, between 14.00 and 14.45 hours with Pilot Officer Halsey in IIB, Z3241.

Flights were cancelled on 1 February due to heavy snow fall and whilst a rapid thaw on the 2nd saw the airmen working hard to clear the runways, flying was limited that day to: '. . . a cross country to Skegness by four aircraft, local flying, local formation and practice flying.' The following day was slightly better with daytime practice, formation and cloud flying but, generally, throughout the month the weather was typical for the time of year limiting night flying and the type of exercises carried out during daytime. On the 7th Stapme attended a lecture on the subject of Army Air Support by Squadron Leader Billy Drake DFC, and the next day the pilots carried out an army co-operation 'beat up' of gun positions before attending another lecture on army air support by Wing Commander 'Sailor' Malan in the afternoon. Malan was, like Stapme, an ace from the Battle of Britain. By the end of the war, he had been credited with: 27 enemy aircraft confirmed destroyed; seven shared destroyed; two and one shared unconfirmed destroyed; three probably destroyed and 16 damaged and had been awarded: DFC and Bar, DSO and Bar, Croix de Guerre (Belgium), Croix de Guerre (France) and French Légion d'Honneur. He was also an outstanding leader of 74 Squadron throughout the Battle of Britain. At the end of Malan's lecture Wing Commander Desmond Sheen DFC and Bar, yet another veteran of the Battle of Britain, 'added a little on tactics and accidents.'

On 9 February the weather was unsuitable for flying and Wing Commander Sheen discussed the problems with Flight Lieutenant Mason. The 10th dawned brighter and the ORB records: 'Practice flying included local formation, aerobatics, low flying, dogfights etc. Co-operation with Havocs and cine gun practice – a very busy day. Capt. Holmes (Searchlights) came to discuss searchlights and arrangements.' The entry for the next day follows on: 'Practice flying by day and night.' The night flying continued until after 02.00 hours and included the searchlight co-operation exercise for which the pilots had been briefed the previous day. Pilot Officer Hogg acted as bomber and Flight Lieutenant Mason searched as fighter.

Stapme flew again on 12 February when he carried out a 'formation and night flying test' in Hurricane IIA, Z2808, between 16.25 and 17.25 hours with Flight Lieutenant Mason in IIA, Z2426. The Squadron ORB records: 'Local formation, camera gun and formation practice carried out during day. N/F [night flying] practice was cancelled as the weather became unserviceable.'

On the 13th Stapme took off at 14.35 in Hurricane IIB, Z3241, on a 'practice formation flying' exercise with his colleague, Flight Lieutenant 'Dusty' Miller, in Hurricane IIB, Z3359. Night flying was cancelled after a mist settled over the aerodrome.

The entry in the 257 Squadron ORB for 14 February reads: 'The day's practice flying included Havoc co-operation and drogue attacks [air to air attacks on towed target]. There was no night flying . . . ' The following afternoon saw cloud and local flying but night flying was cancelled due to poor visibility.

For 16 February the 257 ORB reads: 'A busy day spent in all types of practice flying – cloud; local; formation; cine gun etc.' Stapme carried out a 'dogfighting and camera gun exercise' between 14.40 and 15.40 hours in Hurricane IIB, Z3359, with Pilot Officer Scotchmer in IIB, Z3351. Stapme retains fond memories of Scotchmer who quickly realised that during the mock attack the Spitfire of the experienced Battle of Britain ace was impossible to get in his own gun-sight and also, when roles were reversed, to shake off his tail!

On the 18th Commander-in-Chief, Fighter Command, Air Chief Marshal Sir Sholto Douglas, visited RAF Honiley and chatted at dispersal with Stapme and other 257 pilots. For the following day the ORB reads: 'ZZ Approaches, Havoc co-operation, cloud flying were included in the day's practice flying.' Between 15.10 and 17.00 hours Stapme flew a 'Havoc affiliation/Havoc co-operation' exercise in Hurricame IIA, Z2966, with Dusty Miller (IIC, BN 384), Pilot Officer McDonough (IIA, Z2979) and Pilot Officer Scotchmer in Hurricane IIB, Z3174.

On 20 February the ORB records the weather as being hazy and not much flying was attempted although Stapme flew a 'night flying test' in Hurricane IIB, Z3359, between 17.30 and 18.10 hours.

On 21 February, the ORB reads: 'No flying – weather unserviceable. F/Lt Mason posted to No.79 Squadron and F/Lt Stapleton assumed Flight Commander post.' Stapme's service record confirms he was on 'flying duties' with 257 Squadron as a Flight Commander as of this day. He relished the authority given him and went about his duties with enthusiasm. In many ways the responsibility had been a long time in coming. He was no authoritarian, in fact he preferred an atmosphere of informality in which mutual respect between himself and his pilots quickly developed and added to the efficient and professional way they went about their work.

For the 22nd the ORB reads: 'army co-operation practice and N/F test for a very ambitious programme. The weather closed in however, and night flying was cancelled.' There was no flying the following day but after dark there 'was a series of night flying tests for a large programme, which did not mature, as the weather closed in.'

On 24 February, cloud, formation and night flying tests took place during the day, along with Havoc co-operation. Night flying carried on until 22.30 hours with ten hours flying amassed.

The next day dawned sunny but hazy. Some flying was carried out during the day and after dark and early the next morning a searchlight co-operation exercise took place. The ORB reads: 'The results were satisfactory considering the low cloud and poor visibility, 2-3 miles. Good weather for night flying which was carried on till 0330 hours the next day.'

There was no flying on 26 February due to 'unserviceable' weather. For the 27th the ORB reads: 'Havoc co-operation until 2330 and N/F tests. Major Ricketts of the Durham Light Infantry gave a series of lectures to pilots. Total night flying about three and a half hours.' For 28 February the ORB reads: 'No flying. Pilots went to watch invasion exercise.'

In April the Squadron was re-equipped with Spitfire VBs and on 6 June 1942, sent to High Ercall. Stapme told the author a particular incident during his time there:

> I travelled into Shrewsbury for the day. During the return trip my car broke down and I pulled up by the side of the road. A chap pulled up in his lorry and offered to give me a tow back to the airfield. This he did and even towed me around the perimeter track to dispersal, where he promptly pulled out two bottles of scotch from his cab and we spent the rest of the afternoon

drinking, one each. However, I drank my share heavily diluted with water. The other chap did not. Some days later I heard that the man had died, apparently from the effects of drinking so much neat scotch.

In July, 257 Squadron was once again re-equipped, this time with the Hawker Typhoon IA and B. In preparation for conversion to type Stapme was sent to Napier for a familiarisation course on the Sabre engine. During his stay in London he was involved in an incident following another heavy drinking session:

> In the lounge of the Regent Palace you could sit at the bar or at one of the long tables around which there were chairs and sofas. At one table I recall there was the crew of a B17 Flying Fortress – ten men. At another was the crew of a Lancaster – seven men. One of the RAF crewmen, sitting at the end of one of the long tables, called to a colleague at the other end, deliberately intending to goad the Americans: 'I hear the Americans have got a new fighter.' To which a colleague replied in a similarly loud voice: 'Oh, what's it's name?' 'It's the Flying Fortress,' the RAF chap replied. The ploy worked and one Yank came over and asked: 'What's all this about the Flying Fortress?' To which the RAF lads replied: 'If you can't understand English, go home.' The Yank invited the RAF lads 'outside' and seven of them joined the ten in an alley. I thought the imbalance was unfair and joined the side of the RAF bomber crew and the fight began. It didn't take long for the MPs to arrive, but as there were only three of them we joined the Yanks and turned on them, roughed them up a bit, tied them up and left them in the alley. I then went off to hospital to have an eye wound seen to.

Following the course, most of the period after Stapme's return to 257 Squadron was spent on training. He shared the problems experienced by ex-Spitfire and Hurricane pilots alike as, apart from the increased power of the Napier Sabre engine, the airscrew rotated in the opposite direction:

> The first thing that struck me when I climbed into a Typhoon was you had to get used to the height you were sitting and, as it had become automatic to correct the swing on take-off, we had to unlearn that which had become second nature to us. The result was that early Typhoon take-offs were nearly always in a climbing turn.
>
> Night flying at High Ercall was quite tricky because of the width of the nose. We took off with just two Glim lamps and one glide path indicator. When the occasional German bomber came over, we couldn't use a flare path.
>
> The Typhoon was far more powerful than previous aircraft I'd flown. While based at Exeter I achieved 400 mph on the clock at sea level, it really was a tremendous ground-attack aircraft.
>
> An early mark of Typhoon had twelve machine guns. The front armour of the German tanks was very thick and our cannon shells

were inclined to bounce off. We therefore used rockets against the tanks. Nevertheless, machine guns were devastating for soft-skin targets (vehicles). If there was grass around the target, it was like a wave when the rounds hit the ground and the turf seemed to ripple in retreat. The empty cartridges must have been another source of hindrance to German troops as we strafed, as they fell at a hell of a rate.

There was no recoil when I fired my rockets. Having sighted the target I lined it up and fired just as soon as it disappeared beneath the nose of the aircraft. Using this method I couldn't miss. I found it best to stay low after attack and utilise the speed, rather than attempt to climb away from the target. There was usually too much flak . . . Whilst at High Ercall we had a visit from the King and Queen and two Princesses. Princess Margaret got into a Boston with me and sat in the co-pilot's seat and started to fiddle with the controls. I had to give her hand a little admonishment!

On 21 September 1942, Stapme and 257 were sent to Exeter, with a detachment at Bolt Head, where they attempted to intercept the Fw190s as they attacked targets at low level, beating a hasty retreat before the Typhoons could make contact:

They were nearly always gone by the time we were airborne. However, we did manage to intercept two Fw190s that attacked the RAF hospital (The Grande Hotel) on the sea front at Torquay.

I recall on one occasion, the engine of a Typhoon cut out on take-off from Exeter. The pilot did the right thing by continuing to go straight. If he had tried to turn back to base he would have spun-in. He left the wings behind in the first house he hit, the engine went on and made a hole for the fuselage to go through. The engine continued through the house and onwards through a house across the street and another beyond that! Incredibly, no one was hurt and the pilot walked away from the crash.

We had a satellite at Bolt Head, and the landing strip was 400 feet above sea level, so you had to do a circuit at a higher altitude – 1,500 feet instead of 1,000 feet. On the first occasion we landed there we circuited at 1,000 feet on our approach to the landing strip but as we straightened up we found ourselves looking at the cliff-face!

Some American Airocobras landed there on their way to Gibraltar. They all had long-range tanks and all damaged the nose-wheels of their tricycle undercarriages when they misjudged the height of the landing strip.

On 8 January 1943, 257 Squadron moved from Exeter to Warmwell (with a detachment at Ibsley). Stapme recalled that at Warmwell: '. . . we achieved a little more success during 'Rhubarbs' [ground-attack missions] into France when we successfully attacked a number of supply trains on their way to Brest.' Of the flak, Stapme records:

We experienced a bit of flak during the 'Rhubarbs' over France.

The operations were in support of the attempt to keep Brest isolated. This consisted of blowing up entrances to railway tunnels, things like that, and anything moving would be a target. So we did experience flak but not a lot. We were never afraid of being shot down because you thought it would never happen to you; until it did!

For 7 March the Squadron Form 540 reads:

A state was maintained during the day, and sections were systematically sent off to relieve those whose patrol period was almost expired. The patrol line is between Portland and the Needles via St Albans Head. Sections stay on patrol for approximately 1hr.15mins, when they are relieved by the next section. Practice flying consisted of air-to-sea firing and cine gun practices. F/O Scotchmer returned with a good report of the Typhoon with tear-drop hood. P/O T Clift (Burmese) hit the sea with his propeller during an anti-rhubarb patrol, but did little more than slightly bend the tip. He brought his machine back safely.

At 17.05 hours the following day the Squadron was scrambled for the third time. Stapme was leading A Flight and his friend and colleague, Flight Lieutenant 'Dusty' Miller, leading B Flight when tragedy struck. The 257 Squadron Form 540 reads:

The day was marred by the death of F/Lt. R.S. Miller, B Flight Commander. F/Lt Miller was badly injured when he crashed as he was about to take off on a scramble during the evening. His injuries proved fatal, and he died an hour later. 'Dusty', as he was known to the Squadron, had been with the Squadron since 8.9.41. He took an active part in all Squadron activities, and had done good work as Squadron gunnery officer. F/Lt Miller had become a first rate Flight Commander, an efficient leader of men, and apart from a few weeks when he was posted to No.535 Squadron, he had been with 257 Squadron for sixteen months. He was always keen to meet the Hun, but was never in air combat during his stay with this unit. The standing anti-rhubarb patrol was maintained throughout the day. There were three scrambles, but nothing was reported throughout these patrols.

The Squadron 541 provides more detail of the accident:

8.3.43, Typhoon EJ916, F/Lt. R.S. Miller, Operational, Up 17.05, Down:- Not stated

Scramble 'X' Raid. Pilot was taking off across wind at the same time as a Fleet Air Arm Master was taking off into wind. F/Lt Miller tried to avoid the Master by climbing over it, but stalled and dropped a wing. He crashed on the aerodrome and was seriously injured, dying an hour later. The usual scramble signal – a two star red cartridge – was fired from the dispersal hut, but was not seen by the pilot of the Master. A Court of Inquiry is investigating.

Stapme remained with 257 Squadron until 6 April 1943 when, at the end of his second tour, he joined No.2 Aircraft Delivery Flight (ADF), Colerne. Although he was 'tour-expired', he was infuriated by the loss of his colleague the previous month and believes his own departure from 257 was due to his attempt to apportion blame:

> Following the avoidable accident which resulted in the death of Dusty Miller, I later had an altercation in the officers mess with the Group Captain, Officer Commanding, RAF Warmwell, following which I found myself posted to a delivery flight. The warning flare should have been fired from the duty pilot's office instead of dispersal. One of the chaps at dispersal had seen the potential for an accident and on realising that a flare had not been fired from the correct location, grabbed a pistol and fired the flare as quickly as he could. Although the Master pilot *should* have seen it, Dusty would not have done so because it was fired behind him.

According to the veterans, RAF Warmwell had seen a number of commanding officers come and go in quick succession, with none being particularly effective in the post. The Officer Commanding Warmwell at the time of Miller's death is believed to have been particularly 'useless'. According to Stapme, he had been given the nickname of 'Hirohito' on account of his diminutive stature and appearance.

Stapme's record of service shows that on 23 January 1943 he was transferred to the reserve and retained on the Active List before moving to No.2 ADF* where he spent six hectic months delivering aircraft to various destinations around the country: 'One of the nicest aircraft I flew whilst with the delivery flight was the Mosquito. It was so simple to fly.' During this period, when time allowed, he visited Joan and Michael who were staying with her parents in Chislehurst.

On 1 September 1943, he was posted to RAF Station Kenley as 11 Group, Sector Gunnery Instructor where he found teaching the subject of fighter gunnery very much to his liking. He was also only a short drive from his wife and son. On 27 March 1944, he moved to the Central Gunnery School, Catfoss, Yorkshire, where he continued to expand his own knowledge and skill as a gunnery instructor as well as that of his students. The Officer Commanding, RAF Catfoss (Sept 43 to Dec '44) was Squadron Leader Archie Winskill DFC and Bar, former 603 pilot and friend of Stapme's who helped initiate his move to CGS and who was called the 'Italian Count' on account of his good looks. At that time Stapme's car was an MG Magna of which he remembers:

> In 1934, there were two MGs, the Magnet, which was an under-powered four cylinder, and the Magna, meaning the bigger one.

---

*Formed on 18 March 1941 as Aircraft Delivery Flight, Colerne, it was redesignated 2 ADF from 22 March 1941. Aircraft at 2 ADF included: Boulton Paul Defiant I, Percival Proctor I, Miles Magister, Miles Master III, de Havilland Dominie I, Hawker Hurricane IIC, North American Mustang I & III, Avro Anson I, and Airspeed Oxford I & II.

In 1935, in a TD series Magna with a special body, Goldie Gardener did 202 mph on a German autobahn. They made 12 and I bought one at Roland Smith's, a second-hand car dealer in London.

On leaving Catfoss, Stapme left his car with Archie Winskill who put it to good use. But Joan eventually had to sell it to raise funds after Stapme was posted 'missing' in December 1944.

At CGS Stapme found the work interesting and rewarding:

I had been there previously as a pupil and secondly as an instructor. It was a real eye-opener. We used to get people from various nationalities, including American and Commonwealth pilots. The level of ignorance of where their bullets would go when they touched the gun-button was hard to believe. During instruction, in order to determine exactly where the bullets would go we used a small model of particular aircraft and projected its silhouette onto a screen. With a projector providing the light from behind you'd get an exact angle that the aircraft was at and you'd match it up (overlay it) with the camera-gun footage. So the only thing you had to assume was the target's speed. Of course, if it was at 90 degrees to you, you allowed 100% of his speed. So you can appreciate how impossible it could be to hit the target in those circumstances. We had a '100mph' gun-sight. We worked it out that if you fired and he flew through your pattern, you'd probably only hit him four times, that's all. Your pattern of fire was approximately13 feet high and nine feet wide, like a rugby ball, but only 75% of your bullets would go through that area because of gun chatter. We worked out that the number of bullets fired in the time he would pass through your pattern doing 250mph would be a fifth of a second! So we could calculate how many bullets you had going through him in one fifth of a second, and remember that his aircraft doesn't match the dimensions of the pattern. It was pretty useless. I'm not sure but I think the German fighter guns shot straight ahead.

The reflector gun-sight on our fighter aircraft had two settings: 1). For aircraft you were shooting at (eg., He111 or Me109), and 2). For the distance you were shooting from, which we set at 250 yards, the distance our guns were eventually harmonised to. When firing from behind, you used no deflection. At 30° you had to allow 60% of his estimated speed in order for your bullets to meet him. The greater the angle, the further ahead of him you had to shoot, and to get his 'flying line' right was practically impossible. I didn't realise just how little I knew about gunnery until I became an instructor. I learnt all I know at CGS.

Stapme took great pride in passing on what he had learnt at CGS to other less experienced pilots. He was appointed Acting Squadron Leader on 6 October 1943.

CHAPTER SEVEN

FLYING COMMAND

On 25 July 1944, Stapme was back on flying duties with No.83 Group Support Unit. He returned to operations on 23 August 1944 with 247 (China-British) Squadron, part of 124 Wing, 2nd Tactical Air Force (TAF), flying Typhoons from beachhead code B.6 in northern France. He:

> . . . travelled down to Hurn where, with a number of other Typhoon pilots, I carried out a series of flights to re-acquaint myself, I then did a few more trips during which I fired off my rockets at a target in the sea. From Hurn I flew across to the B.6 landing ground.

On 25 August, 247 Squadron's Commanding Officer, Squadron Leader Robin McNair, who had recently led them in the operation to close the Falaise Gap, was tour-expired and with a Bar added to his DFC, was posted back to England. Stapme took over the following day. Later described by his fellow squadron members as: '. . . a tall South African with blond hair and a Buffalo Bill moustache,' Stapme was recognised as an 'ace' of the Battle of Britain and although his former nickname was known, he was called by the more traditional nickname for a CO: 'The Boss'. Also, on 25 August 1944, the Allied forces liberated Paris.

Flight Lieutenant Basil T. 'Tatters' Tatham, his B Flight Commander, had also only just been appointed and was on his second tour of duty. Stapme developed great respect for Tatters, during what was a particularly hectic period of fighting, which he maintains to this day. Tatters was destined temporarily to take over command of the Squadron when Stapme was reported 'missing'. Having attained the position of commanding officer, this period of Stapme's career was very eventful and could be considered the pinnacle of his wartime flying career.

Shortly after arriving, he had his choice of a logo painted on the starboard side of the fuel tank cowling of his particular aircraft, MP126, code ZY-Y, by the squadron artist Flying Officer 'Spy' McKay. The brightly coloured artwork showed the Nazi swastika with an eagle atop in flames as the result of a sixty-pound rocket which was just making contact with the middle of the swastika. Stapme named it 'Excreta Thermo' but, prudently, Spy McKay didn't include the wording. Spy also designed the squadron Christmas card for 1944, which, as fate decreed, Stapme would miss. In 2001, Spy's daughter visited Stapme and together they enjoyed a chat about her late father, his time with 247 Squadron and the legacy of his artwork.

Based on the European mainland, 247 Squadron initially took part in operations to close the Falaise Gap from their airfield at B.6 (Coulombs), where Stapme took over command. As the allied forces advanced inland, so the squadron followed, first to B.48 (Amiens/Glisy), then B.58 (Melsbroek) and, finally, during Stapme's time with the Squadron, B.78 (Eindhoven). 247 provided aerial support throughout the Arnhem campaign and for his service during that battle Stapme was awarded the Distinguished Flying Cross (Dutch).

In Normandy the pilots had ample supplies of the locally produced Calvados (apple brandy) which Stapme remembers with amusement: '. . . not only did we drink it, we also used it in the paraffin lamps and our Zippo lighters.'

At this time 247 gained two jeeps, one of which Stapme commandeered for his own use. Operational inactivity immediately after his arrival enabled the two jeeps to be used to visit nearby areas that had only recently been vacated by the Germans. The trip round the countryside provided many true pictures of war missed by pilots flying high above the devastation and carnage. The Squadron ORB includes details of this trip but Warrant Officer Michael 'Crusher' Croft kept a Squadron diary of his own and clearly exhibits a talent for observation and writing:

> We passed through towns and villages, which but a week or two back we would have approached from the air with the utmost caution. Of them all, Aunay-sur-Odon proved to be the most pitiable spectacle. We had viewed it often from the air, it was a useful landmark, a great sandy waste, with the gaunt shape of the church, the only surviving building, casting its shadow across the desolate surround.
>
> From the ground the real extent of the destruction could be gauged. Great yawning craters and immense piles of rubble covered the whole area, giving it the appearance of a close-up picture of the moon. Only the church remained to give an air of sober reality to the dreadful scene.
>
> Beyond Aunay we came upon a large field-gun drawn by a huge diesel tractor gun carrier which Jimmy Bryant had destroyed with cannon fire. There was also a Tiger tank which had received a direct hit from a rocket. Entering the hull just below the turret, the projectile had cut right through the thick armour, striking the opposite inside wall of the tank before exploding. The explosion blew the turret off the tank and bulged out the far wall by some six inches.
>
> Further along the road to Thury-Harcourt we discovered the scene of a tank battle, a grim and rather tragic sight. A Sherman and a Panzer Mk.IV sat burned out at some six hundred yards spacing. Both were wrecked and surrounded by the belongings of their late occupants. There were blankets, letters, tinned food, tooth brushes and other worthless little articles, and most significant of all a few tin helmets gored with a jagged round hole. Evidently the Sherman must have been knocked out by the Panzer, which in turn was destroyed by a following British machine.

There were other sights less pleasant. In one lane we were forced to drive past piles of dead horses, literally oozing off the road into the ditches and reeking with putrescence. Dead animals are a common feature of the villages that have suffered heavily from shelling. One often finds the fields and orchards littered with dead cows, bloated out of shape and their legs pointing stiffly to the moon.

These villages smell badly, not only with the reek of dead flesh, but with a strange smell of a far more insidious and subtle nature. One notices it particularly where many of the houses are in ruins, it is a smell of musty wallpaper and decaying furniture, the real smell of utter destruction and desolation.

The wrecked villages are a pitiful sight. Their houses still standing with stark staring walls and gaping sides, exposing with humility their poor secrets upon an unsympathetic world. Or sometimes lying broken and scattered, soiling and crushing the small treasures and simple lives it was their purpose to safeguard and shelter.

We drove until after dark, along roads pitted with craters and lined with graves; past shattered woods and wrecked tanks; past columns of refugees returning to the remains of their homes. It was pleasant to arrive back ourselves; too much sight-seeing makes one morbid.

Whilst operations continued Stapme didn't lead his first patrol until 27 August. The mission was to attack the loading installations and a ferry at Caudebec-en-Caux, on the River Seine. The operation was successfully carried out achieving good results despite some quite determined opposition in the form of flak. All 247 Squadron Typhoons returned safely. Stapme comments:

The Typhoon's eight rockets could be fired in twos or all eight at the same time. The ever-present danger with the low level attack was pulling out too late. In reality the worst thing you could do after a ground attack was pull up. Once you'd dived down to make your attack you stayed down, very little could touch you then, but if you went down and pulled up, they could nail you. I think that's why so many pilots were lost flying Typhoons on ground-attack sorties.

Another of Stapme's memories is of the distance flown from their first few airfields in order to attack the enemy:

From the beachhead we never flew very high because there wasn't the opportunity. Our close proximity to the enemy meant the operations were like 'circuits and bumps' because what we attacked was practically in our flying circuit to the airstrip. We could take off, turn immediately towards the enemy, identify the designated target, carry out our attack firing rockets and cannon, and land in one circuit. It was all over in minutes. Once down we were refuelled and re-armed and took off again.

At one stage before I arrived, the Germans were shelling our aerodrome and the airstrip, and the pilots had to fly the Typhoons back to Hurn, near Bournemouth.

We had an army co-operation officer, whose father had a brewery near Old Sarum. My aircraft was fitted with two 45 gallon long-range drop tanks and then we flew back to England, dropped them at Old Sarum and flew on to Colerne (Wiltshire) where the aircraft were serviced, which would only take a night. The next morning we flew back to Old Sarum, and picked up the two drop tanks full of beer before flying back to France. We were very popular as we were the only people who had such a luxury. It was so simple to get the beer out, all you needed was a little pump because it had all the right connections in order for the petrol to reach the engine. They were brand new tanks that had never been used and later on we only used them officially on two occasions during operations from Eindhoven, as those sorties were slightly longer than the trips from the beachhead.

As our forces moved inland we had a specific area to cover from B.6 and although we were very busy we didn't see much action until we got to Brussels. Because the German army was pulling back so quickly we had to hop from one landing-ground to the next. We used three sites before we reached Brussels and if I remember correctly we stopped at another airstrip briefly before moving to Amiens but this went unrecorded. From Amiens we went on to Brussels. From Brussels, the longer range, higher altitude (8,000 feet) patrols started. There seemed to be very little in between the beachhead and Brussels and until we arrived at the Belgian capital we lived in tents at the airstrip. A section of the ground crews went ahead to establish the airstrip, tents etc., and the aircraft would then take off and make the move. Some of the ground crews remained behind to bring the remaining equipment.

We had quite a character in Wing Commander Kit North-Lewis. He had been in the army prior to joining the RAF and still gave the army salute for which he took quite a ribbing: 'Go and get your khaki on!'

At 07.00 hours the next day, rumours of a move were confirmed when 'A' Echelon of the ground party moved to B.30 at Creton. The short journey of 70km took thirteen hours due to congestion on the roads by the massive number of support vehicles for the advancing Allied forces. In the interim eight Typhoons carried out an armed reconnaissance of the Forêt de Lyons/Cisers area. Unfortunately poor weather negated any possibility of their carrying out an attack and all aircraft returned to B.6. The weather in the Coulombs area closed in and the pilots were unable to join the ground party. Warrant Officer 'Crusher' Croft wrote:

> Since all our kit was packed in the lorries and half the Wing had departed with the road party, life for the next twenty-four hours depended on one's skill and improvisation.

Croft flew with 247 Squadron from B.6 right through to the end of hostilities, the longest serving 247 pilot during that period. Croft was the name of his step-father and post-war he changed his surname back to Shirley, that of his real father.

By lunchtime on 30 August, conditions had improved. At 14.00 hours the pilots were briefed and just after 16.00 hours the Typhoons left B.6 – Coulombs, in sections of four, arriving at B.30 – Creton, after a 30 minute flight. The pilots found their recent wait well worthwhile; their new surroundings were pleasant and the locals welcoming. Croft recorded:

> From the first it was obvious that we had made a very good exchange. The country in the vicinity was much cleaner and fresher, with rolling wooded hills, rich orchards and charming villages. The airstrip was cut through a cornfield and was quite free from the fearful dust which we were forced to tolerate at B.6. The people in the district appeared to be much friendlier than in Normandy – they had suffered more from the Boche and less from the ravages of fighting. After we had arranged our bedding on top of the hay in a huge barn, washed and shaved from water which trickled drop by drop from the drain pipe, we then dashed into the village for our first soaker of French wine. We drank the place dry and returned somewhat hilariously to our resting place in the soft hay.

With the pilots released from duties the next morning they had a little more time to shake off the effects of the previous night, but when the lorries from 'B' Echelon arrived, everyone helped in erecting the tented billeting and squadron offices.

The relief expressed at having a cornfield runway is significant. The landing strip at B.6 had been a very dusty site and the clouds of coarse particles took its toll on engine wear and also penetrated the working components of the guns. Servicing was therefore required far sooner than if they had been using a dust-free strip. The Typhoons returned to Hurn in order for this essential maintenance work to be carried out.

On 31 August, the British 1st Army reached Amiens and captured the Somme bridgeheads. On the 31st General Montgomery was promoted to Field Marshal.

During the evening the Squadron received orders to attack a concentration of German transport near Amiens. Stapme led 12 Typhoons on this mission. The following details were recorded in the diary:

> We forged out at high speed, and found when we arrived over the target area, a road crammed with horse-drawn guns and vehicles. God knows how many times we attacked, or how many of the enemy we clobbered – it was a massacre. With the first attack the horses went crazy and bolted across the fields, the big guns crashing along behind them. Jock Coull dropped a salvo into a bunch of them making for the safety of a wood. They never reached it. There was no opposition and all the aircraft returned to B.30 with ample fuel to spare.

As progress was made by the advancing allied ground force, so 247 was required to move to an alternate airfield site, in close proximity to the frontline.

By 1 September 1944, elements of the foremost allied troops were nearing Belgium and 247 Squadron received information about another impending move, the exact destination unknown. By this time the allied forces had outdistanced the Wing and all that could be done until confirmation of a move came through was to allow essential work on the aircraft to continue. That afternoon the CO of 124 Wing, Group Captain Charles Green [later Group Captain Charles Green DFC, DSO & Bar], accompanied by Australian Pilot Officer Bernie Lee of 247 Squadron, took off to carry out a reconnaissance of their next airfield site, B.48 at Glisy, near Amiens. The next day tents and equipment were loaded aboard the lorries for an early departure the next morning. That night the hayloft in the barn was once again requisitioned for the pilots to sleep in.

At 07.30 the next morning, the ground party left for the new site. At 10.30 the Typhoons took off, watched by the local inhabitants who had turned out in great numbers in order to see them off.

The new site at Glisy was in fact an aerodrome, but having recently been occupied by the Germans the buildings had been almost completely destroyed by the retreating enemy or by the advancing allied forces.

By the time the Typhoons approached the airfield the ground party had already set up the tents. The Typhoons touched down next to the runway and taxied cautiously between the shell craters to dispersed sites, but shortly after they were moved again due to the threat of mines. That afternoon some pilots took the opportunity to visit the city of Amiens, its cathedral dominating the skyline. It was a Sunday and therefore the streets were very quiet. The pilots found the city centre devastated and small wooden huts had replaced the rows of shops that had once stood on the site.

The next morning 30 Douglas DC3 Dakotas flew in with fresh supplies, which included rations, petrol and rockets, for both 124 and 137 Wings.

The four squadron commanders tossed a coin to decide which two units would be released for the day. No.247 was one of the lucky ones and after a quick lunch, wash and change of clothing, the pilots once again headed for Amiens. This time the men found that the city was a little livelier and they were able to purchase various souvenirs. The diary reads:

> After tea the groups filtered back to the Chanticleer where cognac, anisette, pretty women and a piano helped to create a very carnival atmosphere. With Ken Brown conducting, the China-Britons took the stage by storm and gave a fine rendering of 'McNamara's Band'. At one stage in the festivities a sudden quiet fell on the whole place. A batch of German prisoners were being marched along the street outside. It was uncanny that silence; one could feel the atmosphere heavy with malice and hatred. Finally an individual started hissing and booing until within a few seconds the whole crowd had followed suit. Those Huns must have felt quite awful.

The next morning the Wing was on the move and tents, kit and equipment were once more packed and loaded aboard the lorries. This time there was no basis for a comfortable stay outside of the tents, as there were no buildings left standing for miles. A German dugout was later discovered and camp beds were erected for the pilots for when they returned that night from another hectic visit to Amiens. The diary reads:

> Some types went in search of wine, others food and some sought women, while very greedy fellows had a go at the whole set-up. Whatever pleasures gained were soon forgotten in the four-mile drag back to the 'drome.

During this walk four of the pilots had a close shave when, a few minutes after crossing a bridge spanning a railway station and goods yard, an ammunition truck exploded sending shells and bullets in all directions in the area followed by ear-splitting detonations. The cause of this explosion was never discovered.

Stapme had not gone on this trip, but late into the evening he was called to attend a 'house of ill repute' in Amiens where Bernie Lee had become a little too drunk and disorderly:

> There were three squadrons to the Wing, and when we got to Amiens we tossed-up to see who was going to have 24 hours off, and I won. So all the pilots went into the town of Amiens, the ground crew were unable to go because they had work to do on the aircraft. They'd only just arrived anyway by road from the airstrip we'd just left. I chose not to go into town. I had other things to do, including getting maps for Brussels and for the area between Amiens and the Belgian capital, I knew we would be going there in two or three days time, as soon as the Germans had cleared out of Brussels and Melsbroek. There were two aerodromes in Brussels – Brussels and Brussels/Melsbroek – which is where we went. I was busy getting the maps ready for the move, there being three maps, one for Amiens districts, one for between Amiens and Brussels and one for Brussels itself. I wanted each pilot to have copies of those three maps, in case he got separated for any reason at all.
>
> At about 21.00 hours a military policeman asked me if I was the CO of 247 Squadron, to which I replied in the affirmative. He said he and his colleagues were having a problem in Amiens with one of my pilots. I had a BMW motorbike at the time and I said I'd go along on this and bring him back. I followed the policeman down to this place where the MP had to pay his 60 francs for which he received a 'French Letter' in return as well as entry to the establishment. It was a three-storey building and the stairs were chock-a-block. The chaps on the stairs appeared to know what it was all about because Bernie Lee wouldn't come out of his room. He was so drunk it was unbelievable. I managed to find my way past all the bodies up to his room and remind him who I was. He said: 'Yes alright, I'll come out, now I know it's you Boss.' He was passed down the stairs, overhead, by what were mainly army troops who were lying all over the place with the women. I managed to get him on the bike and tied him to me using the belts from our trousers. On the way back to the aerodrome people would shout things at us and Bernie would sway about on the back of the bike, arms flailing, shouting back: 'Go to hell!' and

the like. As he gesticulated towards them, so we veered over in that direction. He would throw his arms about and the bike would wobble off-course. Eventually, we got back to our tents and I helped him to bed.

During the night, Bernie Lee got out of bed and staggered outside to vent some of the large amount of alcohol consumed just a few hours before. As he stood outside his tent in the cold night air he had a moment of panic before discovering, to his surprise, he was still wearing the contraceptive issued at the brothel in Amiens.

On 3 and 4 September 1944 the allied forces liberated Antwerp and Brussels. On the 6th, reveille for the pilots of 247 Squadron was at 04.00 hours and after a quick breakfast and last-minute packing the road party set off at 05.40 hours. Its destination was B.58 at Melsbroek, just outside Brussels. After lunch the pilots were called to Intelligence for briefing. Here Wing Commander Kit North-Lewis informed them that they were assured of a rapturous welcome from the local inhabitants who had only been liberated three days earlier. The Typhoons of 247 took off at 15.15 hours and took 45 minutes to reach the new advanced landing ground. Their arrival was later recorded in the Squadron diary by Warrant Officer 'Crusher' Croft:

> When we circled the aerodrome of Melsbroek, and saw the beautiful capital of Brussels spread out before us we began to wonder if there might not be something in what the Wingco had said after all. As soon as we touched down and were rolling along the strip alongside one of the 2,000-yard runways our doubts were dispelled forever.
>
> We parked our machines on the grass on the southern side of the 'drome and walked over to where we had to pitch our tents, a level strip of ground immediately adjacent to the wire fence surrounding the aerodrome. As we walked across, a rousing cheer rent the air; the far side of the fence was packed with people from the nearby village, all shouting and yelling and waving flags. They were genuinely glad to see us, of that there was no doubt; here was none of the pitiful apathy of the French, or the smug complacency of the English at home. These people had suffered under the Boche, and we had driven the tyrants away, and they were grateful for it.

The ground party arrived half an hour later and was barely recognisable after its drive through the Belgian capital. The lorries were covered with flags and flowers tossed onboard by the eager locals who had filled the pavements in throngs. The airmen were loaded down with offerings of fruit. At the airfield large numbers of boy scouts who had helped to clear the runway now set about the task of helping to erect tents and unpack kit. Children rushed to the nearest village for hot water and returned with fruit and eggs in addition to the hot water. In return the airmen gave them cigarettes and chocolate as rewards. The pilots wasted little time in taking advantage of the local hospitality, leaving behind the appropriate number on standby. The Squadron diary records the ensuing revelry:

We washed and changed as quickly as we could before the admiring gaze of the children and then, boarding a lorry, rushed into the city of Brussels. As soon as we climbed out, having arrived at our destination, we were literally grabbed by the citizens and hustled off in groups to the cafes and night clubs. It was then almost dark but we had seen enough on the way to make us realise that this was indeed a beautiful city and as we learnt very quickly, one containing many attractions.

The people of Brussels were crazy with joy. They thronged the streets singing songs, mostly in English and crammed the cafes drinking and dancing. Wherever we were taken we were cheered and acclaimed as heroes, and our entry into any cafe always without fail caused the orchestra to strike up with 'It's a long way to Tipperary' or the National Anthem.

It all came to an end eventually and we drove back to Melsbroek feeling very happy and pleased with ourselves and with the knowledge that we had made many new friends. Let us hope we remain here for some time.

On Thursday 7 September no operational flying took place mainly due to poor weather. Returning from lunch it was found that the tents in the camp site had blown down and heavy rain made things uncomfortable. It took hours to get things under control in the face of the howling gale. The scouts turned up again to lend a hand, and after weighing down the tent flaps with great rocks it was deemed safe to make another trip to Brussels.

At 10.30 hours the next day ten Typhoons of 247 Squadron led by Flight Lieutenant Jimmy Bryant (who eventually took command after Stapme was shot down) took off on an armed reconnaissance sortie of the Venlo-Wesel area. This was the first mission which took the Typhoons over Germany and in order to increase the range of the aircraft, rockets were not carried. The Typhoons attacked a number of targets on the River Rhine, damaging four barges and leaving two tugs sinking. They also attacked a train, destroying the locomotive. Flak was reported as being thick but inaccurate and all aircraft returned safely to Melsbroek.

That afternoon operations continued when four Typhoons led again by Jimmy Bryant successfully attacked gun positions and following that Stapme led a section of Typhoons in an attack on transport north of Tiel. With little opposition they destroyed four vehicles and damaged another ten. Group Captain Green led the final sortie of the day when eight Typhoons carried out a reconnaissance patrol of the Schelde. There they attacked a number of vehicles on a wharf, starting several fires in the process. The flak was later described as 'one hell of a barrage' but, having assessed the level of success, the pilots managed to depart the situation without loss.

More action followed on 9 September, with cold, clear weather providing excellent visibility – ideal operational flying conditions. The first sortie of the day was an armed reconnaissance in the Flushing/Woensdrecht/Breda area and eight Typhoons took off at 08.37 hours. They located a locomotive pulling passenger coaches and destroyed it with cannon fire. Five E-Boats were also sighted going south along a canal and were attacked and set on fire. A number of barges were also attacked and damaged. At 09.20 hours, all aircraft returned safely. Later in the day a second sortie was mounted with good results, although the weather had begun to deteriorate.

That evening the pilots inevitably made their way into Brussels to enjoy the entertainment and, unlike at some of their previous locations, a plentiful supply of drink. The Squadron diary reads:

> Nearly every other building in the centre of town houses a cafe or a night club, usually with an orchestra. Women are very attractive and very eager to make friends. Naturally one cannot obtain meals in the restaurants. Essential foods are very scarce in Belgium, but there is plenty of fruit at prices that compare ridiculously with equivalent goods at home. Grapes are one shilling a pound, peaches up to sixpence for the finest! One can purchase ice-cream too; most of us haven't had any for over a year. It is such things as bread, milk, cheese and meat which are so scarce.

At 07.26 hours on 10 September seven Typhoons from 247 Squadron left on an armed reconnaissance sortie. They destroyed a locomotive west of Breda and then attacked a road convoy south of Eindhoven.

The second sortie of the day occurred in the afternoon in response to reports of sixty plus MT (mechanical transport), although in the event only 20 vehicles were located and attacked with rockets (rocket projectiles – RP). Sergeant Pilot Sid Jones fired at a stationary goods train with cannon, by which time he was the only one who hadn't exhausted his ammunition supply.

Wing Commander Kit North-Lewis led six Typhoons on the final patrol of the day over the Schelde estuary. Four barges laden with troops and one flak ship were attacked with rockets and cannon.

On 10 September, news came that two DFCs had been awarded to pilots in the unit. One was to Flight Lieutenant Jimmy Bryant who celebrated in style at a Brussels hotel where, for the first time in months, he had a luxurious bath and breakfast in a bed that had fresh sheets. Unfortunately, somewhere along the way he contracted dysentery. Sadly, the other award to Flight Lieutenant Dick Guthrie was posthumous.

Operations the next day were delayed by ground mist but by late morning this had cleared enough for 16 Typhoons of both 247 and 182 Squadrons to take off on a mission to attack 88mm gun emplacements north-west of Tiel. The position of the guns was first marked with red target indicator smoke before the site was pulverised with 128 sixty pound rockets.

Following lunch, two sections of Typhoons left in response to a visual control post/forward control post signal which reported a number of German tanks in the Tiel area (VCP/FCP usually consisted of an armoured car equipped with R/T to direct close air support). Due to low visibility caused by haze the tanks were not located, but a tree-lined road was strafed, in the hope that the enemy were using the foliage as cover.

Haze was again responsible during the third sortie of the day to Axel. With the primary target unidentifiable due to low visibility, B Flight did manage to locate and destroy three barges on a canal. The pilots made it back to base just as darkness closed in.

The next morning saw no flying due to haze, but after lunch a reconnaissance sortie to the Walcheren area saw much action, as recorded in the ORB:

> We were on the look-out for craft of all kinds. Mickey Magee, leading B Flight was the first to go down, taking his No.2 with him and leaving 'Crusher' Croft and Jock Coull, his three and four, up above. The target was a large vessel out in the estuary; it suffered a magnitude of cannon strikes, but nothing happened and it was thought to be unmanned.
>
> Following this, the whole section went down on some barges in the canal, whilst Jimmy Bryant took his section on to some more barges up by the lock gates. Two flamers and three damaged were claimed. Flak was pretty fierce but quite inaccurate.
>
> By the end of the attack, the two sections had become separated, JB (Bryant) moving east and Mickey drifting south. Flushing was passing on the port side (at a very healthy distance) when attention was attracted by twelve Tiffies [Typhoons] bombing a couple of whacking great ships in the Flushing Roads. It was Mickey's opinion that if his section moved in as the bombers moved out, the flak gunners would be caught re-arming.
>
> Happy in this assumption, the four machines turned over and screamed downwards on to the target. Mickey's theory didn't work out very well. No sooner had the section dipped wings than a solid cloud of white flak puffs obscured the ships from view. There was no going back, so in went Blue Section, through the screen of smoke, into the holocaust beneath. Dante's Inferno had nothing on it. Red hot metal was streaking across the straits from both sides, forming a cone with its apex centred immediately above the target. Probably the haze saved the day, for no one was hit. The ships, cause of all the trouble, were raked with cannon fire but rocket firing would have been much better under improved conditions. Pulling away from the attack, the types [Typhoons] were followed steadily by forty and eighty-eight millimetre flak. Still there were no casualties.

The morning of 13 September dawned with conditions good for flying but by the time the crews had been called for operations a rapid build-up of cloud began to present problems. During an armed reconnaissance in the 's Hertogenbosch area pilots observed a V2 rocket climbing into the sky some distance away. This sighting was later reported to the Intelligence Office and was possibly the first sighting of a launch of this fearsome weapon.

Stapme led a second armed reconnaissance later in the day over the Flushing Roads. The Typhoons attacked two stationary 3,000 ton ships and fired a number of salvos of rockets at the first, scoring several direct hits, before scoring a number of strikes with cannon fire on the second. A 2,000-ton ship was spotted moving north-west and was also raked by cannon fire which started a number of fires. Three tugs were also strafed.

There was no operational flying the following day which provided the opportunity to catch up on some of the domestic chores. The adjutant constructed an effective hot water heater from a 45 gallon drum which provided hot water for basic ablutions at least. In the evening the Squadron was released and the men went to Brussels where, despite a bomb explosion in the Plaza Hotel, caused by a booby-trap left by the retreating Germans, everyone had a good time.

The morning of 15 September presented unsuitable flying conditions and it wasn't until late in the day that the Wing Commander led A Flight and the CO of B Flight in an attack on a battery of 88mm guns that were causing problems for the forward troops near Lichtere. Red smoke was laid down as a target indicator and although the guns were not actually seen, the area disappeared under a cloud of smoke from the hail of rocket salvos and cannon fire delivered by the Typhoons.

An early morning reconnaissance of the Turnhout area was ordered for the next morning. Due to nearly ten-tenths cloud cover, the mission was almost aborted but for a small break which revealed two armoured personnel vehicles on a side road which were attacked leaving one destroyed and the other damaged.

In the afternoon the pilots took off on their second sortie of the day but returned to Melsbroek still fully armed after the army failed to provide a smoke indicator of the target as planned.

Success was achieved during the final sortie of the day when the Squadron received information from a VCP of a number of 88mm guns in the Turnhout area. Four Typhoons from B Flight led by Flight Lieutenant 'Tatters' Tatham took off and attacked the guns which were hidden along a tree-lined road, which was duly straddled with rockets. They were met with intense flak but before they could mount a second attack on the guns a fresh report came through ordering them to head for a site identified as a mortar position. In the absence of virtually no opposition the area disappeared under a salvo of rockets. All aircraft returned safely.

CHAPTER EIGHT

OPERATION MARKET GARDEN
AND A DFC (DUTCH)

Between 17 and 26 September the Allied Airborne Army, consisting of the 82nd and 101st US and 1st British Airborne Divisions were dropped at Graves, Nijmegen and Arnhem respectively, in order to capture the bridges over the Maas, Waal and Rhine. Once captured it was intended that the bridgeheads should be consolidated with the arrival of the armoured divisions having progressed up the main road through Eindhoven and Arnhem and that an air-ground thrust across the Rhine be attempted to project the allied advance into the German plain.

At 10.30 hours on 17 September the whole of 124 Wing was called to Intelligence where the pilots were briefed for what was described as a 'very important task'. Stapme: 'General Brian Horrocks gave us a briefing of how we should carry out our missions – from the north-west, going through Arnhem up to Zutphen and a soft approach into Germany.' The operation directed the Wing to attack at low altitude the flak positions that posed a threat to the incoming gliders and parachutists. Each squadron was allocated its own separate position to be neutralised. The mission was the start of what was codenamed Operation Market Garden and consisted of two phases: 'Market' was the seizure of the Eindhoven and Nijmegen bridges by the American divisions and it went to plan. 'Garden', in which the British would gain control of the bridges at Arnhem ended in disaster when the airborne forces came under counter attack by the 9th and 10th SS Panzer divisions which happened to be at Arnhem recuperating from the battle at Normandy. Only the northern section of the main road bridge was taken, but following vicious house-to-house fighting, the British were forced to relinquish it on 21 September. The British Armoured Division (Guards) tried to force its way through the airborne corridor on a 'one tank' front but was held up by fierce resistance and despite reinforcement by the Polish Parachute Brigade, 1st Airborne Division could not hold its positions after 25 September and abandoned them that night. Those that evaded capture attempted to make their way across the Rhine and back to Allied lines.

Just after 11.00 hours, Stapme led the first attack by 247 Squadron to neutralise opposition to the aerial traffic. The force of eight Typhoons left Melsbroek and the first sections to arrive in the area received a hot reception from the German flak units. The first section dived to attack and managed to destroy one site with another damaged. A second attack of a section of four, led by Flight Lieutenant Jimmy Bryant destroyed another site. At 12.40 hours, 12 Short Stirlings arrived over Arnhem and dropped the first of the pathfinder troops, just 20 minutes before the massive airborne assault began.

Stapme led his Typhoons back to base where they were briefed for the next part of the operation. Their next role was to provide support for the armoured columns. The long, straight, white concrete road leading to Eindhoven was to be kept open and clear of any opposition. 124 Wing pilots were told: 'We are prepared to suffer casualties; all attacks must be pressed home regardless of anything.'

At 14.25, ten minutes before H-Hour, the guns of 30 Corps began to lay down a rolling barrage, one mile wide and five miles deep along the Eindhoven road. This was reinforced by eight Typhoons every five minutes, each aircraft making individual strikes with rockets and cannon. The operation appeared to onlookers as a constant stream. Within 30 minutes a cab-rank style back-up of Typhoons had occurred overhead, all waiting to make their attack.

At 14.40 hours, Stapme led eight Typhoons away from the airfield at Melsbroek. Their brief was to attack a German force concealed in woods along the main route of the advance. According to the controller (in an armoured half-track moving with the column) the attack was a success. In order that they be easily identified on the white, pine-tree-lined Eindhoven road, each advancing tank of the Irish Guards carried a fluorescent pink marker panel. The attacks by the Typhoons were so efficiently directed and carried out, they were able to initiate strikes on targets as close as 200 yards from British tanks.

Later, a section of four 247 Typhoons attacked a corner house in the village of Valkenswaard, five miles south of Eindhoven, which had been reported as being a strong-point. The house was destroyed, in addition two nearby flak units were also neutralised. In the evening eight Typhoons were ordered to attack a large building in the same village. The diary reads:

> It was a very impressive show. It was dark, much darker than usual owing to the lowering rain clouds driving in from the west. Only towards the western horizon was there any brightness, where the setting sun cast orange beams which, striking the aircraft, en-haloed them with fire as they streaked across the wild sky. Below, in the earth shadows, numerous fires from burning houses and shattered vehicles flickered dully, illuminating the surrounding gloom with a suffused glow. Into this macabre scene the rockets from the diving aircraft streaked earthwards crumbling the buildings at the north end of the town in pillars of dust and flame, and sparkling cannon shells twinkled their way along the roads and across the roofs, seeking out the enemy who were hidden in the ruins.
>
> Very noticeable were the fluorescent screens used by our troops to mark their positions. We could see the square panels glowing pink along the road from Valkenswaard southwards to the Escaut Canal, where long convoys of trucks and guns eased their way into the enemy lines.

The Typhoon attack enabled the ground force eventually to overcome any remaining opposition and by dusk the Irish Guards had achieved the day's objectives.

Overall, the first stage of the operation over Arnhem was a success due, in part, to the Typhoons of 124 Wing in reducing the threat from flak and providing air cover to any opposition on the ground. Unfortunately, things became a great deal tougher with bad weather playing a major part in keeping the Typhoons on the ground and helpless to support the airborne forces on the ground as they came up against stern opposition.

18 September dawned shrouded in mist with visibility not exceeding 1,000 yards. However, the urgent need to provide air support for the ground forces meant that a mission to attack German tanks which had been sighted in the American Sector near Nijmegen where a counter attack was being made against 505 and 506 Parachute Regiments, had to go ahead.

At 12.17 hours, Stapme led four Typhoons away from Melsbroek and into the mist. After a fruitless search of the Groesbeek area for the German armour, they landed back at Melsbroek after a flight of one hour and 15 minutes. The next day the weather was even worse with visibility down to 500 yards and despite the curtailment of operations by 247 Squadron a large number of allied transport aircraft and gliders just managed to get down at Melsbroek with fresh supplies, despite a number of hair-raising approaches. With the 247 pilots eager to provide all the aerial support they could, but unable to do so because of the weather, they were left feeling frustrated and helpless. The diary reflects this:

> A strange war this. We, forced by the weather to laze about and
> take things easy, whilst away to the north the airborne fellows at
> Arnhem are having the hell beaten out of them, for the lack of
> help which it is our purpose to provide.

With poor weather still prevalent on 20 September, eight Typhoons took off on another fruitless search for enemy guns and troops to the north of Nijmegen. They returned to base having encountered complete low cloud cover over the target area.

Following lunch the Squadron was ordered to prepare for a move to the recently liberated airfield B.78 at Eindhoven in Holland. With all equipment hastily packed away and stowed on the lorries an advanced ground party, consisting of two-thirds of the ground-crew personnel, set off. The Typhoons, their pilots and a basic ground-crew contingent with equipment would receive orders to fly when the airfield had been declared safe and the basic facilities organised. As the progress of the Second Army around Eindhoven had been halted, they were still at Melsbroek the next day when orders were received for one section to carry out an armed reconnaissance to the north of Arnhem. No targets were located and the aircraft returned to base. The pilots of A Flight, led by Flying Officer Bob Walker-Lutz, were more fortunate in finding a target. Unfortunately, the attack had tragic consequences, as the ORB reports:

> The four aircraft of the section were flying in the area laid down
> for their recce when F/O Walker-Lutz called up on R/T to say he
> was going down to attack a stationary truck at E.7484. He dived
> to the target spraying it with cannon fire, his No.2 followed him
> down. It appeared that F/O Walker-Lutz failed to pull out of the
> dive, and crashed into the ground at approximately 350 mph. His
> aircraft immediately burst into flames, the following aircraft

seeing it burning. One pilot reports he thought there was light machine-gun fire from the ground, but it was difficult to ascertain whether or not F/O Walker-Lutz was hit.

Walker-Lutz was buried at the Apeldoorn (Ugchelen-Heidehof) General Cemetery, Gelderland, Holland.

What was formerly a German barracks provided the accommodation for the pilots' final night in Belgium, with the remnants of the Squadron being confined to quarters in the event that an evening in Brussels would be overly taxing. This restriction was overcome for several of the aircrew when a number of girlfriends came to the barracks to say their final farewells. The social life while at Melsbroek left many feeling melancholy when the time came to move on.

Whilst at Eindhoven Stapme recalls:

> When Harry Broadhurst [later Air Chief Marshal Sir Harry Broadhurst GCB, KCB, CB, KBE, DFC*, DSO, AFC, Knight Grand Cross of Order of Orange Nassau and Legion of Merit (US)] visited us he had a beat-up BMW. I had a Wanderer motorcar donated to me by the Eindhoven Phillips works along with a radio. When he saw the Wanderer (an open tourer like the Humber Super Snipe) he said: 'I'll have that, you can have mine.' And that was that, he was a higher rank than me, what could I do!

On Friday 22 September the weather had improved and the Typhoon pilots were able to unleash the fire power of their aircraft during several armed reconnaissance operations. During the first – over the Reichwald Forest/Gleve/Goch area – a large number of stationary German transport vehicles were attacked.

With all aircraft landing safely back at Melsbroek, the remaining men were briefed at 13.00 hours for their flight to Eindhoven. In the event it was delayed until 17.10 when all four squadrons of the Wing departed, carrying out an operation en-route. The departure of a whole Wing was an impressive sight, with the roar of the Napier-Sabre engines as they weaved from side to side along the perimeter tracks in one long line and the pitch of the engines increasing with the volume of sound as they accelerated along the runway. Once airborne, they formed up in loose Wing battle formation, before setting course for Gemert. As they approached the designated target area the Wing split into squadrons, then sections, before weaving at low level in search of the target. As they looked they were met by flak arcing its way skywards from various locations. A staff car was observed by Flying Officer Magee, as it pulled up outside a large barn, which was duly attacked with rockets and cannon fire completely destroying the barn and a number of vehicles which had been hidden inside. During this mission German transport was also attacked as it sheltered in a wood.

Poor weather returned during this sortie and with a lowering cloud-base and visibility down to about three miles there was some confusion with so many aircraft airborne in the same area, as the diary confirmed:

> Jonah, who was following the Wingco, became isolated in some flak, Stan [Stanley] became isolated among some dive-bombing

Typhoons; all of which left Crusher [Croft], the Wingco's No.3,
completely by himself and quite unaware of his position. His only
landmark was a burst of Bofors which periodically smutted the air
whenever a kite lingered near the area. Crusher was still orbiting
the smudge at a healthy distance when Mickey Magee turned up
and led the way home. Tim Lloyd had a narrow escape when a
twenty mil' shell burst inside his fuselage, spattering one side
with ragged holes and half severing a control cable.

The 247 pilots managed to land their aircraft between the bomb craters at
Eindhoven. Although the former Luftwaffe airfield was a vast expanse, on
landing the pilots couldn't help but notice the large number of artillery pieces
positioned on the northernmost boundary of the landing ground. This sight
prompted memories of the sleepless nights they had experienced earlier in
Normandy.

During the previous sortie Warrant Officer Jack A.D. Meechan had reported
a drop in oil pressure and pulled out of the formation and put out a 'Mayday'
call on his radio. Turning south he steered his stricken Typhoon, ZY-C, towards
the British. He then chose to go against normal procedure of turning speed into
height and finding a suitable landing site, and simply maintained course
towards his own lines in the hope that he had enough forward speed to make
the distance. When the engine seized completely he put his aircraft down in a
field and, thinking the Typhoon was about to burst into flames, he clambered
from the cockpit and ran for cover still wearing his parachute. When the dust
cleared and he realised that his aircraft was not about to catch fire he returned
to the Typhoon and set his guns to 'safe', as they were pointing at a nearby
farmhouse. Undecided as to which way to head, Meechan noticed a number of
soldiers making their way towards him from the adjacent field. Drawing his
revolver he realised the futility of any hope of fighting his way out; he was
practically surrounded. The rag-bag soldiers were actually a number of
Dutchmen in civilian clothing armed with a variety of weapons and wearing
German helmets and orange armbands. Initially suspicious of Meechan, they
were assured of his identity after a brief, although limited, verbal exchange. He
was relieved to learn that he had landed in No Man's Land, with the retreating
Germans three kilometres to the north and the British somewhere to the south.
He was taken to a nearby farmhouse where he washed and ate. Some of the
Dutch welcoming committee departed to contact forward units of the army
whilst the remainder stayed with Meechan. After a short while a lorry arrived
to take Meechan back to Eindhoven and [the Dutch] were surprised to see the
pilot open a wing panel [on his aircraft] and remove a camp bed, blankets,
pyjamas and his washing kit.

Back at Eindhoven the squadron tents had been erected alongside a pine wood
flanking the airfield perimeter. The diary reads:

> Rumour had it that there were still some Huns abroad in the
> wood, but since it was obvious we were not going to get any sleep
> from the noise of the guns, we couldn't care less.

For 22 September it reads:

The fellows up at Arnhem seem to have had their time: the foul weather which kept our aircraft on the ground has enabled the enemy to bring up strong reinforcements. Our position isn't exactly pleasant, we are surrounded on three sides by the enemy, by a matter of a few miles east and west and about one mile to the north, in short – anything might happen!

On the 23rd the weather was not ideal for operational flying, but two armed reconnaissance missions were carried out with Stapme detailing Pilot Officer Bernie Lee to lead a section to Gemert on the first flight. Following their return to base having spotted no worthy targets, Flying Officer 'Tatters' Tatham then led his section at low level over the Reichswald Forest area. On investigating smoke coming from a wide track, the pilots discovered a vast line of trucks parked end to end along a clearing. The Typhoons peeled away to port and dived to attack, as they did so they were met by heavy flak and although there were several near misses, all aircraft returned to Eindhoven.

The same day a Wing operation took place just before dusk. German positions north of Arnhem were attacked in support of the many marooned paratroops. On returning to their airfield late into the evening the 247 Typhoons had to delay landing as a number of Typhoons from 137 and 182 Squadrons had crash-landed on the airfield. That evening Jack Meechan was returned to his Squadron in style by the Dutchmen with whom he had spent the previous night. He was driven onto the base in an ex-Wehrmacht (German Army) Mercedes staff car, in the company of a nurse and an armed escort. Meechan recalled:

It was great to be back, if a little bit of a put down to find that the nurse and the Mercedes were considered the important arrivals! There was a quick pooling of any spare chocolate, oranges and fags to be given to my Dutch escort, and they roared happily away.

With Operation Market Garden all but over, the afternoon of 24 September saw Generals Horrocks and Dempsey make the decision to withdraw the 1st Airborne Division, having failed to meet up at Arnhem. It was to be another seven months before allied forces entered the town. It had been a most valiant effort, and many courageous acts punctuated what was ultimately a defeat. For his leadership of 247 Squadron during the Arnhem campaign, Stapme later received the Distinguished Flying Cross (Dutch).

The Allies were held in deadlock for the next four months due mainly to stiffening German resistance, bad weather and logistical problems. The winter months of 1944/45 saw a number of small advances with limited objectives. The fighting was bitter, drawn out and took place in poor conditions.

During this period 247 Squadron played their part in preventing German reinforcements reaching the frontline units to the north and east of Arnhem. Locomotives and trains were the principal targets and on Sunday 24 September, Flight Lieutenant Jimmy Bryant led eight Typhoons on what was to be the final operation of his first tour (which comprised 131 sorties when the usual length of a tour was 100). He led an attack on two stationary locomotives with steam up and 20 trucks in tow, near Griete. Flight Lieutenant McKenzie's aircraft was hit by flak and had to force-land at Eindhoven. During the attack, the Typhoon pilots were informed that a force of 50+ Messerschmitt Bf109s was in the area, but none were seen.

During the morning attack Wing Commander North-Lewis managed to stop a train loaded with vehicles. In the afternoon a second attack was mounted in an attempt to destroy the train and its cargo. Unfortunately, by the time the Typhoons reached the site the Germans had cleared the trucks of its vehicles, perhaps in anticipation of further attacks. The pilots destroyed the locomotive and trucks, and in addition attacked and claimed three more trains as probably destroyed, before heading back to base. Flak had been intense throughout the sortie, particularly during the final attack during which Flight Sergeant Tim Lloyd was killed. Flight Sergeant Al Lye described the loss in his report:

> Near Gelden a train was seen and Pilot Officer Lee, leader of the section, dived down onto the target. Flight Sergeant Lloyd followed, going into a dive firing his cannons. Suddenly his starboard wing appeared to catch fire but went out. Almost immediately the port side of the fuselage burst into flames and he shrieked through the R/T that he had been hit. His aircraft, a flaming mass, plunged towards the ground, and the pilots who passed over the target shortly after stated they saw it burning.

Lloyd was 21 years old. He was buried at the Reichwald Forest War Cemetery, Germany.

Wing Commander North-Lewis also led the final attack of the day going in search of two ferries reported to be operating across the river at Arnhem. On reaching the location the pilots found that the ferries were not operating and, under directions from the army, they attacked a section of railway north-west of Nijmegen instead. The Typhoons also attacked what was thought to be a mortar position in a wood north-west of Arnhem and during the flight back to their airfield they strafed a locomotive at Griete.

Mist and rain once again prevented flying on the morning of 25 September, and the pilots sat around at dispersal. Later a meeting was held at Intelligence, which involved all Wing pilots. The subject of the discussion was which tactics should be adopted in light of the increasing threat by the Luftwaffe. The Squadron diary noted that during the morning:

> A rocket from one of the aircraft sailed across the dispersal, sending all of its occupants to ground. This was just as well because it put the fellows on their mettle, so that when a few minutes later a Messerschmitt Bf109 streaked across, spurting cannon shells all over the place, the types were biting the dust almost before the first shell landed. One of the shells went through Mickey's (Magee) dream kite, much to his annoyance.

Early that afternoon eight Typhoons attacked a number of mortar and 88mm gun positions at Boxtel, having first marked the site with red smoke indicators. As had been the case in the days of the action at B.6 in Normandy, the action could be seen from the airfield. The matinee was followed by a later performance when eight Typhoons from 181 Squadron along with four from 247, attacked a factory near Best, just four miles from the airfield. The factory was being used by German machine gunners which were holding up the advance of the ground forces. The attack was a success with the building being completely destroyed.

247 Squadron made the final attack of the day at dusk when Stapme led an attack against self-propelled guns to the west of Arnhem. It was at this time that the airborne troops were preparing to make their withdrawal under the cover of darkness. Apart from one large explosion, little was seen of any results achieved due to the fading light.

The next morning saw a slight improvement in the weather and Stapme detailed 'Tatters' Tatham to lead a section in an attack on German troops and a machine-gun position in the village of Beng which the army had come up against. No red smoke target indicator was evident on arrival in the area but the control car (VCP) insisted on an attack which Tatham duly initiated. On his return to Eindhoven he was met with a message of congratulations from the army unit involved.

At mid-day orders came through to mount an armed reconnaissance in the area between Arnhem, Zutphen, Keppel and Reichswald Forest. Several vehicles were shot up with cannon fire and rockets were fired into the railway sheds at Gennep, causing a number of loud explosions. Generally the mission brought about limited results.

At 14.00 hours Flight Sergeant Barwise arrived as a replacement pilot and was immediately involved in the action when he flew on the last sortie of the day. Their brief was to attack German troops and guns in the village of Schijndel, about ten miles from Eindhoven, which were resisting attacks by the allied forces. The Typhoons took off at 17.25 hours, arrived in the area at 17.45 and orbited the site until the red smoke target indicator appeared. They then dived to attack. The ORB reports the event:

> On arriving over the target Flight Lieutenant McKenzie, followed by his No.2 dived down to release rockets and blazed away with cannon. Flight Sergeant Barwise followed with Blue 4, (Pilot Officer 'Pinky' Pincombe) on his tail, both releasing rockets and blazing away with cannon. Flight Sergeant Barwise was seen to go into a steep climb weaving all the time to avoid flak – this was the last thing seen of him – he did not call over the R/T, nor was seen by any aircraft to have been hit.

Flight Sergeant Barwise was reported as 'missing'. His time with the Squadron had been brief, just four hours. Some months later the unit received news that he was a POW and had apparently spent some part of his incarceration at Stalag Luft III at Sagan, Poland – scene of the 'Great Escape'.

CHAPTER NINE

'ENJOY TODAY, FOR TOMORROW WE DIE!'

Early on the morning of 27 September the duty pilot roused his colleagues and informed them that as from 06.00 hours they were on 15 minutes readiness. Forty-five minutes later, having been briefed, Stapme led his Typhoons away from the airfield on a sortie to the Arnhem/Zutphen area, where they attacked a barge, a tug and a number of petrol tanks. On its return to base the pilots had their first glimpse of the new Me262 jet fighter/bomber as it streaked across the sky pursued by a number of Spitfires hoping, in vain, to catch it.

The next sortie by 247 consisted of a close-support attack against tanks and troops in a wood near Wijbosch. The next target of seven tanks in addition to assorted transport vehicles at Barnweld was not found, but their alternative target, an SS Headquarters, was razed to the ground in the subsequent attack when the pilots unleashed both rockets and cannon. The final sortie of the day was at Gerwen when the Typhoons attacked troops and guns. Red smoke was laid down and the area devastated by rockets and cannon fire.

The 15th Scottish were facing stubborn resistance from Germans in the pocket near Best. Loud speakers were rigged and the Germans told their situation was hopeless and that they should surrender but, if they did not, a squadron of Typhoons would attack their position. A final attempt to clear them out was ordered and at 18.00 hours on 28 September, seven 247 Squadron Typhoons took off to make their attack. Two large petrol fires were started as a result of the rockets fired but no movement was observed. During this sortie tragedy struck. Flight Lieutenant McKenzie noticed a small panel come away from the aircraft of Pilot Officer Bernie Lee during the attack. The whole tail unit then fell away and the Typhoon spun into the ground. (A weakness in the tail section was a particular problem with the early production Typhoons resulting in a number of fatal accidents. The tail sections of those and subsequent marks of Typhoon were reinforced to rectify the problem.) Lee's aircraft was seen to go up in flames by several pilots, which was confirmed by McKenzie during his second circuit. Regaining control of the aircraft would have been impossible and the altitude was too low to bale out – a constant danger during low-level attack. Australian Bernie Lee, the star of the Amiens brothel, was dead. He was 24 years old.

The German resistance finally succumbed when they surrendered after a further attack by the Typhoons of 137 Squadron two hours after the attack by 247. German prisoners were later visited by a number of the 247 pilots. It was later recorded in the diary:

> They were impressed to see how shaken the Huns were. They said
> that they hadn't experienced anything so terrifyingly dreadful.

They also insisted that many of the troops would have given themselves up earlier had it not been for the Officers and NCOs shooting them down as they came out of cover.

The final two days of September brought limited success against a number of barges, but the weather and serviceability of the Typhoons curtailed full-scale operations.

It was during this period that Stapme met with a slight accident:

At Eindhoven we took over a nunnery which the Germans had used as their officers mess. It was quite comfortable and we had a room each. Both squadron commanders had a jeep and each evening we used to go to the officers club where we had our ration of a bottle of champagne each. One damp, misty night Squadron Leader Vincent and I were returning through cobbled streets in Eindhoven when I ran out of petrol. The four-gallon Jerry can on my jeep was empty. Fortunately, Vincent was behind me in his vehicle, but as I climbed out of my jeep and tried to stop him, he saw me too late in the mist and couldn't stop in time on the wet cobble stones. I jumped out of his way and hit my head on the kerb. Vincent pulled over, poured the four gallons of petrol he had in his Jerry can into the tank of my jeep and off I went to see the doctor. He put eight stitches in the wound. Prior to the return journey Vincent said: 'You go ahead and if you don't feel right just slow down and let me know.' So off we went with me in the lead. When we got back to the officers mess there was no sign of Vincent so I turned round and went back to discover his jeep had hit a pile of 25lb shells which had been stacked at the side of an elevated section of country road. The jeep had gone down a bank of eight feet or so and I picked Vincent out in my headlamps, standing on the side of his vehicle. As I came round the corner all I could see was his head. I picked him up, took him to the doctor who wasn't amused as it was by that time quite late, about 00.30 or 01.00. Vincent had four scratches on his face which went across his eye, but they were superficial so didn't need dressing, but the doctor thought it necessary to put a patch over the eye. Later, Tedder [Marshal of the Royal Air Force Lord Tedder] came to visit and after he finished his talk we asked him a number of questions we had been primed to ask. He spotted Vincent with his eye patch and me with my stitched eye and called out: 'I see you chaps have been in the wars!'

The protective plaster over Stapme's right eye is evident in a number of the photographs taken during this period.

On Sunday 1 October 1944, the weather kept the Typhoons on the ground until early evening. In anticipation of 247 being at Eindhoven for some time to come, the day was spent improving the dispersal area, making it more permanent. A hut was erected for the duty pilot complete with stove in preparation for the seasonally cold weather to come. A brick-built pathway was laid linking the various squadron 'offices' and a mound of grass was established proudly displaying the squadron number using more of the bricks, but painted white. On completion of the work a number of group photographs of the pilots were taken with the '247' featuring prominently.

At 17.15 that evening Wing Commander North-Lewis led an attack against various concentrations of mechanised transport, infantry, and armoured vehicles which were making a counter-attack near the village of Huissen, to the south of Arnhem. The pilots faced intense flak over the target but managed to fire their rockets on target, aided by the red smoke target indicator. The Typhoons also attacked a number of the flak positions and the crew of a 20mm gun were seen to be wiped out. During the attack the wing commander's aircraft was hit but all aircraft managed to return to base.

The pilots were at readiness again by 06.30 hours the following morning but it was not until 08.30 that the first sortie of the day took off – an armed reconnaissance in the Arnhem/Kranenburg area. The Typhoons opened fire on three vehicles on the road south-east of Elton, destroying one and damaging another. They also attacked a camouflaged building at Amersfoort which they suspected concealed petrol bowsers, but were unable to assess the results.

During the next sortie Stapme led eight Typhoons in an attack on field guns that had been harassing forward British troops. Both rockets and cannon left the site in a pall of black smoke. One of the undercarriage legs of Warrant Officer R.G. McGregor's aircraft dropped down during his dive on the target which put him off his aim. The leg would neither drop into a locked-down position, nor raise fully up. On returning to Eindhoven McGregor carried out a successful wheels-up landing.

A concentration of German troops in the tiny hamlet of Huissen provided the target for the final sortie of the day. The presence of the enemy soldiers was witnessed by the Typhoon pilots when they arrived over the site and small arms fire was observed from the windows of the houses. Within minutes the village was reduced to rubble by both rockets and cannon fire.

The next day operations were limited due to poor weather, although one armed reconnaissance was mounted and a train attacked. During this sortie one section became lost but eventually returned to Eindhoven where it was calculated that they had inadvertently flown over an area of the dreaded and heavily defended Ruhr valley at just 2,000 feet. Fortunately, they experienced no anti-aircraft fire.

The weather on the morning of 4 October provided improved operational flying conditions and a sortie was mounted against a strongpoint located in a large factory. The site was marked with green smoke target indicators and the building attacked with rockets, which collapsed the structure. The ruins were then raked with cannon fire. Later a sortie was mounted against a similar target which produced equally successful results. The diary recorded:

> The army types who were less than a mile away must have had a grandstand view of the attack. We have heard though that a lot of them are just as scared as the Huns and take instant cover if we attack anywhere in their vicinity.

On this day Flying Officer James Watchorn, RAAF, was killed. He was buried in Brookwood War Cemetery. He was 22.

The next morning saw the Squadron released for maintenance and in the afternoon an armed reconnaissance was mounted but no movement was detected in the area of the target. Later in the day a more successful attack was carried out by eight Typhoons on a concentration of tanks and troops south-east of Velp, on the eastern outskirts of Arnhem. After scouring the area for some time the pilots found only three lorries heavily defended by 20mm guns. During the attack one truck disintegrated in a huge flaming explosion and the other two were wrecked.

The next day the following entry appears in the Squadron diary:

> Yanked out of bed on a cold, clear, frosty morning, the first team, led by Tatters, found themselves at 06.00 ruefully contemplating the prospect of an armed recce in the Apeldoorn area. Recces are never greeted with fervour at any time, but under these circumstances the thought of a recce leaves one feeling very uncomfortable indeed. However, for a change this one proved quite interesting as it caught the Hun railways still busy after the night's activity. At first a loco hauling about 60 trucks out of Apeldoorn claimed attention, but rocket firing was a bit duff due to the strong wind and only cannon strikes were observed. Hauling away from the fury of light flak Tatters espied another engine and train belting away down a branch line at full steam. A direct hit on the engine sealed for all time its life as a loco and left a cloud of billowing steam soiling the crisp morning air. A third attack was begun but broken off in the face of intense and accurate flak, all the guns in the neighbourhood having opened up on us by this time.

The Typhoons were airborne again by 09.32 having rearmed and refuelled. The target was again the railways and two trains were attacked and damaged near Deventer. After returning safely to Eindhoven the aircraft were once more rearmed and refuelled before another armed reconnaissance took off at 12.22. This time a passenger train was attacked as it headed towards Hengelo, damaging the locomotive and destroying four carriages.

At 15.45 a two squadron operation took place when fifteen Typhoons took off on a mission to attack what was described as a large white factory building on the river west of Nijmegen where infantry activity had been reported. Whilst no initial activity was reported by the pilots the attack went ahead and the buildings were reduced to a mass of blazing wreckage. A few German troops were seen running from the building and were picked off with cannon fire as they made for cover.

Soon after breakfast on Saturday 7 October, the Squadron was brought to 15 minutes notice. The pilots idled around, some waiting in Intelligence for the inevitable news of their next operation. At 11.38 it came in the form of an armed reconnaissance to the Apeldoorn/Amersfoot area to search for rail activity and V2 sites. Shortly after, Stapme led eight Typhoons away from Eindhoven in search of prey. The designated targets were not found but a small convoy of three vehicles were strafed, destroying two and damaging the other.

Soon after lunch, eight Typhoons took off on an armed reconnaissance into Germany where they attacked around a hundred ammunition trucks at the marshalling yard at Coesfeld. Approximately 40 of the trucks were destroyed causing many small explosions and fires as the contents ignited. At the same time as this operation was carried out, a large force of Avro Lancasters bombed the towns of Kleve and Emmerich, which according to the 247 Squadron diary:

> . . . provided Tatters and Company a spectacle of frightful and mighty proportions. They could see the great heavy bombers forging slowly and inexorably through the evil smutted ack-ack puffs; and could see the bombs winging their way down towards the town beneath, already heaving and writhing under the impact of the first missiles. Smoke and dust fused into a massing cumulus nosing its way upwards into higher levels where the fighters wheeled and circled around the bombers, protecting them from the enemy attacks. However, as surely as they [the 247 pilots] could have dealt with the marauding foe, they were powerless to prevent the flak clawing its victims down, and at least two of the bombers were seen to fall from the sky. It is not a pretty sight to see a great and beautiful machine suddenly plunge earthwards trailing the sky with tendrils of flame and oily smoke; still less to see it splatter bloody flames upon the ground beneath.

The last operation of the day for 247 was directed against ferries on the Pannerdensch Canal. No such vessels were spotted and the pilots strafed horse-drawn transport before returning to Eindhoven. The flak had been intense but all aircraft escaped serious damage. The following four days saw no flying of any kind due to poor weather although a Douglas DC3 Dakota flew low over the airfield escorted by three Thunderbolts. Two of the fighters broke off in an attempt to land. Conditions were such that the 247 pilots awaited the inevitable crash. One of the Thunderbolts pulled round in a steep turn in an effort to keep the landing ground in view. Undercarriage and flaps were lowered and the pilot tried to line the seven-ton 'Jug' with the runway. At 50 feet the fighter stalled and made contact with the airfield, port wing first. It then flipped over and slid along the ground upside down. Fortunately, although the engine had caught fire on impact, it had broken free from its fuselage mountings and had been left further back along the landing strip. The wreckage was hardly recognisable from its former state as it lay inverted on the grass, engine gone and wings smashed. Amazingly, as the fuselage was lifted by crane the pilot scrambled clear, bruised and shaken but otherwise unhurt.

With a lull in operational flying, the airmen improved their dispersal area, with work on a wooden dispersal hut started to replace the marquee that had become a little too draughty and uncomfortable. The Typhoons also received some cosmetic attention when they were washed, scrubbed and polished. By that time, each pilot had been allocated his own aircraft and their own choice of name/logo was painted on the fuselage of their respective steed. At one time personalising aircraft had been considered as inviting bad luck but as those who held this belief had either been killed or listed as 'missing', they thought the superstition without foundation and went ahead regardless. Stapme had no such misgivings.

By mid-day on 11 October, the weather cleared enough for the Squadron to be placed on thirty minutes notice. During the afternoon B.78 received a visit from His Majesty King George VI and Field Marshal Montgomery. The ORB recorded: 'All personnel were turned out to greet them, but organised shouts and cheers are seldom a success.' Stapme has confirmed that the event was stage-managed.

Just before dusk 247 received orders for an operation. A factory at St Agathe, a German strongpoint, was attacked with rockets and the target area was left on fire with smoke rising from the site.

Early the next day the sky was bright and clear and by 08.22 the pilots were airborne for an armed reconnaissance over the Arnhem/Zutphen/Neede/Groenlo area. With no activity seen from the air, despite careful scrutiny of the ground, they fired their rockets at a stretch of railway track. After a rapid turn round back at Eindhoven, the Typhoons took off again with orders to attack a wood at Overloon* reported to be hiding German tanks. No flak was reported over the site but Warrant Officer S.R. 'Taffy' Thomas carried out a forced landing south of Gemert following a glycol leak. In doing so Thomas's head struck the gun-sight of his Typhoon causing slight injury, but thankfully, he had landed in Allied territory.**

The Squadron carried out two further operations that day, against ferries, bridges and barges in the Venlo area. The pilots found no targets on the river but they strafed two lorries near Horst with cannon fire, destroying both.

The diary records the activities that evening:

> At 20.20 ENSA gave a show in the Airmen's Mess and the cinema show having been cancelled (no doubt to discourage those who do not appreciate ENSA) there was no option but to attend. However, miracles evidently not being confined to spirits and other supernatural bodies, we actually found ourselves enjoying ourselves. It was unbelievable. So often in these daily chronicles after a visit by ENSA it has been necessary to fill these lines with words of such vitriolic nature that the paper has all but burned up. It gives great pleasure to say that all present at the show spent a perfectly wizzo evening. Evidently ENSA have one good variety show at least!

At dawn on 13 October eight Typhoons carried out an armed reconnaissance in the Arnhem/Emmerich/Xanten/Gelders area. Blue Section went in first, destroying an armoured car. Both sections then combined in an attack on a concealed railway yard in the centre of Doetinchem. The site had been effectively camouflaged and only a tell-tale puff of smoke from a locomotive gave away its position. The Typhoons carried out several attacks and as they left the area a number of the railway trucks were seen to explode and burst into flames with a large fire also burning in the biggest of the workshops. Before setting course for Eindhoven, a barge was attacked on a river near Wesel. Whilst no hits were observed it was last seen to be out of control.

Stapme led a second armed reconnaissance which had equally successful results when a locomotive and coaches were destroyed in Venlo, as was a tug on a nearby river.

---

*Today Overloon is a tank museum.
**Warrant Officer Thomas's son is aviation artist, historian and author, Chris Thomas, who co-wrote a comprehensive history of the Typhoon with Christopher Shores.

As soon as the Typhoons had landed the pilots were debriefed while their aircraft were rearmed and refuelled for the next operation. In the interim all members of the Wing reluctantly gathered for a visit by the Secretary of State for Air, Sir Archibald Sinclair. Following what was described as an interesting speech, the pilots had lunch before the appointed group of pilots were briefed for an attack on a Panzer headquarters at Ouistrum.

At 14.39 hours eight Typhoons took off with the wing commander leading. During the flight to the target, Warrant Officer K.H. Brown called up on his radio to report that his aircraft had suffered loss of boost pressure and that he was having engine trouble as a consequence. He eventually turned back towards allied territory and a short while after he reported that he had managed to land and was unhurt. Unfortunately, he had failed to regain allied held territory and was taken prisoner by the Germans. The attack went according to plan leaving the Panzer HQ destroyed and black smoke curling up into the sky.

For Pilot Officer Osborne this had been only his second mission. During the attack one of his fuel tanks was punctured by flak and he turned for home with vaporised fuel streaming from the damaged tank. Osborne made a perfect forced landing at a water-logged landing strip just inside the allied lines.

At mid-day on 14 October, Stapme led his pilots over the lines at Venray where, in co-operation with the forward control point (FCP), an area of woodland reported to be an enemy strongpoint of mainly German troops was attacked.

The Squadron spent the rest of the afternoon repeating this operation, with sections of four aircraft queuing to attack in cab-rank fashion over the Venray target area. As the various targets were outlined by the FCP, the Typhoons swooped to attack. In response to this operation, Major General Whistler, commanding the Third Division, sent a note of congratulations for the excellent co-operation received from the Wing. These successful attacks on the enemy strongpoints and observation posts paved the way for subsequent allied advances.

Fine weather conditions on the 15th allowed flying operations to continue and at 10.30, orders came through for another 'cab-rank' operation to go ahead. A short while later two sections were airborne led by Flight Lieutenant Dave Crawford and Crusher Croft. The pilots received instructions from the control post to block the cross-roads in the town of Vierlingsbeck near Boxmer. Red smoke was laid down as a target indicator exactly on time and the Typhoons dived to attack. The ORB records:

> An example of complete co-operation between ground and air forces which had as its reward the successful completion of its purpose. The road was not only blocked by craters, but also by the burning rubble of a large building on the edge of town which received direct hits and immediately burst into flames.

In the afternoon Stapme was detailed to lead eight Typhoons on an armed reconnaissance over the River Maas and the Roermond/ Mönchengladbach/Geldern area. During the search for targets, about ten vehicles were spotted in the village of Bruggen and the Typhoons peeled off one at a time and dived towards the targets. Firing rockets and cannon the pilots left several large fires in the village centre and a number of lorries destroyed.

Two more vehicles were attacked in the Geldern area before they returned to Eindhoven, landing at 15.07 hours.

Poor weather prevented operations over the next two days but by 18 October it had improved enough for four sorties to be flown. The first three were carried out in support of a push by the army in the Venray area and entailed the now familiar 'cab-rank' build-up over the target area as each pilot waited his turn to attack. Stapme took the first section to attack a strongpoint in a wood. Although all rockets were seen to explode in the target area, no real results were observed apart from German troops who were throwing themselves into the shelter of ditches.

The next section to attack was led by Warrant Officer Meechan, their target being a road and railway junction marked with red smoke. The rocket strikes were seen to be concentrated in the target area. The section led by Flight Lieutenant Dave Crawford attacked gun positions in a wood but as was usual with that sort of terrain no results were observed due to the effectiveness of the enemy camouflage.

The last operation of the day was an armed reconnaissance of the Utrecht/Hilversum/Amersfoort area. However, thick cloud obscured the whole region and after a 46 minute flight during which the pilots made four or five sweeps of the target area hoping to find a break in the cloud, the two sections returned to Eindhoven with a full war load.

Poor weather the next day meant operations were again suspended and at 10.00 hours the Wing was stood down for 24 hours. Lorries conveyed the pilots and airmen to the theatre in Eindhoven where entertainment was once again provided by ENSA in a production of George Bernard Shaw's *Arms and the Man* starring Richard Greene. Afterwards, some went to the local cinema to see *Gentleman Jim.*

On the morning of 20 October the weather was still bad but the cloud base was sufficiently high for operations to resume. Eight Typhoons took off from the airfield at Eindhoven with Stapme and Flight Lieutenant Dave Crawford leading. The aircraft were directed to a small wood marked with green smoke to the north-east of Venray which was occupied by a force of German troops. The Typhoons were greeted with intense and accurate flak but managed to fire their rockets into the designated area and then carry out a second attack during which they strafed the area with cannon fire.

The next operation was led by Flight Lieutenant 'Tatters' Tatham and directed against a stationary train reported just south of Zwolle. The pilots located the train which consisted of approximately thirty open carriages carrying fifteen tanks and small cars. The engine appeared to have been damaged and several of its trucks derailed.

The Typhoons dived down to attack the target with rockets, although strong winds made accuracy more difficult and as a result a number of the rockets undershot. At least five direct hits were reported and the whole length of the train was raked with cannon fire several times. Several large explosions were reported after the attack.

Operations the following day consisted of attacks against the enemy railways. The first was an armed reconnaissance against a stationary train between Roermond and Rheindahlen (post-war, Rheindahlen became Headquarters, RAF Germany). The target was located and destroyed. Another target was spotted, as recorded in the diary:

> The Squadron roared down on a horse-drawn vehicle which
> turned out on closer inspection to be a milk float. It was not
> attacked. For some strange reason the float was defended by a
> forest of light flak guns, which made the attack still less
> worthwhile. A belt of 88mm fastened on to the Squadron as it
> turned for home and though no-one was hit, life was rather
> fraught for a few hour-long seconds.

During the second operation, another armed reconnaissance, a damaged train
consisting of about forty goods wagons was spotted near Amersfoort and the
remaining undamaged trucks were destroyed. The Typhoons also fired rockets
at a rail-road crossing in the same area. The final operation of the day consisted
of an armed reconnaissance in the Dordrecht/Gouda/Tiel area and although
little movement was seen, the pilots fired their rockets at the rail-road crossing
at Leerdon.

Early on the morning of 22 October saw the beginning of a push by allied
ground forces in the 's Hertogenbosch/Tilburg area. An armed reconnaissance
was requested, but the weather was not suitable and the pilots awaited an
improvement in conditions. Later in the morning a window of opportunity
came with a slight improvement in the weather and at 10.49 eight Typhoons led
by the wing commander roared away from the airfield at Eindhoven.
Unfortunately, ten-tenths cloud cover at 1,500 feet over the target area meant
that the operation had to be abandoned and the Typhoons returned to base after
what was a 30 minute flight.

Late on the morning of the 24th saw an improvement in the weather and in
response eight Typhoons took off at 11.27, their objective being to provide
close support over the 's Hertogenbosch area. The forward control point was
soon in touch with the pilots, and the target was a concentration of mechanised
transport in the small town of Loop op Zand. A number of trucks were
observed and attacked and after the attack at least two were seen to be on fire,
although confirmation of damage caused was difficult due to haze. From this
attack Flight Lieutenant Paul 'Shorty' Langston, did not return. Warrant Officer
Thomas followed the New Zealander into attack but lost contact in the thick
haze. No one saw him crash or any identifiable wreckage of his aircraft. It was
assumed that as there was no flak he must have suffered engine failure or hit
debris. His body was never found and his name is recorded on the Runnymede
Memorial. He was 22 years old.

The last operation of the day was an armed reconnaissance over the
Gorinchen area. No road or rail activity was observed but a few barges on a
canal were attacked. The evening's entertainment was recorded in the diary:

> The evening was spent in the most uproarious way in the Officers'
> Mess to which the members of the Sergeants' 'Mess' were invited.
> A serious beer drinking contest resulted with all and sundry
> becoming wonderfully happy. The Boss amazed the whole
> assembled throng by downing a pint in five seconds without
> spilling a drop [At 82 this feat is probably still not beyond his
> capabilities!]. The party finished with all the squadrons
> competing in efforts to make the biggest splash on the ceiling.

> Naturally we waited until the others had finished and then wrote a huge 'Chu-Feng' across the one part of the ceiling untouched; the part which no others could get to.

The following morning the entry in the diary brought the event to a conclusion:

> Upon rising this morning it was found that a really solid 'clampus dilecti' had descended upon the world, and as a consequence there was much chortling and smug satisfaction on the part of the pilots, who, although never lacking in keenness to smite the Hun, always welcome a day on the ground, if only as a tonic for tired nerves.

The poor weather continued for the next four days keeping all aircraft on the ground. Three pilots were granted 48 hours leave and the remainder toured Eindhoven. Although Eindhoven was a modern town, at that time an air of lifelessness hung over it, not surprisingly due to the conditions under which its inhabitants had existed under occupation. The shops were devoid of all but the cheapest of goods and there was not even fruit or vegetables. Traditional Dutch clogs were worn due to the shortage of shoes and many children walked barefoot. Rubber was not available as it was being used in the Nazi war effort. Reflecting this, the majority of bicycles had no rubber tyres and were ridden on the rims.

Exactly as forecast by the meteorological office the poor weather was replaced by clear blue skies on the morning of 28 October and for the squadrons from 124 Wing, operations began at first light. 247 Squadron were last in order for operations and they did not take off until 09.05 hours, the target being a four-emplacement artillery position near 's Hertogenbosch. The ground was white with frost and in the clear atmosphere the pilots could see the guns from 8,000 feet. The Typhoons dived at the target and destroyed the guns with rockets. As the aircraft carried out this initial attack, the Germans were seen running from their positions and gathering around a white flag which was being waved frantically. One pilot later recorded: 'What they expected to achieve by this act of surrender behind their own lines it is difficult to imagine, but whatever it was they were doomed to disappointment.'

The next section dived steeply towards the target and with the guns already destroyed, they directed their fire at the gunners, wiping them out in a welter of 20mm cannon fire.

At mid-day Stapme detailed Dave Crawford to lead six aircraft on an armed reconnaissance of the Amersfoort/Hilversum/Utrecht area. A number of transport vehicles were spotted in a side road and three attacks destroyed them all. Next, all six aircraft attacked a train with rockets but their accuracy was not as good as it could have been, although a direct hit on the trucks by one pair of rockets was observed. Flying Officer Jock Wallace, one of the new pilots, was forced to head for Volkel after his aircraft was hit by flak during the attack. There he made an excellent wheels-up landing without injury to himself.

That afternoon an attack was directed against a footbridge spanning a canal at Meijel that was being used by German troops. Two sections took off from Eindhoven; the first led by Flying Officer Mickey Magee found a gap in the cloud and climbed to 7,000 feet while the other section, led by Tatters Tatham, were unable to do so and approached the target at an altitude of 2,000 feet. However, this section was deterred by intense 88mm anti-aircraft fire and returned to base. To have attempted an attack at that altitude would have been suicidal. The other section also returned to base having failed to find a gap in the cloud through which they could have attacked the target. As they returned to their airfield two Fw190s dived out of the cloud on Red 2 and 4. Fortunately, the Luftwaffe fighters only made one quick pass before disappearing into the cloud from whence they came. Although shaken, the pilots returned safely.

During a long-range operation on 29 October, 143 Wing were to provide anti-flak cover. The diary recorded details of the sortie:

There was panic in the air this morning when the team was roused at 06.30 and hustled to Intelligence for briefing. On arrival it was obvious that it was not the usual early morning armed recce that had caused them to be summoned from their beds; representative teams from the other three squadrons were already present and the air was filled with mutterings and swift growing rumours. These quietened as the Wingco found his way up to the map, and were replaced by little gasps of indrawn breath and whistles of mingled awe and astonishment as the full weight fell on the ears of the assembled throng.

It became clear that upon those present had fallen a task of great importance; participation in an attack designed to breach the lock gates of the Dortmund/Ems Canal at Beveren, east of Rheine. Nos.137 and 247 Squadrons with the Wingco leading were to silence the flak positions around the target to facilitate the work of twelve Canadian Tiffies with two thousand-pounders each who were to do the actual smashing of the lock gates. Half an hour later, Nos.181 and 182 were to carry out a similar task in support of a further twelve bombing Typhoons.

At 08.00 the boys took off and, joining up with 137 Squadron, set course for their target, 115 miles distant. From a comfortable height of 11,000 feet they were able to look down on 137 who at 6,000 feet were having hell bashed out of them with light flak. They were running into thick belts of the stuff which was bursting in bands of white puffs. Approaching the targets, heavy stuff began to ferret around but the two sections with Dave Crawford and Crusher Croft in the lead, were well spread out and no damage was done.

Visibility was perfect and there was no difficulty in picking out the targets, although owing to their being concealed in woods the flak positions were virtually invisible. These woods, however, were subjected to a continuous stream of cannon and rocket fire which seemed to have an effect for the flak was wild and scattered. The bombers arrived on scene a shade too early and one at least suffered as a result. He was seen to dive smack into the centre of the canal. There was a brilliant flash followed by a billowing mass of turgid fire which ballooned into the air. It was a quick death with bombs still on.

After all the ammunition had been exhausted, the kites made a speedy return to base; the target was too near Rheine and Hopsten aerodromes for comfort. During the attack, the Spits and

Tempests doing top cover could be heard reporting jets taking off, but they did their jobs well and there were no incidents.

On 29 October, aircraft from 247 made a return visit to the foot-bridge at Meijel. On this occasion the weather was perfect and the Typhoons were able to make a long steep dive at the target from a good height. Flight Lieutenant Johnny Crossley scored a direct hit, destroying the bridge completely. As expected the flak was heavy and Warrant Officer L.H. Brown's aircraft was hit in the engine. After crash-landing a few miles from Eindhoven, his aircraft burst into flames before he could scramble clear of the cockpit. By the time he managed to free himself he had suffered slight burns to his neck and one eyebrow was burnt off. A large piece of shrapnel smashed through the canopy of Warrant Officer Terry Lewis's aircraft. It was his first operation. Lewis was unhurt but the hot, lethal shard narrowly missed his neck.

The final operation of the day was an attack on a German Army HQ at Dorn. On take-off, the Typhoon flown by Flying Officer Osborne suffered a burst tyre and the aircraft crashed alongside the runway. Immediately afterward the Typhoon flown by Warrant Officer S.L. Williams suffered the same fate, blowing the wheel off completely. Williams managed to get his aircraft airborne and flew to the bomb line and jettisoned his rockets before returning to the airfield where he carried out a perfect wheels-up landing. Warrant Officer Jock Coull was the next to be prevented from going on the mission. While taxiing, his aircraft suffered a puncture of the tail-wheel. By now it was clear that the airfield was littered with a number of sharp objects. As a consequence three out of nine aircraft had to abort the mission. Those who did manage to take part were easily able to locate the target and the building was severely damaged with five direct hits being observed.

Poor weather returned again for the final two days of October and the low cloud and mist kept the aircraft on the ground. The diary reads:

> The clamp continues and with it the life of laziness and boredom which at this time of the year is the only life we know when we are not bashing the beastly Boche. About the only task completed during the day was the completion of flying time in the log-books for the usual monthly summary, and that was hardly a considerable task.
>
> Of great value in passing the time during a clamp or interim periods between 'ops' is the comfortable weatherproof crew room with its wonderful amenities – open fireplace and wireless. The latter is not as useful as it might be; Arnhem radio station is too near. As a result all the British programmes are relayed by courtesy of Arnhem who cunningly include phoney news items and frightful invidious propaganda.
>
> The adjutant, convinced by the inclement weather that a tent is not the best place to toast bread and brew tea, has followed our example and commenced work on a wooden hut to house himself, his corporal and his piles of bumph. When it is completed the dispersal will have the appearance of a shanty town of the gold rush period.

On 30 October, the funeral of Pilot Officer Bernie Lee took place. He was buried at Eindhoven (Woensel) General Cemetery, Holland. The advancing allied forces had come across his aircraft in the Tilburg area where it had gone down (see page 128). Bernie Lee was still strapped into his seat amongst the wreckage and it appeared he had died of 'multiple head injuries'. Flying Officer Kay, Pilot Officer Fricky K. Wiersum, Warrant Officer S.L. Williams and Warrant Officer Lye attended the funeral as bearers. The adjutant, Flying Officer Kay later wrote:

> It was a cold and unpleasant end, and Bernie's 'Devil may care' attitude to life had met the sudden death he always expected – as he said so many times: 'Enjoy today for tomorrow we die.'

The improvement in the weather forecast by the met office for the beginning of November was not forthcoming and the overcast conditions continued thicker than ever. Later in the day, they improved when a slight lull in the clamp allowed a replacement Typhoon to fly in from Amsterdam, where it had been stranded, having been diverted from No.83 GSU at RAF Thorney Island on the Sussex coast. Warrant Officers Taffy Thomas and L.H. Brown left for 83 GSU in an Avro Anson to collect two more replacement Typhoons. No other operations were ordered.

Despite the night being clear, the clamp had rolled in again by the next morning. Nevertheless, operations brought the Squadron to readiness at 09.30 hours, in anticipation of any clearance in the weather.

After lunch the weather was deemed to have cleared enough for an armed reconnaissance to be carried out. Flight Lieutenant Tatters Tatham led six Typhoons away from Eindhoven at 14.20 hours for the Gorinchem/ Utrecht/Amersfoort/Tiel area. Just as the aircraft crossed the lines over Gorinchem an 88mm gun opened fire and scored a direct hit on Tatham's aircraft. The engine of the Typhoon took most of the blast and stopped as a consequence. Tatters was still at sufficient altitude to enable him to glide back over the allied lines and carry out a forced landing near Tilburg, without injury. The other Typhoons were able to continue the operation but saw nothing and landed back at base at 15.30 hours.

Cold dreary weather on 4 November quickly developed into a clear windy day. Stapme led an armed reconnaissance during which several barges were spotted on the canal east of Gorinchem and attacked with rockets. Three were destroyed and another three damaged. Two rocket strikes were also seen when a floating platform or wharf was attacked in the same area.

The next attack against the Reichskommissar Headquarters at Apeldoorn, was led by the wing commander. Despite several accurate rocket and cannon shell strikes against the building, the Reichskommissar survived. Flak was not particularly heavy, however, Flying Officer 'Jock' Wallace was lost during the attack. The ORB recorded:

> Flying Officer Wallace only arrived on the Squadron on 17.10.44, but although his stay was short, his rich Scots accent and ready wit made him popular. Flying Officer Wallace was detailed to fly No.2 in Red Section with the target a German Army HQ at Z8804 NW of Apeldoorn. On arrival of the formation over the target, the Wing Commander leading, dived down to attack with Flying Officer Wallace following him, from about 7,000 feet. At about

2,000 feet Flight Sergeant Coull, who was flying Red 3, saw Flying Officer Wallace do a roll and then go straight into the ground at about 500 mph. He burst into flames immediately. Other pilots of the formation are of the opinion that Flying Officer Wallace was hit by the light flak that was coming up, and they are quite certain that he did not bale out, but must have been either killed before his aircraft hit the ground, or if not, then certainly when it crashed.

The first operation of 6 November was also directed against a German Headquarters, at Isselburg, where General Student, commander of the 1st Parachute Army was thought to be attending a conference. All three squadrons of the Wing took off on the mission but it was aborted due to low cloud cover over the target area.

The second operation of the day was against a storage dump and Stapme led six Typhoons away from the airfield. En-route two of the Typhoons suffered engine problems and returned to base. The four remaining pilots, with Stapme still leading, located the target and attacked with rockets and cannon fire. The dump was left burning after a number of direct hits. Flak over the target area was accurate and a piece of shrapnel went through the radiator of Flying Officer Dennis Orriss's Typhoon, who was flying his first operation. He managed to return to base safely.

The pilots returned from the sortie and as was usual reported for debriefing in the duty pilot's hut. The diary reads:

A very unpleasant occurrence shattered the normal tranquillity that reigns in the dispersal. Two bombs fell! First warning of the descending missiles was a hushed roar in the heavens which was presumed to be a runaway rocket. When the whisper changed into a whistle and rose to a shrieking crescendo the awful truth registered in the waiting minds. Instantly the door of the hut burst open and seven bodies hurtled through the space and flung themselves into the mire in various undignified and self abasing postures. Pinky [Flying Officer J.A. Pincombe] alone remained standing, whether due to implicit faith in the Hun's inaccuracy or merely the slow registration of the facts upon his Canadian brain box it would be hard to say. When the bombs landed he was heard to say, 'Well they were going away from us anyway.' As they failed to detonate this of course confirmed nothing.

The final operation of the day was directed against frontline German infantry mortar positions south of Meijel. Cloud cover over the target was complete but for a small hole through which the Germans were directing the flak in anticipation of the attack. One section dived through the hole but were chased back through it a few moments later, returning to the blue sky above the cover of the cloud. The attack was aborted and all aircraft returned to base.

During the evening members of the Squadron went into Eindhoven where they watched a production of Noel Coward's *Blithe Spirit* with the full London cast appearing. Warrant Officer Taffy Thomas, whose sister was appearing in the play, secured front row seats for everybody. After a relaxing evening away from the rigours of combat flying, the men were soon feeling the stresses of war again when a V1 flying bomb flew low over the Mess before diving to earth and exploding a few miles away.

Squalls during the morning of 7 November gradually gave way to reasonable flying conditions, apart from the gale which blew at 90° across the runway. Dakotas and Harrows of Transport Command landed with fresh supplies. The cross-wind plagued these aircraft as they tried to land; some required two or three attempts to get down but fortunately and with all credit to the pilots, there were no mishaps.

Flying Officer Dennis Orriss had a miraculous escape on 8 November when his Typhoon suffered an engine failure over Eindhoven town centre. He managed to crash-land his aircraft in what was a very restricted space close to the railway yard. On impact the wings were torn from the fuselage which then inverted. Nevertheless, he managed to scramble clear of the wreckage with only slight shock and concussion.

Tragically, the same luck was not forthcoming for Flying Officer 'Ozzie' Osborne as he ferried a replacement Typhoon from No.83 GSU the following day. With low cloud cover and poor visibility he was forced to fly low on a day when he shouldn't have been flying at all. As he reached the Belgian town of Aalst his aircraft developed engine trouble and witnesses reported that the pilot seemed to make every effort to land clear of the village of Niewkerken. As Osborne tried to stretch the glide to take him to an area clear of the village, the Typhoon stalled and spun in from a height of 50 feet. The large oblong block of the Napier-Sabre engine was thrown clear on impact and the fuselage and wings crumpled and smashed. Ozzie Osborne died of multiple fractures and deep wounds. His body was recovered later by army personnel and buried in the Aalst Communal Cemetery, Holland. He was 22 years old.

On 11 November five Typhoons, led by Wing Commander Kit North-Lewis, took off on a mission to attack a German observation post. Directional finding was carried out for the first time in conjunction with a mobile radar control post. Although the system was more suited to bombers, if the trial was successful it would enable the Typhoons to approach a target obscured by cloud cover, as directed by the radar control post, and then when above the designated area they would dive through the cloud for a visual sighting. Although cloud was a frequent problem at that time of the year, the system saw little tactical success and was rarely used. On this occasion the MRCP directed the Typhoons over the target although there was little significant cloud in the area and the church steeple near Venray concealing the German observers was easily spotted and destroyed with rockets. An adjacent building was also set alight.

Poor weather was a regular feature during November and operations were again cancelled over the next six days. The following comments were recorded in the diary:

> If this weather is to continue, it will pay to have a rubber stamp made of the opening paragraph of the daily record of events. After the first two days of a prolonged clamp it becomes very difficult to find a fresh way of introducing the fact that the weather is non-op. One can write of the first day: 'A clamp has set in', followed 24 hours later by: 'The clamp continues'. The third and fourth days find the page adorned with: 'Still a clamp' and 'Clamp

again'. After that one has to lapse into wild metaphors and useless epithets in an endeavour to record for posterity the fact that the 'drome is shrouded in mist, deluged with rain or overcast with cloud, fourth, fifth, eighth or ninth day in succession. What a life!

During the morning of 17 November, the weather improved slightly and pilots were briefed for a reconnaissance of the Wesel area. The operation was due to be led by Flight Lieutenant Johnny Crossley, but after 15 starter cartridges and a great deal of cursing his aircraft would not start and Pilot Officer Johnny Porter therefore took command. Over the appointed area the Typhoons met a thick haze and heavy flak as they followed the route from Geldern – Wesel – Borken – Bocholt. They attacked a goods train, which damaged the locomotive and three box cars and then went for another train with covered trucks, which was spotted moving east. Having damaged a number of the trucks they landed back at Eindhoven just as the 'clamp' rolled in once again. The break in the monotony had been brief.

The diary entry for 18 November included:

> At last a vista of clear blue skies greeted the types when they ventured out this morning and though the Squadron was third off, it was not long before they were called to briefing. The first show was a recce in the Geldern-Kempen-Suchtelen-Roermond area, designed to deal with any locos or transports that might be met with.
>
> In accordance with our recent policy, a variant of a fluid six was flown, Dave Crawford with Red Section, flying at a comparatively low altitude with Jack Meechan and Jock Coull flying as top cover with Blue and Yellow Sections respectively. The show was unfortunately abortive, no movement whatever being observed.
>
> Within half an hour of the first team pancaking, the next team was called to readiness, and disposing of lunch as quickly as possible, rushed off to the gen room. Here another recce awaited them, necessitating the use of eight aircraft. Movement had been reported in the Erkelenz sector and it was the purpose of the sortie to seek and destroy any troops or guns observed in the area. The Boss [Stapme] was to lead Red Section and Crusher [Croft] Blue Section, but Crusher had to fall out with a faulty engine and Fricky [Wiersum] took his place. The intensive activity was conspicuous by its absence and so a devastating rocket and cannon attack was made against the seemingly undefended village of Wurm, with obvious results. This was Ginger Horn's [Flight Sergeant D.C. Horn] first introduction to operational flying. One could not wish for a more pleasant do.
>
> At 1600, just when we were anticipating being released for the day, a team of eight pilots was called to briefing, there to be informed that the Wingco would be leading them on a recce around Geilenkirchen, to inspect some tanks he had observed earlier in the day. Approach to the target was made without incident, Johnny Crossley leading Blue Section with Pinky as

number 3; calling upon the types to make individual attacks on anything they saw, the Wingco commenced his dive. This act of seeming aggression brought about a speedy mass withdrawal of Teutonic digits and within a few seconds the air was filled with streaking 20mm which showed up with distressing clarity in the gathering gloom. One of the ground gunners received a dose of medicine more potent than his own when Crusher and Johnny Porter diverted their attack and pranged him with a salvo of rockets and cannon shells. Although no claims were made, it is thought that at least one tank was knocked out, a number of pilots seeing a red flash followed by a dense cloud of oily smoke. All our machines returned unscathed.

In a message of congratulations from Headquarters of 20 Corps, the claim of *one* tank destroyed was later confirmed as being *four*. 20 Corps were also able to take some prisoners after the attack.

A repeat operation against the village of Wurm took place the next day when 12 247 Typhoons were joined by eight from 137 Squadron. The pilots were briefed to attack enemy movements in the area. Pilot Officer Fricky Wiersum had to return to base shortly after take-off due to engine trouble. The problem deteriorated before he could make the airfield at Eindhoven and he carried out a forced landing without injury to himself. The operation went ahead and a number of the village buildings were destroyed and left burning, having been attacked with rocket and cannon fire.

In response to orders from Group control centre, Wurm was the target again during early afternoon. On arrival over the village the weather conditions had deteriorated with a heavy rainstorm and a cloud base of only 4,000 to 6,000 feet. 88mm flak also greeted the Typhoons. The weather and flak made flying very difficult, but conditions became even more dangerous when a formation of Boston medium-range bombers drifted seemingly aimlessly across the target area. The Typhoons duly retreated from the target area and the raid was abandoned.

On 20 November, poor weather prohibited any operations and the pilots sheltered from the mist, rain, wind and low cloud in the dispersal hut. In the evening the boredom was lifted with a visit to the camp cinema where they watched *Princess O'Rourke* starring Olivia de Havilland and Robert Cummings.

The next day Wurm was again the target along with Beeck. Both villages were in close proximity to each other and were about a mile from the forward troops at Geilenkirchen and known to be still occupied by German troops, tanks and transport. 181 and 182 Squadrons would be led by Wing Commander North-Lewis and were directed to attack Wurm, while 247 and 137 were to attack Beeck, a total of 47 machines. The weather and bad luck were against the Typhoon pilots right from the start when both tyres of the wing commander's aircraft burst on take-off and his Typhoon blocked one side of the Eindhoven runway. With only a single strip open, the Typhoons took off one at a time, thus doubling the time it would normally take to get all aircraft airborne. Whilst 137 and Red and Blue Sections of 247 Squadron managed to get airborne, and just as Yellow 2 was rolling down the runway, flying control intervened to stop any more aircraft taking off until a number of Typhoons on a reconnaissance operation and short of fuel had landed. The remainder of Yellow Section, Crusher Croft and Jock Coull, were left at the end of the runway with 182 Squadron. The 182 Typhoons took off first but those of Croft and Coull had to return to dispersal to refuel as each aircraft had used over 40 gallons of petrol in 25 minutes of idling. Of the aircraft that had managed to get airborne, Warrant Officer Ray Stanley had to return to base with R/T failure and the remaining nine landed again shortly after as the weather over the target was deemed unsuitable for an attack.

That afternoon an attack was mounted against infantry positions at Maasbree, west of Venlo. This time take-off went without incident with 247 Squadron last to leave the airfield. The clear patch of weather that had allowed the first aircraft over the target to initiate their attacks had disappeared by the time 247 were in position and the frustrated pilots returned to Eindhoven.

The diary for 22 November reads:

> Extremely bad weather today, as it has never stopped raining from before dawn. Definitely no flying. This part of Holland seems to be groaning beneath the overwhelming tonnage of water that has descended these past two weeks. Mud, slush and dampness are the order of the day. The landscape provides but a dreary solace to the service type, who is far from home, wet, cold and cheesed. For those who work on aircraft it is wet, clammy, metal surfaces to the touch, and for those who work within the walls of the shanty dispersal, it is the drip, drip, of searching rain. And yet, in the absence of aircrew types at their messes, there is an atmosphere of peace and calm, and the maintenance 'erk' progresses on his leisurely way without the onerous need to have the job in hand completed by a specific time. What a pleasant sight – a ground type with unlimited time and little work. The aircrew part of the dispersal presents rather a humorous, if forlorn aspect. It is a sea of mud, out of which rises, triumphant, Johnny Crossley's two mosaic brick pathways. But, unfortunately, they both lead to nowhere. In the fullness of his talented enthusiasm, he spent many back-breaking days in building one from the marquee to the adjutant's tent, and upon its completion, was aghast to see the pilots building themselves a small wooden duty pilot's hut. Upon its completion it became the centre of No.247 ground/air activity. Not to be daunted, he built another from the adjutant's tent to the new hut, but retired from business when, a couple of weeks later, the adjutants moved from the tent to another constructed shack. Now the pathways lead to nowhere, whilst the streaming throng of feet between pilots' dispersal and orderly room, squelch in their muddy by-way.

A Squadron party was to be held in Eindhoven on 23 November, and with the continuing clamp prohibiting operations, the pilots were released to prepare for the evening's events. During the day the cat adopted by the sergeants mess was found dead under the bed of Warrant Officer S.L. 'Bill' Williams. The diary reads:

> Bill either would not or could not explain its presence there. The

wretched animal has had the smell of death about it for days and
no doubt considered Bill's bed as good a place as any to park its
body while its spirit departed for the cats' Valhallah.

The squadron 'do' got off to a slow start but the men warmed themselves
through the effect of beers, wines, music and women, who outnumbered the
men. By the end of the evening a few had progressed beyond the happy stage.
The adjutant mounted the dais and, using the microphone stand as support,
began to conduct a mass strip-tease on an elimination basis. Bill Williams,
apparently mourning the death of the cat, sank into deepest sobriety and was
taken 'home' by Stapme in the Opel, who put him to bed. Flying Officer Sherry
McWhirter apparently spent the evening being marched around the town by
two orangemen with his hands above his head; he was unwilling to reveal the
reason for this treatment. The 'do' was declared a success.

During the afternoon of the 27th a weather reconnaissance was carried out
with four Typhoons flying from Nijmegen – Mors – Calgar – Geldern. News
reached the Squadron that Pilot Officer Fricky Wiersum had force-landed in a
replacement aircraft he had collected from No.83 GSU. He managed to land in
a cabbage field close to the centre of Brussels without injury. The total of
Typhoons written off whilst being ferried to 247 in November was now four,
with one pilot killed. Great concern was expressed at the servicing practices at
the support unit.

The 28 November dawned bright and clear and an armed reconnaissance
over the Munster area was ordered. Flight Lieutenant Mickey Magee led the
three aircraft of Red Section while Warrant Officer Crusher Croft led the
foursome of Blue Section. The Typhoons were met by a barrage of flak as they
flew over the Reichswald Forest but once clear of this area things quietened.
Two locomotives were spotted by the pilots in the Coesfeld area. One, which
was travelling north, was brought to a halt and damaged during the attack. The
other suffered a similar fate. The Typhoons also strafed a signal box and a
railway bridge with rockets and cannon fire.

Six aircraft took off from Eindhoven on the second operation of the day led
by Stapme. The brief was the same as in the morning. The aircraft were met by
intense flak but they managed to destroy a locomotive, and the trucks it was
pulling exploded in a large red flash. They also set a building ablaze. Crusher
Croft returned to base ahead of the others after his aircraft suffered mechanical
trouble. He had also witnessed the demise of a 184 Typhoon when it was blown
out of the sky over the Reichswald Forest. He said it reminded him of sitting
in the dentist's waiting room listening to the howls of the previous patient.

A heavy downpour resulted in the cancellation of further operations that
afternoon. The rain continued through the night and into the early hours of the
following morning. However, by dawn it had stopped and the skies were bright
and clear. An armed reconnaissance of the Munster area was ordered. The diary
reads:

> The first sortie was a complete flop from the start to its very
> premature finish. Of the seven kites to take to the air, four landed
> almost immediately with mechanical faults of various kinds, and
> the other three, feeling rather under strength and lonely, followed
> them in only a few minutes later.

Equipped with new machines, the same team set off for another valiant attempt to blast the Hun. Tatters, who was leading, had to return with low oil pressure and Cliff Monk followed a close second with a rough running engine. Johnny Crossley took over and the Squadron surged on, intrepid and undaunted – only to have their good intentions thwarted by a veil of strato-cumulus.

At mid-day, six Typhoons took off from Eindhoven for another attempt at the Munster area. Flight Lieutenant Mickey Magee was leading. On arrival over the target area, no movement was seen so the secondary target, a railway yard in the village of Xanten, was attacked. As Flying Officer Sherry McWhirter pulled out of his dive, having fired his rockets, he alerted his colleagues that his engine was cutting out. Mickey Magee advised him to prolong his glide and head for allied lines, or at least get to the British side of Maas. Unfortunately, his engine cut completely while he was still several miles short. McWhirter called up to say he was about to carry out a landing with undercarriage still retracted. The next message was to inform his colleagues that he was down and about to start running. He was soon captured by the Germans and made a POW.

At dawn on 30 November, 247 Squadron was the first airborne when six Typhoons took off for an armed reconnaissance of the Bocholt – Munster – Rees – Wesel area. With Stapme leading the operation, the murky weather over the aerodrome necessitated a further assessment of the day's work in other operational areas. As they headed towards the Rhine, no movement was seen on the roads or railways and three factories were attacked and set on fire which prompted a fierce reply from the German anti-aircraft gunners. Late in the day, progressively thickening fog prompted the abandonment of the planned sortie and the aircraft returned to base.

On 1 December, the pilots awoke to continuing bad weather and sat around the fire in the warmth of the dispersal hut. Their relaxation was interrupted when they were summoned to the camp cinema to watch a tank recognition film. Following that the medical officer carried out eyesight tests. In the afternoon a football was kicked about and in the evening the pilots drove into Eindhoven to see the film *This is the Life*.

On 2 December, 247 attacked a factory to the west of Venlo which the Germans were using as a strongpoint. Despite poor weather conditions, 16 Typhoons of 181 and 247 Squadrons accurately hit the target with their rockets. As they left the area the building was burning fiercely with several loud explosions heard.

On 3 December the diary reads:

> Soon after nine an armed recce came up and six aircraft led by Mickey Magee set off for the Roermond/Krefeld area. Deteriorating weather conditions prevented penetration beyond Wesel and a return to base was made. Mickey spotted a loco at Neuss and pranged it successfully with cannon. Later, a second call to fifteen minutes readiness came through although the weather was then almost impossible. The Boss [Stapme] and Pinky [Pincombe] took a section each to attack a battery of 88mm guns at Straulen but were unable to ascend higher than 1,500 feet and so were forced to blow off the attack. Rockets were dumped

in the village of Welden which promptly disappeared under a cloud of smoke.

The first operation on 4 December was also aborted due once again to poor weather conditions over the target. When the cloud cleared slightly in the early afternoon, Mickey Magee led six Typhoons on an armed reconnaissance and over the Metelen area a number of trains were attacked: The ORB 'Details of Work Carried Out' recorded the following claims:

> 1 loco and 15 box cars attacked at A6896, loco destroyed; 1 loco and 4 goods trucks at V7003, loco destroyed; 1 loco at V6503, damaged; 1 loco and 12 trucks at V5403, loco damaged; 1 loco and 12 open trucks containing troops sprayed with cannon, troops were seen to scatter, many being killed.

At 08.45 hours on 5 December, two briefings were held simultaneously. One was for an operation to provide army support while the other was for an armed reconnaissance. Flying Officer Magee led four Typhoons away from Eindhoven at 09.49 hours to attack a gun emplacement near Neullaaren while eight more Typhoons led by Stapme and Flight Sergeant Jock Coull took off to attack a section of railway between Borken and Dorsten.

Flying Officer Magee located the gun emplacement which appeared to be empty. Nevertheless, all five Typhoons attacked the target with rockets and cannon. Meanwhile, Stapme led the attack on the railway track, despite some heavy flak which made them seek other targets. They came across five horse-drawn vehicles and two motor transport near Bucholt which they attacked. The outcome was described: '. . . with pleasing results, although it must be admitted that one always has pangs of regret for the luckless animals.'

The third sortie of the day was led by Tatters Tatham and was to the Ahaus – Coesfeld – Dorsten area. The pilots flew the outward leg of the flight above the cloud which nearly resulted in disaster. On descending they discovered to their horror that they were over the extremely heavily defended industrial area of the Ruhr. They rapidly recovered the cover of the cloud. The next time they dropped down through the cloud, they were over the Haltern area and three locomotives were spotted. The Typhoons attacked these and the adjacent yards four times in quick succession.

The final operation of the day was over the Munster area which ultimately provided a number of targets. One locomotive was destroyed and a vehicle left on fire. A factory was then attacked and left on fire and belching smoke. Another factory was then targeted and its tall chimney seen to collapse and lastly, a lone caravan was annihilated with a few rounds of 20mm cannon fire. Whilst flying at low level over gun positions near Rhede, intense and accurate flak was encountered. Blond-haired Dutchman, Fricky Wiersum, reported over the R/T that his aircraft had been hit. As he pulled into a steep climb, it was seen by the formation leader, Mickey Magee, to disappear into the cloud trailing a stream of glycol. Over the R/T he reported that he thought he could make it back to base and went to button 'C' on his radio for a homing. Unfortunately, failing to make the distance, he force-landed near Bucholt and was captured.

After yet more poor weather, operations resumed two days later on 8 December, when three sorties were made over the Munster area. At 07.00

hours the briefing for the first took place and after a hurried breakfast Mickey Magee and Jock Coull led two sections away from Eindhoven. Jock Coull would not return. The diary reads:

> Just after attacking a train, the formation leader spotted a second train about four or five miles away, coming in the direction of the formation. At that time, thick flak started coming across from the town of Letie, and to escape it the formation went down to nought feet. Flight Sergeant Coull was the only pilot in a position to attack the second train, and as they were then below tree-top level, he had to pull up a little to get sufficient deflection for his cannon. As soon as he gained a little height (400ft) the flak poured into him, side on, and the aircraft pulled abruptly up as if the pilot had been hit, and then crashed into the ground at 300 mph scattering flaming debris across the green fields.

A number of sorties were carried out on Sunday 10 December but the weather made the task difficult. In the afternoon three field guns were the target but poor visibility negated any possibility of carrying out the attack. During the search for the guns Mickey Magee's Typhoon was hit by a large piece of shrapnel which tore off the back of his canopy and grazed the back of his neck. A lucky escape indeed.

Twelve Typhoons from 247 Squadron were also very fortunate the following day when they were attacked by four P47 Thunderbolts. The Typhoon pilots had been trying to locate their designated target of a number of gun positions when the Thunderbolts made two passes during which they opened fire. No one was hit, mainly due to what was later described as the poor tactics of the American 'Jug' pilots.

For the next week the seasonally inclement weather continued and prevented practically all flying. The Germans took full advantage of this and launched a counter-attack which began on 17 December, against a weak American division which was situated at the point where the British and American forces met in the Ardennes. The diary for 18 December reads:

> In view of the German counter-attack near Aachen, it was no surprise to be greeted at dawn with a general panic and an allowance of fifteen minutes in which to make Intelligence. Weather was pretty foul and not having had breakfast the team wasn't feeling very happy about flying from Dusseldorf to Cologne [Köln] at 2,000 feet on an empty stomach. Our shortage of pilots was so acute that we couldn't raise a standby team, so No.137 had to take over whilst breakfast was attended to. On return from the mess both squadrons came to thirty minutes [readiness], at which state the morning passed.
>
>   Briefing eventually took place at 13.00 and half an hour later eight machines led by Dave Crawford and Crusher Croft set out on a recce in the Köln – Bonn area. Weather was pretty poor except for one small area west of Köln where ceiling reached 10,000 feet. No movement was observed, which was not surprising considering the large number of allied aircraft in the air.

From a very comfortable height the types watched a flight of Thunderbolts playing very expensive games with a small railway station. For some unknown reason it was heavily defended, light flak was streaming up from all corners. Seemingly oblivious to the opposition the Thunderbolts continued cruising around in circles at two thousand feet. One, a ball of fire, descended in a flaming curve to shatter into fiery pieces, to be followed in a few minutes by a second, which, belching white smoke, flicked into a spin and spiralled into the ground. The others still circled optimistically.

Feeling much less like pressing on regardless, the Squadron turned its attention to the peaceful little town of Euskirchen and loosed off its rockets from a very discreet height. A few rounds of accurate flak was experienced.

While this was on, Group Captain Green, the CO of No.124 Wing, and Cliff Monk carried out a low level penetration into Luxembourg, destroying one tank and three half-tracks, and also damaging one lorry and one half-track.

CHAPTER TEN

'UNT HOW IS SQUADRON LEADER STAPLETON, UNT HOW IS 247 SQUADRON?'

Today, Stapme remembers the many characters in 247 Squadron during his short time as CO and the sadness that so many were killed. He also remembers it being very busy, even though they found the time for the occasional night out. In many cases these were taken when perhaps the pilots should have been resting, but Bernie Lee's saying 'Enjoy today, for tomorrow we die!' tends to explain the attitude of some of the men at that time.

A colleague of Stapme's during his time at Eindhoven was R.J.E.M. Van Zinnicq Bergmann, who flew Typhoons with 181 and 182 Squadrons, also in 124 Wing. He later became Winston Churchill's ADC during a visit to the area. Stapme reflects on the kindness shown to him by the Dutchman: 'While at Eindhoven Van Zinnicq Bergmann took me to visit his father at their home in Vucht, on the outskirts of Eindhoven. His father gave me the gift of a bracelet made of tiny three-penny-bit-size coins. I gave it to Joan but it was later lost.' Post-war Van Zinnicq Bergmann became Equerry to the Queen of The Netherlands and retired with the rank of Air Commodore in the Royal Netherland Air Force.

As a veteran and 'ace' of the Battle of Britain, Stapme has no trouble avoiding comparisons with that period of his flying career and his days as a Spitfire pilot. His favourite aircraft is to this day the Spitfire Mk.Ia despite the fact that the Mark IX had the essential 20mm cannon armament. Stapme thought that the weight of the extra armament spoilt its flying characteristics. The combat flying from his time with 603 Squadron as opposed to his time with 247 bears no comparison. 247 Squadron was part of the Tactical Air Force, and carried out ground-attack operations only. His days of air-to-air combat were over and while other aces continued to add to their score of aircraft shot down, he was never given the opportunity to increase his score, but he knew his role as a Typhoon pilot was vital and he had been happy to move on.

The next operation by 247 Squadron was not until 23 December. The morning was 'clamped' with thick cloud and haze and so a 'hilarious' game of football with few rules helped pass the morning. Fortunately, injuries were light and at 14.00 hours the pilots were called for briefing when an armed reconnaissance was called for. Sixteen Typhoons of 247 and 137 Squadrons led by Wing Commander Kit North-Lewis took off from Eindhoven with instructions to search between Aachen and Blatzenheim for fifteen-plus tanks forcing their way into the American sector. The weather over the target area was very poor, the ground being hardly visible from the air, even from low altitude. As the aircraft searched for any breaks in the gloom it was fortunate that there were no collisions, conditions were that poor. Having been unable to locate any tanks, Wing Commander North-Lewis ordered the individual squadrons to split and continue with the armed reconnaissance. The only target that the 247 Squadron pilots managed to locate was a locomotive in a factory siding near the town of Modrath. Stapme took his section down and destroyed it with rockets, but it was during this attack that Stapme – the Boss and CO of 247 Squadron – disappeared from view.

The 247 Squadron ORB for 23 December 1944, takes up the story and concludes with a poignant reference to Stapme:

> Blatzenheim area and 15+ tanks at F.2251. The tanks were not located owing to heavy ground fog, and the Wing Commander, who was leading, continued with the armed reconnaissance. A loco in a factory siding at F.2842 was attacked with R.P. and destroyed. Shortly after this attack, S/Ldr B.G. Stapleton, D.F.C., called up to say he was unable to make base, and is believed to have crash-landed behind enemy lines. Up at 14.49 hours and down at 16.09 hours. Very duff weather today and visibility very low, in fact the trip was so fraught that 16 aircraft were dicing around at 200 feet in thick mist – fortunately none collided. The following is the circumstantial report prepared in respect of S/Ldr B.G. Stapleton, D.F.C. missing: S/Ldr Stapleton was detailed to lead a formation of eight aircraft to attack 15+ tanks at F.2251, in conjunction with eight aircraft of 137 Squadron, the two squadrons being led by W/Cmdr. North-Lewis, D.F.C. Owing to the thick haze the target could not be located and so the Wing Commander gave instructions for the two squadrons to split and to proceed independently on armed reconnaissances. Within a mile or so of the town of Modrath a train was seen, and S/Ldr Stapleton went down to attack it firing rockets and cannons. Direct hits were seen by his No.2, F/Sgt. D.C. Horn, who was of the opinion that sufficient damage had been done and so he did not attack with rockets but merely sprayed with cannon. F/Sgt. Horn followed S/Ldr. Stapleton up in a steep turn to the left of the train, and it was not until they had done a complete circuit of the target that S/Ldr. Stapleton called up over his R/T to say that his revs had gone completely off the clock, and that he would have to go down. Next his glycol tank burst and he made a gradual descent into a thick murky haze which completely enveloped him. Next he called up to say he had no idea where he was, but that when he landed, he was going to run like 'hell'. No more was heard. The exact location of the forced landing is not known, as the haze was so thick everywhere, that the pilots had only very general ideas as to their whereabouts, but think that S/Ldr. Stapleton must have landed somewhere within a radius of 15 miles of Elsdorf. No 'flak' was seen during the attack and it is believed that S/Ldr. Stapleton was hit by his own debris when attacking the train. The loss of S/Ldr. Stapleton, or, as he is

affectionately known to the Squadron, 'The Boss', will be heavily
felt by all.

Although it would have made no difference under the circumstances, in pulling
up in a steep turn to the left of the train, Stapme had gone against his usual
practice of staying low. Years later Stapme recalled the events of 23 December
1944. He had been flying Typhoon MP189 and, on spotting the train, he lost
altitude and followed the railway tracks behind the engine until he was in range
to attack with rockets. He believes that one of the rockets went straight into the
firebox. The engine blew up and he couldn't avoid flying through the debris: 'I
remember hearing the debris hitting my aircraft, I could hear the Tikka, tak,
tak!'

The damage was severe. The radiator had been punctured causing him to
force-land two miles inside German lines near Mönchengladbach. He was
posted 'missing (Flying Battle)'.

By its nature, the method of ground attack left little room for error and when
hit there was little or no chance of gaining enough height to bale out. It was all
over so quickly and the pilots remember that many were hit during the
attacking dive. If the aircraft and/or pilot were seriously hit, they invariably
continued to lose precious height until they flew into the ground. Stapme
reflects ruefully:

> I suppose I shot myself down when I flew through the debris. I
> managed to use my radio and request a bearing to get me home
> and stuck to the route until my engine finally gave out and I had
> to put her down. The visibility was very poor and I was lucky to
> come down in a clear area of farm land.
>
> Two very old German soldiers came up to the aircraft, I think
> they were the German equivalent of the Home Guard [*Volkstrum*].
> I climbed out onto the port wing having set the explosive charge
> on the IFF to destroy the system. One of the old soldiers climbed
> up and peered into the cockpit just as the charge detonated. It
> frightened the German so much that he fell off the wing. The
> other chap started laughing, and I started laughing too, and there
> were the three of us laughing our heads off.
>
> I was eventually taken to a rear echelon platoon HQ, not big
> enough for a regimental HQ, where I met a young German officer
> Flight Lieutenant [Hauptmann] in his early twenties, rosy
> cheeked, spoke perfect English and was quite respectful. I was
> then driven to a Luftwaffe aerodrome where I was paraded before
> and questioned by several very well-dressed Luftwaffe officers –
> apparently top-echelon characters – who made me feel a bit
> scruffy as I was a bit mucky by this time. I just crossed my arms
> and said nothing and we just looked at each other. I thought to
> myself at the time: 'Hey! I'm bigger than they are, there are four
> in all and I could beat the lot of them!'
>
> From there I was taken to the station from where I was to go to
> the interrogation centre at Oberursel. I had a two guard escort but
> the trip was interrupted due to an air raid on Cologne. It wasn't a
> heavy raid, it may have been a diversionary raid. There were a lot

of civilians in the shelter but they didn't seem to recognise me for what I was and I did have the two guards who were equipped with rifles. We got on the train and settled down in the goods van where there was a female guard smoking. In those days I used to smoke cigarettes and although I had cigarettes on me I wasn't going to let on, so I asked her for a cigarette and she gave me one. We arrived at Frankfurt and moved on from there to Oberursel where I was interrogated. I remained there through the Christmas period.

Later, 247 received news that their CO had been taken prisoner. Flight Lieutenant Tatters Tatham temporarily assumed command of the Squadron until the arrival of a new CO. He recalls:

Stapme commanded 247 from the Battle of Falaise through to Brussels. We didn't have much time for anything except eating, sleeping, and flying. He was shot down in December '44 when I was on leave. I came back to discover this and find I was in temporary command.

Flight Lieutenant Jimmy Bryant eventually took over command.

Dulag Luft, Oberursel

Durchgangslager der Luftwaffe (Transit Camp of the Luftwaffe) was always known by the prisoners of war by its abbreviation, 'Dulag Luft.' The camp was established in countryside to the west of the village of Oberursel, on the road to Hohemark and lies seven-and-a-half miles (12 kilometres) north-west of Frankfurt-am-Main, the nearest German city. Situated on a narrow lane leading northwards off Hohemarkstrasse to Eichwäldchen and the Oberstedter Forest, Dulag Luft was surrounded by sparsely wooded grassland which gradually sloped towards the foothills of the Taunus mountains. The camp initially consisted of just one farmhouse, with a number of small outlying buildings, surrounded by barbed wire and designated *Offiziersdurchgangslager* (Officers Transit Camp). The interrogation officer was initially an elderly reservist and he and his guards were billeted in local guest houses. With the RAF operating over western Germany the camp was taken over by the Luftwaffe and renamed 'Dulag Luft' in *Wehrkreise* (District) XII of the *Oberkommando der Luftwaffe*. A directive was issued stating that the nearest Luftwaffe base to where a prisoner was captured was responsible for transferring the individual/s to Dulag Luft before any initial interrogation had taken place. That responsibility rested with the staff at the camp. Despite repeated attempts by the SS Reichsführer, Heinrich Himmler, between 1940 and 41, to take over control of Dulag Luft, the camp managed to remain under the control of the Luftwaffe for most of the war and provided accurate intelligence on the RAF.

The first RAF POW to arrive at Dulag Luft was Wing Commander Harry 'Wings' Day (later Group Captain Harry M.A. Day GC, DSO, OBE), the Commanding Officer of 57 Squadron and part of the Air Component of the British Expeditionary Force. His Blenheim had been shot down by Me109s on 13 October 1939 during a reconnaissance mission over France. His crew perished. On arrival at Dulag Luft he was the first RAF officer to be asked to fill in a form headed 'International Committee of the Red Cross in Geneva.' It was obviously a bogus Red Cross form and Wings Day returned it having only noted down his name, rank and number.* Following interrogation, Day was initially moved to Oflag IXA/H, at Spangenberg, run by the army. Interestingly, the Germans had already gleaned comprehensive information on RAF airfields and squadrons during the lead up to the war using a variety of sources including: spies, monitoring of newspaper reports, Empire Air Days, and General Wenninger, the pre-war German air attaché in London. This information was supplemented by photo reconnaissance carried out by Heinkel 111s in civil airline regalia equipped with cameras undertaking 'civil route-proving' flights. Information was less forthcoming after the outbreak of war but it soon became clear that the main source of general information on the RAF was from captured aircrew, much of which was divulged unwittingly.

On November 1939, the Dulag Luft Kommandant was Major Theo Rumpel. One of his greatest successes at Dulag Luft was gathering intelligence on 'Identification Friend or Foe' (IFF), a device which allowed RDF plotters around the British coast to identify if an incoming plot was the enemy. As a consequence, the Germans successfully developed their own system. Rumpel's interrogation reports were frequently detailed and bulky, copies of which were flown to Berlin by Fiesler Storch aircraft, which took off from the aerodrome at Eschborn, situated nearby.

At Dulag Luft in December 1939, a 'permanent staff' was formed and consisted of 15 of the older more senior British and French officer POWs who had recently been sent back from Spangenberg. Their task was to help with the acclimatisation of newly arrived POWs and maintain discipline within the establishment. In return Kommandant Rumpel promised to provide a comfortable lifestyle for his permanent staff, including a generous daily ration of German Rhine wine. The concept ultimately generated considerable ill-feeling from those prisoners in normal locations. Following his return from Spangenberg, Wings Day was one of those selected. In 1940, the British and French 'permanents' had an enjoyable Christmas. Having received their first Red Cross food parcels since capture, the Kommandant also allowed them wine. On the evening of 24 December Rumpel joined the celebrations, bringing with him two bottles of schnapps. He later agreed to allow prisoners out on lengthy cross-country walks, albeit with an armed escort. During the return journey they stopped off at one of three Biergärtensituated along the route. These privileges were given for a very good reason, as the staff were ever keen to coerce the POWs into inadvertently passing intelligence to their captors.**

---

*In addition to his name, rank and service number it asked for: 'trade, date of birth, where born, profession, religion, married, how many children, home address, next of kin, what was your payment during the war, when shot down, who by, where taken prisoner, who by, squadron, group, command, station, station number, letters and number of aircraft, type of aircraft, how is your health, wounded, members of the crew.' Such details were of no interest to the Red Cross and the form was in contravention of Article 5 of the Geneva convention.

**Privileges also had their drawbacks. On one occasion Rumpel brought Wings Day a cat for a companion which Day named 'Ersatz' after the awful German coffee made from acorns. A photo of Day and Ersatz appeared on the front page of *Der Adler* and was later used as evidence against him by some less well-off members of his own side who tried to level accusations of collaboration against him.

Dulag Luft soon became Nazi Germany's most important centre for the interrogation of RAF and later United States Army Air Force (USAAF) aircrew prisoners of war. As with so many who were escorted into the camp as prisoners of the Germans, Stapme has never forgotten his time in Dulag Luft. Eventually, Allied aircrews were made aware of the existence of Dulag Luft from the 'escape and evasion' lectures back in Britain. Rumours also added to the trepidation they felt on arrival; rumours of temptation – dinner parties, drinks in the local inn, prostitutes and skiing trips to the Taunus mountains to collaborators and torture, including physical abuse, of which there were surprisingly few incidents.

Following the German invasion of Norway in April 1940, a new prisoner compound was opened and the POWs were moved from the converted farmhouse. The new compound consisted of three single-storey wooden barrack huts (East, West and Middle Blocks) surrounded by inner and outer barbed wire fencing, in a rectangle with a perimeter of no more than 160 yards. The fence was floodlit and overlooked by three 40 foot high guard towers equipped with machine guns and spotlights, each occupied by two guards at a time armed with rifles. To the south of the prisoners' compound was the recreation ground, also fenced off with barbed wire. As with the farmhouse, West Block had hidden microphones.

Around this time the permanents decided to pool the Red Cross parcels (whether they were addressed to individuals or otherwise) in order to provide new arrivals with extra rations and allow them to become used to the camp diet before being moved on to a permanent camp. Any escape attempt would be given escape rations from the stock of Red Cross parcels. This apparent hoarding of the parcels was another aspect of life as a permanent which antagonised other prisoners particularly when the older perishable rations had to be eaten by them rather then left to go off.

Following the fall of France, a listening post was established at Wissant, Northern France, by the German Interceptor Service (part of 'H' *Kompanie*) under the command of Hauptmann Horst Barth. By tracking the radio traffic between RAF pilots and plotters the listening post learnt the number, call sign, leader and base of every RAF squadron. Numbers of aircraft in the air at any one time and intended targets could also be determined. This information could be used to good effect when sending fighters to intercept the incoming RAF aircraft. They could even determine how many they had shot down.* In an attempt to counteract the advantage the Germans had at that time, the RAF eventually adopted a system of coding their radio transmissions; in the interim, satellites of Dulag Luft were established in Paris, Chartres, the former Carlton Hotel in Amsterdam and North Africa, to allow the interrogation of aircrew brought down over enemy occupied territory to be carried out at the earliest opportunity. Barth was later sent to Dulag Luft to take over as head of the Fighter Interrogation Department. Many of his staff went with him, including 'Blackie' Schwartz who came to know Stapme.

---

*Horst Barth came to know the voice of Squadron Leader Douglas Bader during missions and was listening the day he was shot down. He alerted his superiors that Bader had come down over France and, not knowing if he was dead or alive, they eventually confirmed he had been captured and was in hospital in St Omer.

During the Battle of Britain the interrogation centre was renamed. With a similar operation in the east called *Auswertestelle-Ost*, the Luftwaffe Intelligence and Evaluation Centre at Oberursel, became officially known as *Auswertestelle-West* (Evaluation Centre – West) whilst the transit camp continued to be known as Dulag Luft.

During the summer of 1940, more prisoners became 'permanents' including: Major Johnny Dodge DSO, DSC, a relative by marriage of Winston Churchill, who was awarded the DSC following service in Gallipoli in WWI. Although in his forties, he rejoined the army in 1939, and had been captured at Calais. He escaped but was recaptured by the Luftwaffe, which explains why he was sent to a Luftwaffe interrogation centre; Flying Officer John Gillies, son of Sir Harold Gillies, distinguished plastic surgeon and cousin of Archie McIndoe; and his commanding officer Squadron Leader Roger Bushell, a 30-year-old South African-born barrister who had been commanding 92 Squadron, flying Spitfires, in operations over France when he was shot down. Life at Dulag Luft for these men was particularly comfortable compared with the outlying POW camps. As well as the aforementioned 'luxuries' they also dined with the camp Kommandant in his own home. Later, although it would seem rather bizarre at this stage of the story, Wings Day and Roger Bushell were part of a larger group which tried to tunnel out of Dulag Luft, were caught and sent to Stalag Luft* I, Barth, where Stapme was also later to be incarcerated. At Stalag Luft I they received a far from pleasant welcome from those who recognised them from Dulag Luft. In June 1940, Pilot Officer 'Jimmie' James (later Squadron Leader James MC, RAF (Ret'd) joined their number at Dulag and was also sent to Stalag Luft I, from where a group including James, Day, Dodge and Bushell were later sent to Stalag Luft III, Sagan, Poland. In March 1944 they were prominent members of the 'Great Escape' team, with Bushell ('Big X') being one of the fifty murdered by the Gestapo.

As Britain faced the threat of invasion, and despite the privileges given to them as permanents, Day and his colleagues became increasingly concerned that escape should be given greater priority in order that they could contribute further to the war effort. Even if there was a negotiated peace they would remain in captivity and as older, experienced leaders they had an important part to play. Escape was given priority and in addition to a well-organised administration, Day appointed Roger Bushell as officer in charge of intelligence, supply and escape. They had the advantage over their captors as an escape attempt had yet to be made from Dulag Luft and nobody thought the permanents would be interested in getting out.

During the summer of 1940 a tunnel was dug from West Block in the new compound, and out under the wire, a total of 180 feet. Digging was halted over the winter period when the ground flooded.

By the end of the year approximately 800 RAF and Fleet Air Arm (FAA) POWs had been interrogated at Dulag Luft and sent to other camps, most to Stalag Luft I at Barth, which had been opened in July 1940 and features later in this story. The superior lifestyle enjoyed by the permanents continued to rankle with many of the ordinary prisoners and, having lived six to a room

---

*Stalag is short for *Stammlager*, meaning 'permanent camp.'

(Day had his own room while the other permanents were two or three to a room) resentment continued. Feelings were such that even the senior RAF officer at Barth sent a letter through German channels accusing Day of 'diverting' Red Cross parcels for use by himself and the other permanents. Day found the tone and nature of the letter disconcerting but decided against replying. The matter did not end there. Details of what was going on in Dulag Luft reached RAF Intelligence who instructed two squadron leaders at Stalag Luft I to carry out an enquiry into the conduct of those at Dulag Luft and others who had passed through the camp. Six months later the report was complete and found very much in favour of the permanents, fully vindicating Wings Day and his staff. Sadly, both accusers and accused were not informed of the outcome of the enquiry and a cloud remained over the British permanent staff at Dulag Luft.

Although work on the tunnel didn't begin again until March 1941, detailed preparations for the escape attempt had continued throughout the winter. The tunnel was completed by the end of May and the escape took place at 21.00 hours on Sunday 1 June. The eighteen who escaped included Day, Bushell, Dodge and Gillies. All were quickly recaptured by a force of some 3,000 men mobilised for the man-hunt and were prohibited from returning to Dulag Luft. Day Bushell and Dodge were sent to Stalag Luft I. Amongst their rations for the train journey was a crate of champagne given '. . . with the compliments of Major Rumpel.'

The mass escape (five or more constituted a mass escape) almost ruined the career of Kommandant Rumpel and the running of the camp was nearly passed to the Gestapo. Whilst Hitler and Himmler wanted Rumpel removed from his post, Hermann Göring was keen to keep the camp under the control of the Luftwaffe and defended the camp Kommandant. As a compromise Göring suggested the appointment of someone to carry out an assessment of security and intelligence systems at Dulag Luft and make recommendations for improvements. Here the story has an interesting twist. Göring chose Hauptmann Franz von Werra to carry out the task. Having been shot down by Stapme on 5 September 1940, he had escaped from a POW train in Canada and returned to Germany via USA and Mexico and was welcomed home a national hero.

Von Werra's report on the security set-up and intelligence gathering systems at Dulag Luft was mostly derogatory and he recommended the British methods, which had worked so well against him at RAF Intelligence, Trent Park, Cockfosters, after his capture in 1940. In the main, his recommendations were implemented. Thereafter, existence at the camp became more difficult and the interrogation team increased in number and experience. Unless the new arrivals co-operated during interrogation, they would be denied fresh air, exercise, Red Cross parcels, reading and writing materials, washing facilities and contact with other prisoners. One unpleasant aspect sometimes occurred when a POW refused to complete the Red Cross form. Staff threatened not to inform the POW's family whether he was dead or alive. Once the form was completed, concessions were made. Use of violence went against policy but the threat of psychological oppression was fearsome. Nevertheless, despite von Werra's recommendations, escape attempts continued.

In November 1941, as a legacy of the earlier escape, Major Rumpel, seen by many of the Nazis as an appeaser of his prisoners, was finally replaced. Promoted to Oberstleutnant he was sent to take over the Luftwaffe HQ at Görlitz, the command centre of flying training aerodromes. His replacement was Oberstleutnant Erich Killinger who ordered the erection of an additional barbed wire perimeter fence around the entire camp with guard towers.

Representatives of Frankfurt Gestapo (*Auswertestelle-West* also had its own Gestapo liaison officer) were occasionally allowed to interrogate prisoners in their own building on the camp, known by the POWs as 'The Bunker'.

Another of Killinger's first major tasks was to order the construction of a 'cooler' consisting of 103 solitary confinement cells, first-aid room, communal showers, toilets, laundry and guardroom. Each room was thoroughly insulated with a four-inch-thick snug-fitting door, also insulated, and a powerful heater under the window. With little or no airflow into the room, the insulation and heat source was used against prisoners as part of their interrogation on a number of occasions as life in the camp became tougher, most likely as a consequence of pressure put on the regular staff by the local Gestapo. When Killinger found out about the illicit use of heat against the prisoners he took action against those reponsible.

A number of POWs were actually 'turned' by their interrogators to good effect, as informers within the camp, or given even greater tasks on behalf of the Reich.

By now the old farmhouse was no longer occupied by prisoners but was used to house their own branch of 'H' *Kompanie* of the signals corps where experts in wireless communications worked. On the first floor was the wireless/telephony room (W/T) where staff listened in to aircraft to aircraft, aircraft to base, R/T and BBC broadcasts, the contents of which were vetted and sometimes used during the interrogation of prisoners. Next door was the photographic room where any film found on prisoners or recovered from the wreckage of their crashed aircraft could be processed.

In November 1942 work started on the construction of a new administration unit. The information held in the *Kommandantur* (Headquarters) was divided into individual categories with each given its own room. These included:

Document Evaluation Room – which produced 80% of *Auswertestelle-West*'s intelligence by scanning newspapers, books, magazines and materials found on captured aircrew.
Yellow File Room – where biographical information on allied personnel was collected from newspapers, magazines, POW mail and radio broadcasts and recorded on yellow index cards for easy reference.
Squadron History Room – where information on RAF and USAAF squadrons was kept, including past and current stations, details of senior personnel, addresses and special equipment used.
Map Room – where a large number of detailed maps were kept for reference by interrogators and document specialists.
Attack Room – displayed maps with air operations by the British and Americans during the previous twenty-four hours showing targets, routes flown and results gleaned mostly from German radar tracking and observer reports but updated with information

acquired during interrogation.

Situation Rooms – one for the RAF, and another for the USAAF detailing raids and air movements by the individual forces.

Press Evaluation Room – where a staff of translators worked through allied newspapers and passed any relevant information to the Squadron History Room and the Yellow File Room.

Technical Room – to assist interrogations this room contained data on allied equipment, with some physical examples.

Crash File Room – where all RAF/USAAF crash details were filed. Interestingly, details concerning the missing and dead were passed to the Red Cross from this room.

The full extent of the operation at *Auswertestelle-West* was not known by the RAF for the duration of WWII, in fact it was years later before the full significance of the camp was known. What the prisoners didn't realise was that information gathered from the crash site of their aircraft was often sent by teleprinter to the interrogation centre prior to their arrival and could also include personal effects including letters and photographs. Such information was certainly useful to interrogators in gaining the upper hand over the prisoner. In the *Kommandantur* there was also the archive of documents, reconnaissance photographs, maps, squadron histories, personality profiles, crash files and newspaper cuttings to refer to. Collectively, the interrogators were part of a very professional set-up which worked efficiently throughout the war, to the extent that the Luftwaffe were later able to fend off a complete takeover of its operations by the Gestapo.

Kommandant Killinger became increasingly concerned by the threat from air raids, on average the air raid siren sounded in Oberursel once every three days during WWII. The town was bombed on a number of occasions with the threat of falling shrapnel from the anti-aircraft guns adding to the dangers. Whilst the camp had not been hit, nearby Hohemark suffered, and as the number of incidents increased Killinger had the letters 'POW' painted on the roofs of the camp buildings.

By the second half of 1943, an average of 1,000 prisoners were passing through *Auswertestelle-West* each month. The POWs were suffering from severe overcrowding and conditions continued to deteriorate. The intelligence staffing level had risen to 50 and by the time of Stapme's arrival it had reached 65 with approximately 100 other ranks and 250 administrative staff (comprising: one Luftwaffe construction company and one guard company). Due to the continuing increase in the camp population, yet more building took place during the autumn of 1943.

On 10 September 1943 the transit camp at Oberursel was closed and the operation moved to Rothschild Park, Palmengarten, near the centre of Frankfurt-am-Main, just a mile to the north-west of the mainline railway station. It was a vulnerable position considering Frankfurt had been heavily bombed on numerous occasions and it soon became clear that while the main reason for moving the prisoners to Frankfurt had been due to overcrowding, it was also done in an attempt to deter bombing of the city. Following the move to Palmengarten, *Auswertestelle-West* continued to be used for interrogation and evaluation, after which, prisoners were sent in groups to Palmengarten to await transfer to permanent POW camps.

During this period the treatment of prisoners by their interrogators deteriorated, with violence inflicted during interrogation if information was not forthcoming. Apparently, such treatment also included the awful staged mock executions whereby prisoners were 'shot' by firing squad, just out of view of their stubborn colleagues. Nevertheless, such treatment failed to bring about the desired affect and the soft approach was soon re-established.

During this period a newly qualified interrogator arrived at *Auswertestelle-West*. Gefreiter (Corporal) Hanns-Joachim Scharff was 36 and from Greiz, East Prussia. Between the wars he married the daughter of WWI British fighter ace, Lieutenant-Colonel Claude Stokes DFC, who had been shot down and killed by a pilot in Manfred von Richthofen's (the Red Baron) squadron. Before the outbreak of WWII he had spent eleven years living in Johannesburg where he was Overseas Director for Adlerwerke, an industrial giant in Germany which manufactured cars, aircraft, tanks and other items for peace and war. During the company summer holiday of 1939, Scharff and his family returned to Germany but with war looming his exit visa was revoked and he was pressed into service with the Wehrmacht. Initially a *Panzergrenadier*, Scharff was transferred to *Dolmetscher Kompanie Nr.XII* (Interpreter's Company No.12), Wiesbaden, where he began training as an interrogator. Trainees were required to be intelligent, worldly wise and have an excellent understanding of the English language and Great Britain and, in January 1944, having gained his Red Certificate of qualification as a *Vernehmungsoffiziere*, he was sent to Dulag Luft, where he joined the team responsible for the interrogation of American fighter pilots. Scharff was also transferred from the army to the Luftwaffe. Although he had received no training in the interrogation of POWs, the depth of information available to Scharff was to his liking and, as part of a larger team, he soon achieved great success as an interrogation officer with a very gentle approach. As an army corporal he was advised to adopt the title of 'Mr' not 'Corporal' and not to be intimidated by the senior rank of many of the prisoners he was to interrogate. Scharff was catapulted from team member to senior Interrogation Officer after a Fiesler Storch reconnaissance aircraft carrying his friend and senior interrogator crashed in woodland after developing an engine fault after taking off from the local aerodrome of Eschborn. Everyone onboard was killed. By the time of Stapme's arrival, Scharff dealt with all those captured in north-west Europe and was fast developing the reputation as the Luftwaffe's 'master interrogator'. As well as speaking excellent English, 'Stone Face', or 'Poker Face' as he was known to some, also had in-depth knowledge of Zulu and Afrikaans, something he shared with Stapme, which is significant as it was Scharff who interrogated Stapme following his arrival at *Auswertestelle-West*/Dulag Luft.

During 1943, USAAF fighter pilots were still a novelty at Dulag Luft but by February 1944, the majority of permanent staff at *Auswertestelle-West*/Dulag Luft were Americans and the overcrowding problem continued. Despite moving many to Palmengarten, the monthly intake doubled to 2,000. This figure peaked in July when an astonishing 3,000 Allied aircrew were processed through *Auswertestelle-West*. The capacity was only 200 at any one time but this exceeded 250 on most days with up to five airmen sharing a solitary confinement cell. The hospital at Hohemark was also overcrowded and could no longer cope with all cases.

Following the bombing of the new transit camp in Frankfurt in March 1944 (killing one prisoner, but no Germans), it was moved again to a bigger site at the cathedral town of Wetzlar, 30 miles to the north of Frankfurt.

Later in the year Kommandant Killinger and his staff endured increasing pressure from the resident Gestapo officers for their apparent 'Anglophile tendencies, defeatism and transgression of service rules,' accusations which had also been directed at Killinger's predecessor. In an attempt to take over the running of the camp, the head of the Frankfurt Gestapo tried to concoct a series of charges against Killinger including 'fraternisation' and 'defeatism'. Killinger's immediate superior managed to stall his appearance before the awful 'People's Court' and was instead tried by a Luftwaffe tribunal. In November 1944, Oberstleutnant Erich Killinger was acquitted and remained in the post, although his adjutant was replaced.

And so it was into *Auswertestelle-West*/Dulag Luft that Stapme was escorted for Christmas 1944. After leaving Cologne (Köln) he eventually arrived by train at Frankfurt station from where he was taken by local train to Oberursel railway station in Nassauer Strasse. Opposite was a car showroom and garage with petrol pumps. Stapme and other POWs remember it for the prominent metal Coca-Cola signs, the freshwater drinking fountain and the elderly woman who harangued and threatened with her walking stick any prisoners who attempted to drink from it. He was then taken out of the village by local tram (the station was right opposite the mainline station), for the short journey, crossing Nassauer Strasse, along Arndtstrasse (now Berliner Strasse), stopping at Portstrasse before continuing along Hohemarkstrasse to Kupferhammer where Stapme got off, crossed the road and walked into Siedlungstrasse for the short walk up the slight incline to *Auswertestelle-West*/Dulag Luft.

By the time Stapme arrived, the procedure for new arrivals had been honed since its initial implementation by Dulag Luft's *Vernehmungsoffiziere* under Major Rumpel in 1940. Initial contact was made by a member of staff who introduced himself as the 'receptionist' and gave Stapme the standard but bogus Red Cross form to complete. Stapme gave only name, rank and number while the German made an initial assessment of the new arrival. Any objections to providing answers to some of the other questions were met with gentle prompting that their wife or children could be informed they were safe and no longer 'missing' thus allaying their fears. This weak attempt to prey on the emotions of the prisoner was often greeted with a terse 'fuck-off!' Later, any observations which might prove useful when trying to coerce the prisoner were noted on the back of the form before it was passed on to the next stage of the process. It was not unusual for the prisoner to be asked to fill in more than one Red Cross form. Some of the new receptions were even given a card to fill in, asking for details of their qualifications and previous employment, in order for the Germans to assess the kind of work the prisoner might be suited to when the war was won. Many replies rendered the prisoner unsuitable for work in post-war Germany due to the surprising number of 'lion-tamers' and one comedian even claimed he was a 'planer and shaper of square-heads'!

Stapme's interrogation by Hanns-Joachim Scharff took place in room 47 of *Auswertestelle-West*. Interrogation consisted initially of general conversation to get the prisoner in a more relaxed frame of mind, subjects being: wife, family, sport and personal interests. If the prisoner wasn't keen to 'open-up', talk of politics would be the next stage. The interrogators were knowledgeable on the subject of politics and their perception of the political knowledge of RAF and USAAF aircrews was that it was generally commonplace and weak. Questioning on the subject therefore served to reduce the prisoner's confidence. Interrogation of a prisoner might run to several sessions a week, from one to six weeks, or until the staff were satisfied there was no useful intelligence to be gleaned. In many cases the prisoner's state of mind was poor, feeling lonely, humiliated, hungry, dirty, in need of fresh clothes, and possibly still in shock from being shot down and captured. Stapme recalled his own chat with his interrogation officer:

> During interrogation they wanted to know about 'G' but I knew nothing about 'G' which I later learned was a navigational aid for bombers. I was at Oberursel for a while because they thought they could learn something from me.
>
> Just after Christmas 'Blackie' Schwartz, one of the guards at Oberursel, asked me if I wanted to go to the Opel shooting lodge, to which I of course replied 'Yes.' We were being held in solitary confinement and it was an opportunity to get out. As we approached the lodge with our armed escort I recall the smell of pine logs on the fire. When we got there they produced real coffee, not Ersatz, and apple strudel, which made a welcome change to the usual diet. They also tuned their radio into the BBC and we listened in. They sat there watching us with a smile on their faces.

Blackie Schwartz was one of Hauptmann Horst Barth's cronies from 'H' *Kompanie*, the radio listening organisation at Wissant. Now Schwartz worked under Barth in the Fighter Interrogation Department at Dulag Luft. The solitary confinement cells to which Stapme refers were in the section completed in October 1942. Although reasonably comfortable, they became sweat-boxes in the hands of the more unscrupulous interrogators. Stapme saw a number of familiar faces:

> Whilst at Oberursel I met Charles Green, Group Captain I/C of our Wing. He was walking down a corridor towards me but we pretended not to know each other. He had been badly beaten by the SS. That is also where I saw Fricky Wiersum, who happened to be flying my aircraft when he was shot down. He had been badly beaten up by the Hitler Youth. When Wiersum was brought into the room where I was being interrogated by a German corporal, he entered and saluted the corporal. I dressed him down: 'An officer in the RAF does not salute NCOs in the German air force!' Fricky seemed badly traumatised by events prior to our meeting. During his own interrogation he never said a word. The photo of me standing against the cockpit of my Typhoon was taken by Fricky.

The fact that Stapme refers to his interrogator as a corporal confirms it was

Scharff, whom he recalls was dressed in his trademark grey suit, rather than his uniform. Some prisoners believed him to be an officer and treated him accordingly, although not all were fooled. It would have certainly given officer POWs an advantage to know they were being questioned by a subordinate but, as Scharff preferred to lull prisoners into a false sense of security, this too may have put him in an effective position to extract information. He was a master of his trade who used to greet the prisoner with a courteous: 'Come in, please. I am your interrogator.'

Tatters Tatham recalls an alarming story of an incident whilst Stapme was undergoing interrogation which highlights just how efficient the intelligence gathering operation at *Auswertestelle-West* was:

> A photograph of most of the Squadron (247) had been taken (illegally) at Eindhoven. I was on three days leave at the time and I do not appear in it. When Stapme was being interrogated the Hun greeted him with the words: 'How is Squadron Leader Stapleton and how is 247 Squadron? I have a good photo here, from which I see Flight Lieutenant Tatham is missing and was on leave at the time.' The German proceeded to show it to Stapme, who whipped it out of his hand and tore it up. The Hun grinned and produced another copy from his desk drawer!

Over the years Stapme and Tatters have kept in touch and between them confirmed the accuracy of this story.

One of Scharff's many useful interrogation aids was the camp's photographic archive containing many photos taken at allied airfields, showing aircraft, markings and many of the squadron pilots. It was not difficult for Scharff to discover the name of a well known fighter pilot. A simple ploy could bring about the desired result: 'Isn't that a great picture of Hubert Zemke?' 'No' came the prisoner's reply '. . . that's not Zemke, that's Francis Gabreski.' Hub Zemke and Frank 'Gabby' Gabreski were outstanding American fighter pilots with Gabreski finishing the war as the top-scoring US pilot in Europe. Both were shot down over enemy occupied territory. Gabreski was taken to Oberursel where Scharff recognised him among the new intake. Stapme later came to know Hub Zemke in Stalag Luft I.

CHAPTER ELEVEN

STALAG LUFT I, BARTH

In July 1940, the first contingent of RAF POWs had been sent from Oberursel to a new permanent camp run by the Luftwaffe, Stalag Luft I, near the village of Barth Vogelsang (which lay within sight of the camp to the south) near Pomerania's Baltic shore. Rostock lay to the south-west while Stettin lay further away to the south-east. Some of the earliest prisoners transferred to Stalag Luft I were from Stalag 8B, Lamsdorf. By the time of Stapme's arrival the camp contained thirteen thousand British, Commonwealth and American prisoners.

From Dulag Luft*, in late January 1945 Stapme and a number of other prisoners were taken by train to a transit camp 50 miles north of Berlin, before moving on to the German capital where they were transported by train from Stettiner station to Barth Vogelsang. (It is possible the transit camp was a former Wehrmacht barracks near Prenzlau.) From the station in Barth Vogelsang Stapme and his companions were escorted on foot to Stalag Luft I, where Stapme spent the remaining five months of the war.

Pomerania, in which Stalag Luft I was situated, is an ancient Baltic province of Germany. It was once inhabited by Slavonic tribes (the name originates from the Slav words 'Po' meaning 'by', and 'more' meaning 'sea'). Between the sea and the flat agricultural land to the south lies an area of flat salt marshes, rivulets and sand dunes interspersed with dark pine woodland. Whilst this area would be suitable for summer holidays, in winter the area becomes an icy desolate place open to the mercy of the freezing winds coming off the Baltic. Stapme felt the full brunt of the winter during his stay. Apart from a pine wood which lay to the north and restricted the view to the Baltic Sea, the surrounding landscape was dreary and flat. The nearby coastline was popular with German yachtsmen and the tips of the masts could just be seen from the camp. Rising high above the roof tops to the south-east was the steeple of Marienkirche. On another side of the camp was a brick-built training centre for Luftwaffe anti-

---

*On 19 March 1945, Oberstleutnant Erich Killinger, Kommandant of *Auswertestelle-West* and other members of his staff left the camp and travelled to Nürnberg-Buchenbühl, burning most of the records before leaving and taking the remainder with them. *Auswertestelle-West*, Oberursel and Hohemark was occupied by American troops on 25 March and found to be no longer in use. The American forces also used it as a POW camp. Killinger and 200 guards were captured on 16 April when Buchenbühl was taken by the 45th Division. The original site of Dulag Luft later became 'Camp King', and an American NATO transport depot when the interrogation block became the officers mess. At the time of writing, apart from the listed buildings, the site was due for demolition and cleared for housing development having been purchased by the town of Oberursel.

aircraft recruits whose initial training routine provided a source of amusement to the POWs as the German recruits were seen floundering in the mud during their physical training. By Christmas 1940 there were three single-storey huts in the compound in which 2-300 POWs lived. In such a confined area the men soon got to know each other. A barbed wire fence, with a gate which was usually left open, separated them from the rest of the compound containing: the cookhouse, the parade ground where *Appell* (roll-check) took place each morning and evening, and the main gate to the *Vorlager* which contained the *Kommandantur*, various administration huts and the *Arrestlok* (cooler) where prisoners were sent for solitary confinement. Prisoners (known as kriegies) in normal location close to the cooler would shout encouragement to those being punished but were soon driven away at gunpoint by the guards. A system was devised by which prisoners would call out encouragement to those in solitary during football matches, when their comments were masked by exaggerated cries from the touchline supporters. Few of the guards understood English and those who spoke a smattering of the language wouldn't have understood the mixture of RAF slang and obscenities!

From the time when Stalag Luft I was first opened the one German the Kriegies decided had to be watched and treated with caution was Feldwebel Hermann Glemnitz, the German's chief 'ferret'. This very professional German soldier had travelled the world and had fought as an infantryman in the army during WWI. After the war he became a pilot, and a machine operator for a steel company. He was also a competent linguist. A serious mistake by any kriegie was to believe Glemnitz would actually relax whilst on duty and allow himself to be influenced. Although he was compassionate and had a distinctive sense of humour, which the prisoners appreciated, he was a highly experienced senior NCO and they quickly realised that despite his seemingly casual air and friendliness he and his team of ferrets were always alert. He was respected and feared, his excellent understanding of colloquial English learnt during the years spent working in England made him a formidable foe. If there was one man who could understand the mind of a British POW and collect and sift through intelligence in order to reveal intentions of tunnelling or other questionable activity, it was Hermann Glemnitz. Nevertheless, despite the dedication of Glemnitz, production of escape equipment continued and there were many escape attempts. While some resulted in success, others ended in tragedy.

Dour Scotsman, Flight Lieutenant Harry Burton, an experienced bomber pilot and former instructor at an OTU, managed to get himself sentenced to two weeks in the 'cooler' for possessing escape equipment. He succeeded in escaping from Stalag Luft I by sawing through the bars of his cell with a hacksaw blade. Once outside the cooler, he was initially caught in the sweep of a searchlight beam but froze against the wall of a cell block. He was not spotted and managed to get to the *Vorlager* gate. Although the gate was guarded, the sentry had a regular beat and when he left his post Burton scoured a trench under the gate. After a nervous period of digging and dashing back into the shadows whenever the sentry returned, Harry Burton managed to squeeze under the gate and walk out of the camp. He walked to Stralsund and across the island of Rugen to Sassnitz, a distance of 50 miles. From Sassnitz he smuggled himself aboard a ship flying the Swedish flag and by 31 May 1941 he had reached Trelleborg, Sweden, and eventually he made what was the first RAF 'home run'. The previous September, Burton had seen the build-up of the German invasion fleet at St Malo and when he arrived back in Britain he was debriefed about all he had learnt while in captivity, by which time Operation Sealion had long been cancelled (Harry Burton was awarded the DSO and eventually retired from the RAF as Air Marshal Sir Harry Burton).

Burton's colleagues back at Stalag Luft I felt elated by his achievement and were quick to mock the guards. The news had made a pleasant change, as reports of German success in the conflict were broadcast via the camp PA system. The sinking of HMS *Hood* by KMS *Bismarck* was particularly grim. As a consequence of any escape the kriegies faced hours on the parade ground while the huts were searched. Security was also reviewed and what few privileges they had were withdrawn. Serious offenders also faced being sent to concentration camps.

Nevertheless, tunnelling continued through 1941 and it was only the cold, hard frost of January 1942 which brought the latest project at Stalag Luft I to a halt. So Flight Lieutenant 'Tommy' Thompson took a break from hooch-making and managed to get into the NCO's compound. With Sergeants Johnny Shaw and Evans he attempted to escape by crawling across the football field and through the wire under white sheets, which provided camouflage against the snow. They were spotted by guards and Johnny Shaw was shot dead by a guard in the nearest tower. The others were rounded-up later. Shaw's colleagues, as well as the German staff at Stalag Luft I, made every effort to give him a full military funeral. On his coffin were placed two wreaths; one from the RAF, the other from the Luftwaffe and at the graveside a party of ten Luftwaffe personnel fired a volley across the grave in salute. Whilst the Kommandant was a kindly man, he made it clear to the POWs that escaping was not a sport, but a deadly gamble. Nevertheless, the aforementioned examples are presented here in tribute to the numerous, ingenious and courageous escape attempts from Stalag Luft I, during its time as a POW camp.

Stapme recalls his arrival at the camp:

> We were treated well but food was in short supply. The first thing they did was to shave every hair from my body, including round my backside, and then spray us with disinfectant powder.
>
> There were four goon towers to a compound, one at each corner. There was also a sort of parade ground, quite a big one, on which we were counted each morning.
>
> The camp Kommandant was a very good chap. He told Zemke [Colonel Hub Zemke, the most senior ranking American in the camp] and Charles Green, my wing commander and (as far as I was concerned) the senior RAF officer on the camp: 'I don't mind you bartering with my soldiers for fresh fish in exchange for the cigarettes and coffee you get in your Red Cross parcels but tell my guards not to let the fish tails hang below the bottom of their greatcoats!' There was also a major who was a Nazi and nobody knows what happened to him after the Russians arrived and liberated the camp. Whether they 'disposed' of him or not I don't know but there wasn't any love lost between the Luftwaffe personnel and the Nazis.

The senior officers had a room to themselves, not our own rooms but rooms of four officers at one end of each block. All the other chaps were six to a room. We had a batman but he wasn't required to do much as we used to do most of it ourselves to keep busy. He did bits and pieces. We had a stove and he did the cooking.

The camp Kommandant was Oberst Warnstedt, who spoke English. Every morning and evening Apell took place on the parade ground under the scrutiny of Kommandant Warnstedt and a small squad of armed guards. The men lined up in two ranks to be counted. The guards (all members of the Luftwaffe who in the main behaved well towards the POWs) were referred to as 'goons' by the prisoners and the sport of 'goon baiting' was pursued with great enthusiasm by the younger prisoners. At dusk each evening, the doors of the barracks were bolted from the outside and the shutters fastened over the windows, thus increasing the feeling of confinement. The usual routine of reading, card games or simply 'bunk bashing' followed but later organised conjuring shows and theatricals helped cheer up the prisoners.

During the early days at Stalag Luft I, the delivery of Red Cross parcels had stopped due to the Nazi Blitzkrieg across the Low Countries and France. The ration for an officer in the camp became that of a non-working civilian and consisted of a cup of ersatz coffee (made from acorns), a bowl of soup (usually sauerkraut) with a few potatoes at mid-day, one fifth of a loaf of traditional black bread with a pat of margarine, and a small piece of sausage or cheese in the evening. This was supplied per room and divided up by the 'stooge' of the day (this was carried out with great accuracy as his room-mates had first choice of the portions). These rations amounted to just 800 calories a day, which is less than half the minimum requirement for an adult human being. Prisoners were forever hungry. By the time of Stapme's arrival the daily intake had risen to 2,000 calories, which was an improvement but still not enough to maintain good health. Shortly after, the delivery stopped. Stapme again:

> To start with we had one Red Cross parcel per person, per week, which was enough to keep us alive. The Germans used to give us very little red meat but we did get potatoes and cabbage. We mixed that with the tinned fruit we got in the Red Cross parcels and made a hash of it. That was in the beginning but from about March '45 the Red Cross parcels started to dwindle and we got one a week, for four people to share! That was when we started to lose weight. Didn't do us much harm I don't think because it didn't go on for too long. I think I lost about twelve pounds, which I could afford to lose. However, the thin chaps couldn't.

'Jimmie' James spent 21 months at Stalag Luft I having arrived in the summer of 1940 from Dulag Luft, Oberursel. Although he left Stalag Luft I well before Stapme's arrival he later recollected conditions in the officers' compound:

> . . . there seemed only a remote possibility of escape from the cramped and dusty little compound to which our small party of 20 were the first to arrive. The two wooden barrack blocks were

surrounded by a double row of eight-foot barbed wire fencing six feet apart, with Dannert wire packed into the space between. A low warning fence about six feet in from the main wire further restricted our freedom of movement. This dreary rectangular area, about 100 yards by 70 yards, was covered at all times by guards with machine guns and searchlights mounted in the watch towers at opposite corners, with perimeter lighting at regular intervals.

There was one gate on which a sentry was posted, leading into the wire-enclosed *Vorlager* containing the cell block and a few other buildings, and beyond this was the administrative area. The NCOs' compound with six wooden barracks was adjoining.

Jimmie also notes the mind-numbing inactivity of a POW:

War has been defined as: 'long periods of boredom interspersed with short periods of tension and terror.' Prisoner of war life was a minor extension of war. There seemed to be no end to the boredom which stretched out endlessly into the grey future. We were all young men cut off in our prime from normal life, and forced to live a spartan, closely knit, communal existence, hemmed in by barbed wire, guard boxes, machine guns, patrolling sentries and dogs. In the early days most of us were regular officers and flying had been the reason for our existence. To be forcibly grounded in such circumstances, with all prospects of promotion and career shattered, worst of all being no further use to the war effort, was a heavy burden to bear.

While at Stalag Luft I, Jimmie became a member of the first RAF team of WWII to dig a tunnel out of a POW camp. During the summer of 1941, Wing Commander Wings Day, Squadron Leader Roger Bushell and Major Johnny Dodge arrived at Stalag Luft I from Dulag Luft, Oberursel. With Wings Day in charge the organisation of further escape attempts was elevated to a higher level. However, under the supervision of Hermann Glemnitz, Jimmie James, Day, Bushell and Dodge were part of a large group sent to Stalag Luft III, Sagan, Poland, in April 1942. At Stalag Luft I, they left behind an astonishing 45 tunnels in the officers compound alone!

During Stapme's time at Stalag Luft I, one of the methods for passing the time was the organisation and attending of lectures:

A chap called Robert Cowan had been a racing car driver before the war and he used to give lectures on the mechanics of motor cars (Robert Cowan was the first person to change his sex when he became 'Roberta' Cowan). There was always something going on – theatricals and Hub Zemke's now legendary boxing contests (Zemke was a winner of the prestigious Golden Gloves Award). There were always people to talk to.

We also made wine which the Germans never found out about. In the Red Cross parcels we used to get prunes, apricots, dried fruit, that sort of thing. We fermented it with sugar, yeast and water and then distilled it, producing an alcoholic drink. In a

barracks containing over 200 men you could always find
somebody who could get what you needed. One of the chaps went
into Barth (usually to carry out a job of work) and traded
equipment/ingredients for producing alcohol with stuff they had
hoarded from the Red Cross parcels. By that time they were
coming through again. In addition they also brought back fresh
eggs, meat and goodness knows what, but they all came back.
None of them actually escaped although some had before I
arrived. The result of such an escape meant the guards got a bit of
a roasting. We established a little distillery within the barracks
and used to ferment the concoction in one of the lavatory cisterns
– the traditional overhead cistern. We took one apart, put the water
in the top, put all the fruit in, added yeast and sugar and let it
ferment. When you wanted to release it you simply disconnected
the down pipe and pulled the chain. We produced about a gallon
at a time. We then passed it on to the Czechs who distilled it, drop
by drop by which time it was a pure clear liquid. I didn't arrive at
Barth in time for Christmas but I was told the guards in one
compound were given a bottle of this clear stuff. When they were
found they had all passed out.

The British and American kriegies at Barth knew allied troops had reached the
Elbe and that the Russians were in Berlin. Stapme recalls there was tension in
Stalag Luft I. Liberation could not be far off but most of the prisoners were
concerned as to whether their war would end with straightforward liberation or
a fight for survival. Colonel Hub Zemke and Rhodesian Group Captain Grant
were informed by Kommandant Oberst Warnstedt that his orders were to
evacuate the camp and march the prisoners west. Zemke and Grant
immediately made their position clear; they had no intention of ordering their
men to move from the camp. Warnstedt responded: 'I will not have bloodshed
in this camp, my men will leave you in charge.' By the afternoon of 30 April
1945, the last of the guards left with Major Steinhauer.

   With liberation near and prior to the Germans leaving Stalag Luft I, a group
of British and American prisoners were formed into a unit named 'Fighting
Force.' A number of army glider pilots captured at Arnhem were co-opted as
instructors and lectures on army fighting techniques were arranged and
covered the use of Wehrmacht weapons and the location and disposal of any
booby traps left behind by the retreating Germans. White armbands with 'FF'
printed in bold letters were issued to each member of the squads and platoons
formed. Meanwhile, as the FF waited in some semblance of readiness, the
Russian advance was monitored by the POWs' home-made radio receiver.
Towards the end of April, explosions could be heard. They continued to come
ever nearer to the camp until they reached the Luftwaffe flak school next door.
Excitement mounted amongst the kriegies but life continued normally in the
camp with the guards going about their duties until the morning of 30 April.
That morning the prisoners rose from their beds to an uncanny silence. There
had not been the usual clattering open of the shutters by the guards followed
by the 'Raus! Raus! Appell, Appell!' As the men staggered from the huts they
noticed the posten boxes were empty, there were no guards in sight, the camp
was bereft of Germans, all that is, except for one. Legend has it that a tall well-

dressed German soldier strode into the office of Group Captain Grant and Colonel Zemke in the *Kommandantur* and, afraid he would be shot if captured by the Russians, asked if they would help smuggle him back to Britain or America. His request was flatly refused and the German left. He was the German heavyweight boxer, Max Schmeling.*

On discovering the camp had been abandoned overnight, the Fighting Force was called into action while the remainder of the prisoners were kept in their respective compounds by their senior officers. The FF confirmed the camp was devoid of guards, gained entry to the *Vorlager*, the German quarters and the nearby flak school putting the recent training lectures to good use as they moved about keeping a lookout for booby traps. They discovered a number of rifles, ammunition and machine guns which they brought back into the camp. The following morning a detachment of the Fighting Force was sent to a nearby Luftwaffe aerodrome to discover if it was still manned and useable. It was deserted and the airstrip littered with live ordnance.

An American officer who could speak Russian and a British officer who could speak German headed away from the camp hoping to meet the Russians. That evening they returned having failed to make contact. They reported back that Barth was empty of all but the very old and children and white sheets and towels were hanging from the windows.

The camp was liberated by elements of the Russian army on 1 May 1945, three days after the Germans had retreated from the area. The Russians queried why black armbands were not being worn as a mark of respect following the death of President Roosevelt! As the Russians came into the camp, the weapons recently obtained by the kriegies were kept out of sight. The next day the Russians arrived in force. Most are remembered by the POWs as being mostly of eastern Asiatic appearance, often drunk, and firing their weapons at every opportunity, terrorising everyone in the area. A runner was sent to inform a detachment of the FF at the nearby aerodrome that the Russians had arrived.

The early success by the Wehrmacht in Operation 'Barbarossa' in June/July 1941 had resulted in the capture of thousands of Russians, some of whom arrived at Stalag Luft I after forced marches of hundreds of miles. The first to arrive were in a terrible state – emaciated and practically starved to death – they had also been brutalised by the Germans and this continued after their arrival at Stalag Luft I. Numerous Russians were still captives in the camp until it was liberated by their own soldiers, many having been forced to clean the camp latrines.

The Russians were tough but friendly and even drove live pigs and cattle into the camp for food; alas, nobody was keen to start slaughtering them. The Russians even organised a full ENSA type performance in the camp 'theatre'.

After liberating the camp, the tanks and armoured columns of the victorious Russian army moved on in pursuit of the retreating Germans leaving the

---

*In 1930-32 he was World Heavyweight Champion having beaten Jack Sharkey on a foul in the fourth round. He lost the re-match. In 1938, he fought Joe Louis and after discovering a weakness in the American's defence, knocked him out. In the re-match Louis overwhelmed Schmeling in the first round. During the war he became a German paratrooper and took part in the invasion of Crete. Postwar he returned to boxing by which time he was over 40 and lost to Walter Neusel. He then retired.

inmates practically to their own devices. As each day passed the kriegies noticed a deterioration in the quality of the Russian army personnel and equipment which passed by the camp until it eventually consisted of poorly equipped troops and women on horse-drawn carts, or bicycles.

Stapme was impatient to return home. He recollects waking to find the guards had gone:

> For two or three days prior to the arrival of the Russians we were virtually free. There was a rumour going through the camp that the Germans we had earlier seen marching past the main gate were retreating in the face of the Russian advance. By this time there was nobody supervising us and in that time myself and two Canadian colleagues made our way to the local rail depot where we found some 80,000 Red Cross parcels stockpiled. No wonder we were hungry! During the preceding weeks the Germans were unable to get them to us probably because the German railway system had been so messed up by the allied bombing that they didn't bother to bring the parcels up to the camp. As they came in they gradually piled up. So we went down there and brought back to the camp about six each – they weighed about 11lbs each and carrying that number was not a problem if you made the right sort of bag (like a ruck-sack) in which to carry them. That was rich currency with which to barter and we were probably the richest people in Germany at that time!
>
> Barth was only about two miles away. While we were busy (there were no soldiers in town at all) we were informed that a local farmer had a car. We went to see the farmer and gave him a Red Cross parcel for his Adler. He could no longer make any use of it and it was in perfect condition. It had been run regularly until recently. He showed us everything we needed to know about the car before we went off to try to find some petrol. This we did in exchange for another parcel (all that for just two Red Cross parcels!). The engine of the car was actually two-stroke which meant we had to mix the oil and petrol. We then returned and collected the car. It was a very similar car to the DKW – the little DKW two-stroke, two-cylinder. We drove it back to the barracks and hid it underneath one of the blocks – the barracks had been built on sand and situated on legs elevating them to a height of three feet above the ground to enable the Germans to see underneath. It was there that we put the car to avoid it attracting too much attention. It was very easy to dig out the sandy soil. We got a lot of the chaps to help us.
>
> We then had Russian uniforms made for us by the camp tailor with the recognisable red tabs in the correct places. He also made us caps with red bands. When the Russians came, they only put one guard on the main gate and so we just drove in and out and he gave us that funny salute the Russian army had. Finally, having helped ourselves to eight Red Cross parcels each, we drove out of Stalag Luft I, never to return. We left just prior to a change of

guard because if we went out just *after* a change, the same guard would have expected to see us return during his lengthy spell on duty. Having not seen us return, our absence may have been noticed. We drove to Lubeck, through Lubeck and on to where the Canadians were situated at that time. They were in the north having moved up from the beach-head, having stuck to the coast most of the way.

Our first meal consisted of six or seven fried eggs each and of course they took the car off us! I was then taken to the nearest aerodrome. I don't know what happened to the two Canadians who had travelled with me. They probably stayed with the Canadian forces. I got to Luneberg and we were flown back to England in bombers, although I'm not sure exactly which airfield we took off from. We landed at Cosford where the officers were instructed to pay for new battledress outfits. We replied: 'Send us the bill!'

Stapme was air-lifted back to RAF Cosford, near Wolverhampton, on 10 May 1945, as part of 'Operation Exodus,' two days before his twenty-fifth birthday. He was given extensive leave before 'rejoining' as he described it.

Meanwhile, back at Stalag Luft I, following a meeting between the camp senior officers and the senior Russian officer it was agreed that members of the Fighting Force could carry their recently acquired weapons. The Russian then instructed the FF men at the nearby aerodrome to clear the ordnance, thus rendering the airfield serviceable for a possible airlift. They were also told to reverse their white armbands and mark them with the letters 'AMEPNKAHEU' (Russian for 'American'). All members of the FF obliged as nobody knew the Russian for British. Two experienced armourers volunteered to defuse the bombs on the airfield. The hundreds of bombs were eventually moved to the airfield perimeter using a tractor and trailer which other kriegies had made serviceable. Left alone by their liberators to complete the task, it was while carrying out this work that the POWs heard that back home in Britain VE Day was being celebrated.

It was decided that the Rhodesian Group Captain Grant, should attempt to reach the allied lines to arrange an airlift for the POWs of Stalag Luft I. He was successful and on 11 May 1945, a message was received that, with permission from the Russians, aircraft would be arriving at the airfield the next day to begin transportation of the POWs to France on the first leg of their journey home. The aircraft were American B17 Flying Fortresses and, despite the fact that the RAF had been the first prisoners at Stalag Luft I and had provided the guard and cleared the aerodrome of the ordnance, the Americans were given priority and the RAF personnel were last to leave. In groups of 24 to 30 the men were transported to RAF Ford in Sussex and by late evening on 13 May all Stalag Luft I prisoners had been repatriated. Group Captain Charles Green, Stapme's wing commander, was amongst them. Like Stapme, he also later went to live in South Africa. Always remembering his time with Stapme with fondness, he died in September 2001.

Stalag Luft I, the first permanent prison camp built for RAF personnel was left in the hands of the Russians. Today, nothing remains of the camp or the Luftwaffe flak training school.

Stapme returned to No.106 Personnel Reception Centre as a supernumerary (ex prisoner of war) on 12 July 1945. He was posted to the Air Ministry Unit on 1 August 1945 and then to the Directorate of Personnel Services on 1 September 1945. His rank of Acting Squadron Leader was relinquished on 12 July 1945 but he was re-appointed Acting Squadron Leader on 1 August, a rank he was permitted to retain when he finally relinquished his commission on 1 July 1949:

> The first aircraft I flew after my return was a twin-engine Percival Q6, a lovely little aeroplane. I didn't do much flying for a while after that. I used to go to the various RAF stations to assess the various problems associated with rehabilitating Afro-Caribbeans because some of them didn't want to go home due to the high level of unemployment in their own countries. Some were returning from America where they had taken the place of land-workers who had gone off to fight. They seemed to occupy about ten stations (RAF). I did this job whilst waiting for my demob.

Stapme's first wife Joan had found life difficult during her husband's time away as a POW and had an affair with an American forces journalist. With Stapme back home again the couple decided to give their marriage another chance.

On 1 January 1946, Stapme's award of the Distinguished Flying Cross (Dutch) for his leadership of 247 Squadron during Operation Market Garden, conferred by Her Majesty The Queen of the Netherlands, appeared in the *London Gazette*. He recalled: 'There was no ceremony. I received notification of the award in the post, a short time later the medal arrived the same way.'

CHAPTER TWELVE

'HAMBA GASHLE/SAHLA GASHLE'*

Believing he had no post-war future in the RAF, due possibly to his no-nonsense attitude and outspoken nature, Stapme left the service on 9 April 1946 and joined BOAC:

> Officially, according to my service record I left the RAF in April, but I'd left some months earlier and joined BOAC, so I had a couple of months on double pay.
>
> Naturally, the flying with BOAC was different, always straight and level, for the sake of the passengers! Before West African Airways (WAA) was formed we started off on DC3s (Dakotas) going from Hurn to Portugal, from Lisbon to Casablanca, to the French town of Rabat in Morocco where, on one occasion, we stopped for an engine change which took seven days. We then went down to the 'bulge' of Africa to Freetown (Sierra Leone) and then we went to Takoradi, which is on the Gold Coast (Ghana) and used during the war as a transit post for, amongst other aircraft, B17 Flying Fortresses flying across the Atlantic. They'd drop in at Ascension Island in the middle of the ocean to refuel before flying on to Takoradi and up to the Middle East where they joined up with the 15th Air Force (it was the 8th Air Force in the UK and the 15th in North Africa). Then BOAC moved its base to Accra, also on the Gold Coast. That was an amazing aerodrome because it only had one runway but the runway was about 3,000 yards long and about 200 yards wide. You could land a Tiger Moth on it across the width. It had been laid for the wartime transit work. Whilst there we stayed at Achimota which had been the police barracks at one time and was then accommodation for BOAC and home to the ground crews. It was very, very comfortable. I met a South African called Andy Andrews there. He was mad on music and we met two girls who had been left dozens of American discs, 12 inch records, including Glen Miller. Andy was a radio mechanic and we started a radio station called 'Radio Ger-Andy' which could broadcast up to 50 miles from Achimota – great fun! BOAC had a beach hut at Labadi Beach. I had a Hudson Terraplane called the 'Silver Bullet' with a 'Dicky'

---

*Old Zulu sayings, often used by Stapme, who is reasonably fluent in Zulu. 'Hamba Gashle' means 'Go gently' and is said to someone who is departing. 'Sahla Gashle', 'Stay gently', is the traditional reply.

seat. At Labadi Beach the local pineapple seller came along selling his wares. We used to cut the top off, scoop out the pineapple, fill it with gin and add pineapple and drink it. Andy and I had a boat hollowed out of a log and we paddled out through the surf towards the local fishing fleet and came back surfing on the waves.

Flights terminated at Accra and the next day you'd fly off to Lagos (Nigeria) before returning to Accra on the return trip.

I only did this journey for a couple of months when West African Airways was formed, feeding the trunk routes from Léopoldville (now Kinshasa) during 1946-48 north to Europe and feeding the South African route up through Nairobi to Europe.

I also flew a Junkers Ju52 from Accra to Port Harcourt and back as the 'King's Messenger' carrying the diplomatic pouch.

The Belgium Congo became Zaire which, in 1997, became the Democratic Republic of Congo, with Kinshasa is its capital. South Western Africa became Namibia. Stapme continued:

We established routes between the east and the west. There was the old service between West Africa and South Africa, they had to get across and then come down because Léopoldville was the terminal point. There was no service down across Angola, Léopoldville and down to Cape Town, so if they wanted to go south they had to go through Nairobi. For this trip we used the four-engine de Havilland Heron. The twin-engine de Havilland Dove was used for local flights from Accra and in Nigeria. The Doves were also used to go up to Kumasi – which was the gold mining area 200 miles north of Accra (Ghana) – and from Lagos (Nigeria) to the Nigerian towns of Port Harcourt, at the mouths of the River Niger; Enugu, Jos, Kano, Kaduna, Karnaya, and Maiduguri. At Maiduguri they had the ground-nut scheme going with huge trucks on the road carrying peanuts to Jos, which was a railhead for the journey south to Lagos. That local route included passengers, goats, chickens, all sorts of things. You had to be very careful landing because all the airstrips in Nigeria were laterite, tiny little iron pebbles.* When you landed you had to lift your flaps up very quickly otherwise they'd make little holes in them. So you raised your flaps as soon as you touched down, but not before! I did this for two years.

While at Jos, Stapme recalls meeting a number of well-known characters. The first was the footballer, Stanley Matthews (later Sir Stanley Matthews), who was on a visit to promote football in the area. Stapme was living in a local hotel at the time when he was approached and asked if he minded sharing his (two-bed) room with another man. He said he would have supper with him before

---

*Laterite: red residual soil characteristic of tropical rain-forests which is formed by the weathering of basalts, granites and shales and contains a high percentage of aluminium and iron hydroxides. As a permeable and infertile layer which inhibits plant growth it was suitable for landing strips.

making a decision. At dinner that night he met the great footballer and shared his room with him for his brief stay. On another occasion he met the best-selling author, Wilbur Smith, who was in Jos to carry out some background research for a novel he was writing.

Whilst at Jos, Stapme also owned and rode his own race-horse called Royal Mail which he actually rode to victory on one occasion. He recalls: 'The handicapping system was simple. The heaviest rider started ahead of the next heaviest, and so on. It was carefully measured.'

Stapme flew Dakotas, Doves and Herons on the West African 'Gold Coast' routes until 1948, when he returned to England.

On his arrival home he learned that the management were eager for him to return to Africa again and, inquisitive as to the reason why, he discovered that once again his wife's attentions had wandered and she had been having an affair with Malcolm Brown, the UK manager of BOAC.

After learning from another veteran of the Battle of Britain, Max Aitken, that the affair was common knowledge to everyone apart from Stapme, he took his family to South Africa to start afresh. He recalled that Heathrow in those days was: '. . . a shambles, it was all shacks and prefab buildings,' but even in those days the BOAC employees were given such benefits as free travel when going on leave:

> I arrived in South Africa with 2/6d [12½p] in my pocket. We stayed with my father and mother in Sarnia, Pinetown, about 15 miles from Durban, 15,000 feet above sea-level, where their house was called 'Thurlby Lodge' after the town in England where my father had been born.

Soon after, Joan gave birth to their second son, Harvey, who grew up to be the image of Stapme.

Initial employment took him to Dunlop Limited in Durban before the company sent him to Johannesburg to take over as their technical representative. The company provided tyres and seals for the agricultural and airline industry. Dunlop made various types of rubber tyres for aircraft as well as the rubber sealing which had a multitude of uses. While living in Johannesburg Stapme was involved in a car accident:

> I was driving my Standard Vanguard down what we called the 'dual highway' which had avenues of palm trees down the central reservation. A black guy in a hat (you could usually identify from where the guy came from by the type of hat he wore) stepped out into the road and in swerving to avoid him I skidded off the road and the car rode up one of the trees. The front end finished several feet up one of the trees. I was lucky, I'd had a skin-full!

Whilst at Dunlop Stapme joined the company cricket team which competed in a Sunday commercial league (against other companies) in Johannesburg. He recalled:

> One team would supply the food, the other the booze. We used to play against a team called the 'Jockey's Owners and Trainers' and during one match against them I was fielding deep by the

boundary and within earshot of the opposition batsmen by the pavilion. I discovered just how much money was resting on the outcome of the game. They were even taking bets on when and where the first boundary would occur. One particularly lusty shot came to me on the boundary but as it came out of the sun I never saw it. It hit me right between the eyes.

Stapme also played league squash, which he continued to do until well into his sixties.

In 1952 Stapme and Joan separated. During Stapme's time with Dunlop Joan's attentions had wandered again, this time with a neighbour and when Stapme became aware of her infidelity the marriage ended for good. It had also been blighted by heavy drinking on the part of both parents. Stapme agreed to let Joan bring up their two sons (Mike was eleven and Harvey three) and moved into rented accommodation in Johannesburg. Joan later married the man she was seeing and he proved a worthy step-father for the boys. Stapme recalled: 'He was a really nice chap who sadly died a couple of years ago.' Joan still lives in South Africa.

Mike Stapleton is a gifted vocalist and enjoyed a very successful pop singing career fronting his band 'Mike Shannon and the Diamonds' (Stapleton was thought to be too long). Together, the band produced seven albums and enjoyed many appearances in their weekly TV show in Australia, where Mike was best-known. It was years later that Stapme walked into a club in Durban to see Mike performing on stage, having not seen him since the breakdown of his marriage. The fatherly influence during the years since had come from his step-father. Reunited, the two were to see more of each other. During Stapme's subsequent time as a tour guide he even contrived to take his passengers to the club where Mike was working in order to provide a little extra business. A rare treat is to hear the two singing together, with Mike taking the lead and Stapme providing the harmony.

It was 1954, and Stapme had been with Dunlop for six years when, in his own words, he 'had a seven year itch' and went to work for Leylands where he delivered vehicle chassis for six months during the summertime:

> Me and a friend called Palmer flew to Cape Town to pick up a couple of Leyland chassis which were to be delivered to the Leyland depot in Johannesburg. On arrival Palmer received a telegram informing him his wife had just given birth to a son. Having previously had three girls it was a cause for celebration and instead of climbing into our Leyland Tiger chassis and starting our drive back to Johannesburg, about 1,000 miles, we parked them in the garden of a friend living nearby and set off to celebrate the birth of Palmer's son.
>
> Leaving the hotel in which we had been drinking, Palmer saw a motorbike and said to me: 'I bet you can't ride that bike?' I took the bet and rode around the block, as it turns out, with a policeman chasing me! Another policeman met me and hit me over the head with his truncheon and when Palmer tried to

intervene he was thrown by another policeman with such force, he landed under a parked truck. He was charged with hindering the police in the course of their duty. The bike I had taken was a police bike and I was arrested and charged. When they tried to put the handcuffs on me they actually punched them closed through the cuffs of my sports jacket. I spent the night in jail and later returned for the court case but, strangely, once in court I was let off the charges because the arresting policeman had not been wearing his hat and had no means of identification. I even gave the arresting police officer a lift home from court to his home in Worcester, a distance of seventy miles from Cape Town. He turned out to be a really friendly chap.

Following the short time he spent working for Leylands, Stapme spent an even shorter spell working in the Freestate Gold Mine. This was fraught with danger:

I was in the mine carrying out a survey. Whilst walking down a 'drive' I had been measuring, a large rock dropped from the 'hanging', and nearly hit me. The surrounding stone was slate and it was oily which probably caused this large piece to shoot out. I was back in Durban twelve hours later!

At that time Stapme owned a small easy-to-maintain car: '. . . a two-stroke car which had a cylinder-head gasket leak. I used to take the plugs out, turn the engine over, blow the water out, put the plugs back and get on my way.' He recalled his next place of employment:

I was working for Durban Corporation for a while as a night-shift bus inspector. I had to ensure all the buses were clean and in the proper place for the morning shift to come on duty. I did that for about three months, it was just a fill-in until I went to Sprite Caravans.

Stapme joined Sprite Caravans in 1954 as works engineer where he remained for seven years:

When I first got there we were making one caravan every four days. When I left them seven years later, we were making 40 caravans a day of the small model we called the '400', a little ten foot caravan, then we made the twelve foot 'Alpine', the fourteen foot 'Musketeer', and the 'Major' which was a sixteen footer.

We had a production line of about 100 yards in a factory that was 50 yards long. The railway line ran in a 'U' shape from the start down to the far end before coming back again. In the centre we built a rubber floor and all the parts that were needed for each station were kept here. Each caravan chassis came from the welding shop and was pushed manually onto the railway line and it would stop at each work station where it would remain for about twenty minutes, depending on the type of van that was being built, the bigger vans requiring more work. All the parts required for the people to do their twenty minutes work were laid out on the rubber mat, before the whole thing was pushed along to the next station. These parts were ordered by the batch in advance. If you knew you would be building fifty caravans of one type you'd have to order all the necessary parts that would go into that particular type of caravan. These parts had to be in the store ready when you switched from building say an Alpine to a Musketeer. You'd get all the stuff in overnight for a changeover and you had all the necessary chaps working overtime. The only thing you didn't put into a caravan on the production line was the upholstery because if you have people working in the van with the upholstery in place there was the risk it would be spoiled. Most of our parts were shipped out from England and we had problems during strike action there and had to resort to sourcing parts locally. In the event work could not be completed the main line couldn't come to a halt so we established a secondary production line and when the parts came in we could complete the work.

Eventually, Sprite was taken over by Caravans International (CI) and I became a human resource – thank you very much. Sprite had been a family business and eventually we became quite successful, making 1,000 caravans a year. We had a separate unit for administration, accounts, that sort of thing and a separate unit for the stores and another for the wood (we called it the wood mill) for the side structures and floors, and then all these units amalgamated with Gypsy Caravans and then the overseas Sprite Caravans were changed to Caravans International. They wanted a works engineer who was certificated, so I handed over to a chap called Parkinson and went on my way.

In the late fifties, Jack Stapleton, Deryck, Marjorie and Stapme were left mourning the loss of wife and mother, Myrtle, who died of lung cancer in her early seventies. She had been a chain-smoker for most of her adult life and the habit had taken its toll over the last few years prior to her death. After seven years service with the company, Stapme left Sprite in 1961, and turned to escorting enthusiasts on photographic safaris.

CHAPTER THIRTEEN

'GOD'S OWN' BOTSWANA

On leaving Sprite Caravans Stapme's next job was in total contrast to life as a works engineer on a production line. He became a guide in Botswana, 550 miles north-west of Johannesburg, a country and period of his life he remembers with great affection.

The Republic of Botswana covers 225,000 square miles. Formerly occupied by nomadic hunter-gatherer groups in the early 13th Century, the area was settled by the Tswana people. Following the discovery of gold in 1885, the country became the British Protectorate of Bechuanaland at the request of Chief Khama who feared invasion from the Transvaal (South Africa) by Boers. In 1965 the capital, Mafeking, was transferred to Gabarone and the following year Bechuanaland achieved independence from Great Britain when its name was changed to Botswana. Throughout the seventies the economy grew rapidly as diamond mining expanded. Today, Botswana is the third largest exporter of diamonds in the world. 70-80% of the national territory is desert with the Kalahari in the south-west, the Makgadikgadi salt pans in the east, the Okavango Delta/swamp in the north and the Chobe Game Reserve north-east of the Okavango. It is the last two areas which feature prominently in Stapme's story. Of the early days in the Okavango, he recalls the hunting trips:

> Apart from the clients, we only allowed observers along on the trips, no others, otherwise if you had people wandering about they'd end up shooting each other. The wives sat around doing nothing while their husbands went off hunting. During the season I had two observers I used to take out on quite a lot of the safaris. You could only go up to the Okavango Delta during the wintertime, not the summer.

The Okavango Delta, probably Botswana's greatest natural treasure, is situated in the north-west of the country and is also known as the Okavango swamp or marsh but delta is preferable as it sounds more appealing to the tourists. The Okavango Delta is where one of Africa's great rivers fans out eventually to lose itself in the Kalahari desert. The Okavango river rises in the tropical highlands of central Angola and flows south-east across Namibia's (formerly South-West Africa) Caprivi Strip, along the Angola/Namibia border, before flowing into Lakes Ngami and Xau.

The Okavango Delta is a place of unforgettable beauty where water and land are interlocked and camouflaged by vast reed beds to the point that it is hard to tell where one ends and the other begins. For 60 miles, the channel of water is curbed between parallel geological faults and in this 'panhandle' the river continues to meander over a relatively confined floodplain, forming hairpin bends as it loops its way through extensive papyrus swamps. At the point where the Okavango flows over the Gomare Fault, it ceases to be a normal river when it breaks into several main channels and a web of smaller waterways and washes over the intervening flatlands, fanning out into a great arc of permanent swamps and seasonally flooded plains. With the arrival of the annual flood from Angola the Okavango Delta fills and feeds a shallow layer of water over 6,000 square miles of countryside, but so slowly (just half a mile per day) that 95% is absorbed by plants or evaporates under the heat of the African sun before it gets to its southernmost reaches, some 100 miles away, where the last of the Okavango's waters are channelled down along the small Thamalakane river where they flow past Maun, the largest settlement in the vicinity, before turning eastwards down the bed of the Boteti river and vanishing into the Kalahari Desert. The Okavango Delta is an incredible feat of nature in that it is situated in the middle of what is almost desert and where life forms including fish, frogs, crocodiles and hippos thrive. The Okavango is the main breeding ground for the crocodile and the upper river is well known for both the number and size of these beasts. Herds of cattle and goats are brought out by the villagers to graze on the panhandle's flood plain during the dry season giving the larger crocodiles the chance to grab a meal from the banks of the main river. Barbel (catfish) and tiger fish also provide an abundant food source for the Panhandle's crocodiles.

The Okavango is a dynamic yet adaptable river system. Once it spreads out over the flat Kalahari countryside the delta is no longer recognisable as the single river it is. Reed beds and papyrus creates a floating carpet on the surface of the water and the perennial swamps of the panhandle and the northern delta are the realm of the papyrus which grows in dense floating mats held together by a submerged matrix of roots. As the slow moving water flows through the sea of reeds and grass, the vegetation filters it, forcing it to drop any heavy silt particles and turning it crystal clear. The small fast-flowing rivers are kept open by the passage of mekoros* (dugout canoes) and hippos but a raft of floating papyrus, an abandoned mokoro or a fallen tree has the potential to block a channel forcing the water to find another route and in a system as unstable as this, every part is subject to change. The annual floods filter down through the delta to reach Maun by June or July, although they may not come at all.

The town of Maun is situated a few miles to the south-east of the delta and is the largest settlement in the vicinity. It is also the tribal capital of the Botswana people and the administration centre of Ngamiland. During this period Stapme lived at a place called 'Crocodile Camp' near Maun. A local guide book provides us with an insight into the locality:

> Located at the southern end of the Okavango Delta, Maun is the safari capital of Botswana. It is more an extended village than a town, with dusky sand tracks weaving between simple modern houses and traditional Tswana family compounds. Maun has the notorious reputation of a frontier town, and it has long been the

*mokoro – singular. mekoros – plural.

hangout for a collection of professional hunters, adventurers, and safari guides. Indeed, quite a bit of partying (or drinking, at any rate) goes on at the handful of watering holes and lodges where the safari crowd gathers. Aside from getting organised for a safari, there is little else to do. Maun's airport is one of the busiest in Africa, with a constant stream of light aircraft coming and going into the bush. You are very likely to fly to Maun on either end of your safari, but may not be scheduled to spend any more time than it takes to connect to an ongoing flight. The only hotel in town is Riley's Hotel. It has a pleasant garden and features Harry's Bar, a favourite local meeting place. The nearby Crocodile Camp is nice and has the best food of all the local lodges [offering] accommodation in chalets, as well as sites for campers. All the lodges rent boats and mekoros and arrange safaris into the delta and the parks. But be wary of water sports around Maun.

Stapme reflects on his time at Maun:

The season stretched for about seven months and in that time I was busy but the rest of the year was quiet. I used to collect all sorts of tourist trophies, like Karosses (patchwork blankets of animal skins). The Africans used to make them, along with all sorts of other tourist carvings and that sort of thing. In that five months I used to sell it to a tourist shop down in Durban called Ivy's which specialised in tourist souvenirs. I used to buy stuff and put on 500% and Ivy's used to put on about another 500%. On one trip I did down to the Transkei, Eastern Cape, there was an African chap with a monkey-fur hat on, sitting, chipping away at a little white wood warrior. A piece of glass and a hacksaw blade were his only tools. He made a little Pondo warrior man, a Pondo woman smoking a pipe (Pondo women used to smoke pipes), and child – three separate carvings in white wood. I bought them from him for about 12 rand, about 10/- (a rand in those days was worth two to the pound – it's worth nine now). I knew I could sell them on for the equivalent of £15 and the tourist shop knew they could sell them for the equivalent of £30 a set because they were unique, nobody had seen them before. I said to the African: 'If I ordered ten from you how much would you charge me?' He said: 'If you want ten, I'll charge you more for each one.' I said: 'Why would you want to charge me more for each one if I'm ordering so many?' 'Because, there's so much more work for me!' He said he had children who used to sharpen his hacksaw blades down in the river on the water stone. So, that's what I decided to do during the off-season.

I also used to paddle up the river (Okavango) in a mokoro. These canoes were made from huge trees. Once felled, they used to burn the middle out. I bought one which was eighteen feet long and three feet wide for £5. I used a paddle, whereas the natives used a (punting) pole, a very, very, long pole. In most places the water was about twelve feet deep and in other places even deeper but they knew their way around using poles. I didn't use a pole because that was something they had learned from childhood. They knew the waterways very well indeed. Their canoes were twenty-five feet long and four feet wide. They loaded their mekoros with reeds from the delta as they travelled downstream at about 2 mph before punting back. When they eventually returned to their settlement each mokoro was loaded to a height of about six feet. Remember, they were only four feet wide! They used the reeds to make the walls of their huts. They then thatched the reeds with grass. The natives also used to move great islands of papyrus reeds on the river (like herding cattle) which were also used to thatch huts.

At that time my home in Crocodile Camp, near Maun, consisted of a hut. Occasionally, when I didn't have anything to do, I used to paddle up the Thamalakane river or the Boteti river [The River Boteti runs west into Lake Xau and from Lake Xau continues west to Lake Ngami and on to the Okavango Delta]. The two rivers came together not far from the camp. I used to set off in my canoe and paddle up-river against the current for maybe three hours. There was a very slow flow because, as you can imagine, the delta was very flat. In certain areas I could just lie in the front of my canoe and pull myself along using the reeds. I'd put a line over (or use a Neptune trident) and catch a fish, which I'd have for dinner when I got back. I'd simply put it in the fire to cook, wrapped in aluminium foil, then eat it. There were bream but no tiger fish which were further north. Tigers were real fighting fish. On the way back I used to just go with the current. This was a most enjoyable period of my life. You'd see all sorts of things there – snakes going through the reeds, not on the water but on the reeds as they were so thick. The water was clear, filtered by 6-700 miles of reeds and you could see all the reeds underwater and how they had collected all the silt. The water was so soft you could wash your hair in it and drink it. You didn't have to boil it – nobody had to because it had been filtered over a thousand miles from Angola without pollution. It was so clear. The Okavango Delta is the largest body of inland water which doesn't run into the sea.

At Crocodile Camp I knew a chap called Bobby Wilmott who had established a business there in which he was required to provide 3-4,000 crocodile skins a year in order to fulfil a contract he had with the Botswana Government. He had about fifteen outboard motor boats and on each of these he had one 45hp motor and a little 'phut phut', a smaller motor in case the other broke down. He used to send his hunters up into the Okavango. These chaps would head off with their provisions in 45 gallon drums in order that nothing could get to them. These supplies included salt for salting the skins, food and fuel. Bobby was an odd character, a very strange man, who had been born up there (his father, Cronje Wilmott, wrote a book about the Okavango), unfortunately, Bobby was killed by a snake bite. He always used to wear shorts while everybody else used to wear longs. The reason why the snake – a black mamba – got him. He was carrying a battery from his pick-up down to a boat because he had one boat which had a battery electric starter while all the others had pull-cords. The snake got him as he walked down to the boat. The black mamba was very long, thin and very quick. Bobby had a son called Lloyd who now has a business up there flying tourists through and around the Okavango Delta. He's now also got aeroplanes in which to take tourists around.

Stapme then spent some time escorting small groups of tourists on photographic safaris around Botswana. Whilst the towns are not particularly appealing, Stapme reckoned the countryside was stunning and used to route the excursions through the Chobe Game Reserve (pronounced Ch-o-bee, it is also known as the Chobe National Park), about 200 miles to the north-east of Maun, where the tourists could see the spectacular big game wildlife. The park itself is one of the greatest wildlife sanctuaries of southern Africa and gives protection to some 4,600 square miles of bush country, but to this must be added thousands of miles of wildlife habitat in surrounding hunting blocks and forest reserves. Attracting game from as far away as the Linyanti Swamps, Nxai Pans National Park and even from Zimbabwe and Namibia's Caprivi Strip, Chobe is a key stronghold for the wildlife of the entire north-eastern Kalahari region. Although Chobe is flat, sandy and not wonderfully scenic, there is a wide range of plants providing natural beauty and niches for a wide variety of animals. Chobe Park is a legendary elephant refuge for the greater part of Botswana's 60,000 plus elephant population which live in the park for at least part of the year. Chobe river is one of the largest in Botswana and game viewing is excellent in the area (because of its proximity to the major regional gateway at Victoria Falls, Zimbabwe, the Chobe river area is the most crowded game viewing area in Botswana), including massive herds of elephants which are regularly seen during the dry season along the river and are almost an icon of current safari lore. Cruises on the river are available. In the woodland can be viewed: kudu, impala, vervet monkeys, baboon, giraffe, roan and antelope. Viewing on the floodplain is exceptional because the country is so wide and flat. Huge numbers of waterbirds and waders congregate on the floodplain where, in the extensive grasslands, cheetah can be found.

Stapme also routed his guests via the Chobe Game Lodge, approximately nine miles from Karane, the nearest settlement. The move was deliberate, as his son, Mike, was manager at that time. Chobe Game Lodge is the only one within the park and the prestigious 47 room luxury hotel overlooks the river flats and is in the middle of a prime game viewing area close to the Serondella area, where lions and other predators can be found. Superstars Richard Burton and Liz Taylor were married for the second time at Chobe Game Lodge. Together, father and son had a number of good times in Botswana. Mike recalled one occasion they were out drinking together:

My father had an American 1957/58 Plymouth [Fury], a great big car with the instantly recognisable wings on the back end. We had had a few drinks, the roof was down and the radio on. In the

middle of nowhere he pulled-up, got out and leaving the driver's
door open, started dancing with the closing edge of the door, his
body swaying to the tune on the radio!

Stapme also has affectionate memories of his adventures as a businessman in
Botswana:

I bought a Land Rover and a six ton, four-wheel-drive,
International. I took customers on photographic excursions into
the Moremi Game Reserve. They rode with me in the Land Rover
and their equipment was carried in the truck. The trips included
'fly-nights' from the main camp (a 'fly-night' was a one night stop
before packing up and moving on to spend the next night in
another place). There was no accommodation so we carried our
own tents, equipment and a team of seven boys.

Sadly Stapme's business venture came to a premature end at a time when life
was good:

We were driving along one day and the road suddenly gave way
plunging both vehicles into the river below. Whilst the passengers
were insured, I didn't have insurance for their baggage, including
all their camera equipment. The reason for this was that their
clothing baggage was usually left behind at the main camp during
the fly-nights and each took just a small denim bag with a change
of underwear, that sort of thing. The vehicles were alright after
they'd dried out, but I had to sell them in order to pay off the
people who had lost their cameras. I subsequently arrived in
Durban where I became a taxi driver for two months before I got
a job with a touring company.

Following the loss of his business Stapme was employed by a company called
Springbok Atlas Tours. It was not a particularly happy time for him simply
because the company didn't provide the support when the inevitable problems
occurred during what were very long trips across great expanses of often
inhospitable open country.

During one trip, his coach was involved in a road accident which resulted in
damage to his vehicle. As he brought his vehicle to a rapid halt, he managed to
stop his tour guide, who had been sitting up-front alongside him, from being
launched through the front windscreen. In the split second he had seen her
propelled forward he reached out and grabbed one of her arms, while he
continued to steer the coach with the other. His action in seizing the girl as the
momentum threw her forwards broke her arm but saved her from more serious
injury. In response to Stapme's gallant efforts but also out of a sense of relief,
the passengers broke out in a spontaneous round of applause. Similarly, on
another occasion he had a German tour guide at the front of the coach busy
providing the passengers with a tour commentary over the PA system when
Stapme was forced to carry out an emergency stop:

The girl flew forward and if it hadn't been for me reaching out an
arm behind her to cushion her impact with the windscreen she
would have gone right through the glass. As it was, the left-hand

panel of the windscreen was shattered and had to be replaced. The German guide was left with a few bruises. The coach business licences were displayed in the windscreen and before I could move off I collected them from amongst the glass on the roadside in order to ensure we continued as a legitimate business.

During another safari:

One of the coach tyres punctured just short of Mbabane, the capital of Swaziland. I changed it for the spare and finished the trip into town where Erickson's, a local company, found the replacement tyre was defective. I had it replaced and I also bought another tyre but the company refused to refund the outlay for both tyres.

During Stapme's final trip for Springbok Atlas Tours, the coach engine broke down just outside Mbabane:

I met a chap who was a Cummings engineer (Cummings was the make of the engine). He re-built the engine and afterwards I said to him: 'If you meet me in Mbabane I'll pay you for your trouble.' We did meet and I gave him twenty-four bottles of beer. When I returned to Springbok Atlas, I handed them the bill for the engine repairs and the beers which they refused to pay, so I left the company. Their coaches broke down during the last three trips I went on.*

From Springbok Atlas Stapme worked for Collins, a more supportive company which also specialised in taking tourists across the country, from one major city to another, in 48-seater Mercedes coaches. This proved a change for the better after Springbok Atlas and he thoroughly enjoyed his time travelling round the country and keeping his customers entertained with his local knowledge. He found the coaches were easy to drive and the company en-route varied, interesting and particularly friendly. The gratitude of the passengers towards the driver who had acted as a tour guide, was expressed in the form of generous tips which exceeded his actual salary:

Collins were fantastic. This was the greatest time of my life, the scenery and the lifestyle being quite perfect. It was great meeting so many different people, from different cultures, with different interests and questions. I had to learn about the wildlife and environment, as well as the history as I went along. I might have a 1,000 mile trip to Cape Town, a 400 mile trip on to the Kruger National Park and then 180 miles from the Kruger Park to Johannesburg where the passengers normally stopped the night before catching a flight the next day, to wherever they were going. There were other trips that we did and one of those was to Lesotho and the battlefields of the Boer War in South Africa. The

---

*During the late nineties a Sprinkbok Atlas coach plunged off the road at Long Town Pass, a notorious accident black spot, during a tour of the Kruger National Park in Kenya. Several elderly passengers lost their lives in the accident. The enquiry blamed the driver.

longest trip I did was from Durban to Cape Town and back to Durban. I did two trips in a month, completing 15,000 kilometres. The buses were easier to drive than cars, you had a sprung seat, everything was powered. I recall only a couple of trips when there were problems while working for Collins. One occurred during the part of the tour from the Kruger National Park to Johannesburg. The generator broke down and having made it to Johannesburg I telephoned the Collins depot to report the unserviceable generator. Young Collins, the son of the owner, picked up a replacement part, drove out to Johannesburg and fitted it by the next morning when we set off on the next stage of the tour.

The other breakdown occurred when one of the fan-belts broke in open country. South Africa Railways had contracted Collins for a ten day trip from Durban to west South Africa to Cape Town. The Mercedes coach had nine fan-belts which powered the generators, air conditioning etc. Unfortunately, the fan-belt which broke was the radiator fan-belt. If you drove during the night in the winter it was cool enough to get by without a fan belt, but this was in the summer. Aware of our predicament, a lady produced a pair of her pantyhose, which I fitted as a temporary replacement for the broken belt, which got us the 32 miles to where I could get another fan belt. I was lucky. We had lunch there while the chaps were fixing it and that took us on to Cape Town where we had to change all nine fan belts (once you've changed one fan belt, you've got to change the lot).

On another occasion Stapme was driving a large group of particularly demanding and arrogant German tourists who had put together a detailed and carefully planned itinerary of their own with scant regard for the plans and superior professional knowledge of their tour guide. After only a few miles he became sick of the 'arrogant and superior autocrats' in his care, but for the entire trip he refrained from expressing his true feelings whenever they were impolite or rude. Finally, towards the end of the trip, hoping to belittle Stapme, one of the group asked loudly in front of the others: 'Vot did you do in ze vor?' To which Stapme replied: 'I was a *bomber* pilot!' The coach continued its journey, and onboard a stony silence reigned. Apart from rare instances like that, this period of Stapme's life was memorable.

On another occasion he was driver/tour guide to a coach party of friendly and enthusiastic American tourists who Stapme found a delight to work with. Sadly, during the trip one of the men had a heart attack and died overnight in Mbabane, Swaziland:

I pulled in and telephoned the American Embassy in Mbabane and informed a lady on the end of the line of the sad demise of one of my group. The lady replied: 'Does he have a return ticket (to the United States)?!' I eventually managed to get the Ambassador on the line who rather apologetically offered his excuses for the insensitivity of his staff: 'We have people like this all over the world.'

The story did not end there: such was the good time they were all having, the wife of the deceased saw the body of her husband off on its lone trip back to the States for burial while she climbed back onboard the coach and continued her holiday!

In 1968, a number of years after a particularly short-lived second marriage had ended and, according to Stapme, best forgotten, he met Audrey 'Abey' Blyton while in the tour-guide business. The Blyton family are from Peterborough, Cambridgeshire, and Audrey had left England to work in Durban some years before.* Audrey joined the Wrens in 1947 and demobbed in 1949 before she was 21. During her service with the Fleet Air Arm she was a mechanic on Seafire 47s at Royal Naval Air Station (RNAS) Anthorn. After leaving, Audrey had a number of short-term jobs before she went on the stage for eighteen months touring the Empire theatres. Initially inexperienced, she was taught the dance routines. She also toured Sweden as part of the dance troop accompanying Phyllis Dixie. They performed in Gotenburg and at the China Theatre, Stockholm. Her other sister, Mary, was part of the same tour. Audrey missed life in the Wrens and re-entered the service in 1951 at RNAS Abbotsinch, just outside Glasgow. One of her proudest memories of her time at Abbotsinch was when she deputised for Marina, Duchess of Kent, for the 'Mock Admiral's Rounds':

> I was so flattered that it had been thought appropriate I should play the role. I was driven around in the back of the Captain's car beautifully attired in a lovely dress, gloves and hat. I was driven to the dais outside one of the hangars by the flagpole where I carried out an inspection of the Wrens in their ranks and was even given a bouquet by one of them. Only my best friend knew it was me.

On leaving the Royal Navy for good, Audrey trained as a nurse and initially worked at a hospital in Leith, Edinburgh, where she became an experienced midwife. Later, she was on a contract as a nursing sister at Addington's Hospital, situated on the resort seafront in Durban, when she was introduced to Stapme. Mike Stapleton recalls: 'If it wasn't for Audrey the drink would have killed him.' The couple married on 8 October 1971 in Durban and have been happily married ever since, Audrey having provided important stability to Stapme's life.

Stapme's father, Jack, continued to live in retirement in Thurlby Lodge which was situated in two acres of land in Sarnia, near Pinetown. During the late 1960s he found happiness and companionship again when he married Cissie Staplee, whose late husband had owned a farm at Tickencote, near Stamford. The Staplee's only child was tragically killed at the age of thirteen whilst out cycling on the Great North Road. With marriage to Cissie pending, Jack divided his land into two one acre plots. On one was situated Thurlby Lodge and on the other he built a bungalow for he and Cissie to live in once they were

---

*It is possible the Blytons are related to the author Enid Blyton. Enquries by Audrey's sister (also called Enid) proved inconclusive.

married. His daughter, Marjorie, and her family subsequently moved into Thurlby Lodge. Of his father's new home Stapme remembers the garden as 'quite fantastic. There were giant avocado trees the size of oaks which produced many pears. Bananas and paw-paw were also grown.' Jack Stapleton died in Sarnia in 1972 aged 87 and is recalled as being '. . . a man of great wit and humour who, to people's amusement, absent-mindedly spoke of rupees when he should have been speaking in £.s.d. and later rands. Those who knew him will remember him as the man in Pinetown with a pipe, solar topee and a spaniel that was his constant companion.'

CHAPTER FOURTEEN

'WILL YOU SIGN THIS PLEASE
SQUADRON LEADER STAPLETON?'

Stapme continued to play league squash and commercial league cricket until he was sixty when he finally retired from sport. Sadly, his time with Collins on the long-haul trips came to a premature end: 'I developed a cataract on my right eye and was unable to continue with my work. I couldn't see properly at night and therefore couldn't drive long haul trips anymore.'

Stapme's next employment came as a tour guide for groups travelling in the Drakensberg Mountains, a 400-mile range of mountains with peaks of up to 10,000 feet. The Natal Parks Board has extensive reserves in the foothills of the Drakensberg Range:

> I used to take small walking parties as far as we could scramble. The wild flowers, the birds and the trees were all of interest. The more I did the job, the more I learned. There were hotels dotted right along the foothills from north to south, until the range went in to Lesotho. During the trips I took the tourists to see the Mont-aux-Sources (10,768 feet), the second highest single waterfall in the world, which was the source of the Tugela river which flowed into the Indian Ocean.
>
> Natal is about the size of England, but with a population of 4 million. It was called the 'garden province' because of the rainfall on the south-west wind which would go over the mountains and drop its load on Natal.

Stapme's next job was as a night-shift worker in a factory in Hammarsdale, between Durban and Pietermaritzberg, making pure wool fur pile for an international market:

> I did that for three years and then, when I turned 65, they had a system of retirement at that age and I was out. I then met Mike, my eldest son, who was running Kloof Country Club. At that time he was looking for someone else to work in the caddy-master's office to look after the boodle because Tim, the caddy-master, an African who was a really nice chap, couldn't look after both, although he had tried to. So I went in with him in the caddy-master's office. I took the boodle and he allocated the caddies to the various golfers. That was quite a job in itself, allocating all the young African caddies to golfing customers.

Despite his eye condition, Stapme did the occasional coach driving job for

Collins, driving children in school buses to and from school during the hours of daylight as the vision in his right eye continued to deteriorate. This was later rectified to some degree when he underwent surgery in a South African hospital to remove the cataract and transplant a new lens onto the eyeball.

Stapme and Audrey lived in retirement at Pioneer Gardens, 18 Stapleton Road, Sarnia, Natal, RSA, where life wasn't as easy as they hoped it would be. On numerous occasions Audrey encountered prowlers in the house looking for valuables. For her to walk into a room in her own home, with Stapme away, was terrifying. Her only reaction was to scream which, fortunately for Audrey, sent the intruders fleeing from the bungalow. At home Stapme kept a child's 'super-soaker' water-pistol which he kept loaded with ammonia, in the event they found another intruder in the house, hardly adequate against the ever-increasing number of firearms offences. For his personal protection when out walking, Stapme drove a number of short spikes into the end of his walking stick over which he placed the standard rubber tip. When confronted he simply removed the tip and thrust the end towards the midriff of his assailant, which proved effective! On one occasion he was accosted in the lane by his home by an irate driver of a BMW who, having roared past at excessive speed, leapt out to confront Stapme after he struck the car across the bonnet with his modified walking stick. Their experience of crime left the couple pondering their future in the town. A more natural nuisance in the neighbourhood were the monkeys which disrupted domestic life and which retreated to the trees in their garden when shooed away. As a deterrent Stapme used a hunting catapult from which he fired steel ball-bearings. These proved lethal and a number of monkeys never returned to steal or make a nuisance of themselves at the Stapletons.

In 1990 Stapme and Audrey travelled to England to attend the 50th Anniversary, Battle of Britain Dinner at London's Savoy Hotel. Sometime during 1993/4, Wing Commander John Young AFC who, like Stapme, had also worked for BOAC, travelled to South Africa to visit friends with his wife, Thelma. During their stay John and Stapme (both members of the Battle of Britain Fighter Association) were reunited and had lunch together in the Lord Charles pub/restaurant, Durban.

On 3 September 1994, tragedy struck when Harvey was left in a coma following a motocross accident in which he suffered severe head injuries. The ground floor of the home of his girlfriend was converted to accommodate Harvey and his life support equipment.

Stapme and Audrey continued to live in Natal in retirement tolerating the threat of further crime until Audrey's health took a downward turn. In December 1994, with an unsure future ahead if they remained in South Africa, the couple moved back to England taking their two cats with them. Michael and Harvey remained in the country with Harvey still critically ill. Whilst still in South Africa, Audrey had attempted to find a home in England for herself and Stapme prior to their departure. She contacted a firm of solicitors in Broad Street, Stamford, called 'Stapleton & Son'. After their return to England they discovered that the founder of the business was Richard Stapleton, Stapme's great uncle.

On 10 February 1995, six months after Harvey's crash, he succumbed to his injuries. He was 48. He left a young son, Cameron (born April 1990). Harvey had lived life to the full and had been a fanatical off-road motorcyclist (interestingly, he didn't ride a motorcycle on the public roads). Bearing in mind the nature of the sport, he had many spills, some of which were serious. Audrey recalls that whenever she saw Harvey it always seemed to be in Addington's Hospital, where she was working at the time, and while he was a patient, having suffered various injuries. Some, as the law of averages dictates, were serious, but he was prepared to take the risks as he loved the sport. Stapme returned to South Africa for the funeral.

In 2001, the transplanted lens was removed from Stapme's right eye in Peterborough District Hospital, after problems developed. Today the vision in his right eye lacks definition leaving him only able to see light and colour. Bright light and darkness pose problems and he considers the eye practically useless. Since returning to England he has also undergone a lens transplant in his left eye at Peterborough. This was a success and he is more or less totally reliant on this eye.

Stapme and Audrey now live in quiet retirement near Stamford, Lincolnshire, the area from where the Stapletons originate. Sadly, their cats died shortly after being released from quarantine but being great cat lovers they quickly adopted two more. In 2000/1, Mike spent some time working in England, during which we spoke of his father. He told me, rather poignantly: 'If there is one thing I would really love to do for Dad before it's too late, it would be to take him back to Botswana, one last time.' Mike has two children, Damon and Tarin, who live in Johannesburg. Mike eventually became a grandfather and by the end of 2000, at the age of 60, a great-grandfather and Stapme a great-great grandfather at 80. At the time of writing Mike is back in South Africa once again working in the music industry singing on advertising jingles and as a voice coach for pop stars. Stapme's brother, Deryck, lives in retirement in Devon on the River Axe. Deryck's eldest son, John, is a pyrotechnist and lives in a castle in Kent. He has produced photographic reconstructions depicting his uncle's adventures on 7 September 1940 and 23 December 1944. Bruce is a farmer in England and recently acquired a vineyard in New Zealand. Having started out as a cameraman, Deryck's youngest son, Oliver Stapleton BSc, is now one of the world's finest directors of photography in the film industry. His latest work at the time of writing is *The Shipping News* starring Dame Judi Dench and Kevin Spacey. Stapme's sister Marjorie (Gétaz) still lives in Sarnia, near Pinetown, with her husband and daughters Olivia, Suzanne and Marion.

* * *

By the end of WWII, Stapme's total combat claims amounted to six and three shared destroyed, eight probable, and two damaged, all while serving with 603 Squadron during the Battle of Britain. Stapme told me that during that period he was more fortunate than others in that he never felt scared:

> While waiting at dispersal I felt butterflies in my stomach, but once in the air I thrived on the rush of adrenaline, the thrill of flight, the sight of the beautiful land below, and of flying alone,

high above the fluffy white clouds. It was exciting, frantic and all over so quickly.

Referring to combat he said: 'We were all so busy just doing our job.'

After the war Stapme remained in contact with a number of his former 603 Squadron friends including: Uncle George Denholm, Ras Berry, Archie Winskill, Tannoy Read and latterly Jack Stokoe and Ludwik Martel. In recent years he has returned to Tarfside, Montrose, Drem and Turnhouse. During the afternoon of Friday 10 March 2000, Stapme and I were guests of the Lord Provost at the reception to mark the reformation of 603 Squadron, RAuxAF, at the Edinburgh City Chambers. Later we returned to the Squadron Town HQ at Learmonth Terrace where Stapme had a drink with some of the ground crew personnel of 1940. The brief friendships from so long ago, during such a tumultuous period, mean a great deal to him; a chance to share memories with kindred folk, as it is only they who can appreciate and understand what he went through. Of the far-off summer of 1940, Stapme just says: 'We were young and our pleasure was flying – in my case at night with a full moon. It was so exciting being a fighter pilot and we had a job to do; but then we grew up . . .'

One anecdote stands out from the trip to Edinburgh. That same evening we returned to our accommodation to freshen up prior to a night out in the Scottish capital, something Stapme hadn't done for nearly 60 years. Dressed in casual attire I knocked on Stapme's door and informed him the taxi had arrived. He emerged from his room dressed in blazer, shirt and tie and, unhappy that he had overdressed, promptly disappeared back behind his door. Moments later he remerged, his blazer and tie gone, his shirt open at the neck (two buttons were undone from the neck and the collar was up) and his hair slicked back. 'Right let's go!' he uttered as he brushed past and made his way downstairs. We initially made for the Café Royale in West Register Street which was unfortunately very busy with no way to the bar. I suggested we went to The Abbotsford in Rose Street and we set off. As we crossed St David's Street we misjudged the speed of a taxi cab coming down the hill towards Princes Street and had to run for it. As I broke into a jog I must admit I left Stapme to take his own evasive action but, much to my surprise, he suddenly appeared at my side running with his chest out and shoulders back in an elegant, high kicking style and made the opposite pavement well before me. We strode into the Abbotsford where, within minutes, Stapme was settled with a pint and a local audience. Not bad for an eighty year-old!

He has also become a member of the 247 Squadron Association and remained in touch with a number of the other members, including Flight Lieutenant Tatters Tatham. Stapme is a popular figure at air shows and is an enthusiastic fund-raiser for the RAF Benevolent Fund and the Royal Air Forces Association. A percentage of his fee for the many print signings he carries out for the various military aviation galleries around the country, is sent to one charity or another.

At the Fighter Pilots Reunion at RAF Lakenheath in 1999, Squadron Leader Paul Day OBE, AFC, RAF, Officer Commanding the BBMF, invited Stapme to visit Coningsby and have a look round 'P7' (also known as 'Baby Spit'): 'Go on, you can take her up', he offered. Stapme travelled to Coningsby later that year. Although he climbed aboard P7, he declined Squadron Leader Day's invitation.

During 2000, the 60th Anniversary year of the Battle of Britain, Stapme appeared in a number of TV news items as well as countless press articles. He attended the RAF Museum, Hendon, where the *Daily Mail* arranged an exclusive photo shoot of the large number of Battle of Britain fighter pilots who had gathered there as part of the anniversary tributes.

During 2000/1 Stapme also went to great lengths to accommodate researchers, directors and producers of TV and film companies, and it is good that recordings of Stapme recounting his wartime experiences have found their way into various archives.

Both Stapme and Audrey appeared in a Battle of Britain 60th Anniversary special edition of *Songs of Praise*, filmed at RAF Halton, Buckinghamshire. At the Theatre Royal, Nottingham, he was guest of honour at a concert organised by RAFA and featuring the Massed Bands of the Royal Air Force. He attended the Royal International Air Tattoo at RAF Cottesmore during 2000 and 2001 – Cottesmore being near to his Rutland/Lincolnshire home. He was also a guest at RAF Cottesmore and RAF Coningsby, at the respective dinners organised to commemorate the Battle of Britain. On Sunday 9 July 2000, along with many members of the Fighter Association, Stapme attended the Battle of Britain 60th Anniversary Memorial Day at the Battle of Britain Memorial, Capel le Ferne, Kent. Since returning from South Africa he has also attended a number of the annual services at Westminster Abbey to commemorate the Battle of Britain. In September 2000 he was present at the 60th Anniversary service with Pat Roe, his brother in-law and good companion. Pat was a former Lancaster navigator who flew 36 missions over enemy territory in WWII. Sadly, Pat passed away in 2001.

At RIAT 2000, RAF Cottesmore, Stapme met former 603 Squadron colleague Ludwik Martel and Luftwaffe fighter ace Hans-Ekkehard Bob who, as a successful post-war businessman, retired as the President and General Manager of Bomag & Co. Ltd, the company he founded. He also owned his own private aircraft. Stapme and Bob spent much time chatting together about their respective wartime experiences as well as posing for the media in front of the Battle of Britain Memorial Flight's Mk.IIa Spitfire, 'P7' (P7350), which was at one time in service with 603 Squadron during the Battle of Britain. Eckhart Bob revealed how his aircraft had been badly damaged during combat with RAF fighters. The radiator had been hit and he knew the engine would over-heat before he could get back to his airfield. He decided the best way to make it across the Channel was to increase the engine revs intermittently, in order to maintain sufficient altitude, before closing it and gliding until the aircraft slowed and started to lose height, at which time he opened the throttle again. Thus he opened and closed the throttle until he made it back safely. When he described his method to his colleagues he inadvertently coined a new expression which was referred to many times before the end of the battle – he had managed to get home by 'bobbing across the Channel!'

Also in attendance was the very likable and humble H. Möllenbrok, a former Dornier Do17 pilot from the Battle of Britain who had been shot down by RAF fighters and badly injured. It is possible he was flying Dornier Do17Z of 8/KG2, U5+GS, when it was shot down by RAF fighters on 15 September 1940. The aircraft crashed in the sea and he was rescued and taken prisoner. Möllenbrok praised the excellent treatment he received from the many British hospitals in which he was a patient during his time as a POW. Apart from other injuries, one hand had been particularly badly damaged. As a consequence he was eventually repatriated through Sweden as part of an exchange deal before the end of the war. At RIAT, he shared his experiences with Stapme. He also recounted that during his time in Britain he compiled a book of small paintings (9″ x 7″) recording some of the most memorable views seen during his stay. He later managed to smuggle his small art-book back to Germany in his trousers. At RIAT, the elderly German veteran took out the now faded book and showed Stapme some of his impressive artwork. Stapme recalled a poignant comment he made before departing. Referring to WWII and, in particular, the bombing campaign against the RAF airfields and London he had been part of in 1940, he said: 'You British are very forgiving people.'

In April 2002, Stapme was one of the guests at the Imperial War Museum, Lambeth, for the re-launch of Gordon Mitchell's *Schooldays to Spitfire* and *Spitfire into Battle*, the autobiography of Group Captain Wilfred G.G. Duncan Smith DFC & Bar, DSO & Bar, father of the Rt. Hon Iain Duncan Smith, the current leader of the Conservative Party, who was also in attendance. (Coincidentally, as a child, Iain Duncan Smith's playmates included Deryck Stapleton's three boys when both families lived in Dolphin Square. Deryck was working in Whitehall at the time.) A journalist from *The Times* interviewed Stapme and asked him to comment on Group Captain Duncan Smith's description of the Spitfire as 'beautiful and frail yet agile, potent and powerful.' Stapme replied: 'I always wanted a lady like that!'

Stapme has therefore had a busy time these past few years and it would be particularly appropriate to mention the reunions of the Battle of Britain Fighter Association which we attended together, in particular the Battle of Britain Fighter Pilots Reunion at RAF/USAF Lakenheath for the years 1997/98/99 and 24 June 2000, which saw the last ever such function. The itinerary was practically the same each year. On the first occasion we arrived on the Friday afternoon and checked into our very comfortable and well-equipped rooms, including a fully-equipped kitchenette. The room also had a fully-equipped bar including a wide range of whisky and bourbon miniatures. At five o'clock we agreed that I would knock on his door at six when we would go to the Officers Club bar for the evening. A few minutes later my door burst open: 'Have you seen your miniature bar?' Stapme exclaimed, to which I confirmed I had. He then stooped towards the bar and, gathering up all my miniatures, said: 'You don't drink, so you won't be needing these,' and promptly left. An hour later, showered and changed, I knocked on Stapme's door and walked in to find him knotting his tie but otherwise ready to go. All the miniatures – his and mine – were empty! We started off for the club with not a waver in his step, returning around midnight, he apparently none-the-worse for the evening's libation.

At the Battle of Britain Fighter Association reunions at Lakenheath, each veteran was provided with a member of the US Air Force as an escort for the weekend. For the 1997 function Stapme had a very attractive young lady who, at the end of the banquet asked the rather ambiguous question of Stapme: 'What did you do in the Battle of Britain?' Stapme pushed back his chair, unfastened his jacket button, assumed a very relaxed pose and, with a pint mug half-full of quality Californian tawny port, looked at her and to the amusement of all around, sang: 'Night and Day you are the one. . . . '

The old man walked slowly and deliberately along the flight
line, occasionally stopping to glance up at the flying display
overhead. The sight of a Spitfire and Messerschmitt 109 in the
air together so many years after his war had ended brought a
wry smile to his face. His wispy white hair blew in the breeze,
his eyes twinkled and his large handlebar moustache bristled.
He paused, took his pipe from his pocket and placed it in his
mouth. Taking a Swan Vesta from its box he lit the match and
placed it in the bowl of his pipe whilst shielding it with his other
hand. After a few deep puffs he pushed the pipe to the corner of
his mouth and walked on. Some of the spectators recognised him
as he went and came over to seek his autograph and shake his
hand. Some thanked him for what he had done all those years
before. Others, unaware of his identity, were curious and felt
compelled to walk over and find out who it was attracting the
attention of the more knowledgeable. The old man had all the
time in the world for those who wished to talk about his
experiences and times gone by. With his signature in a book, on
a programme or a painting, he smiled, shook their hand and
sent them on their way with a good feeling in their heart.
As the roar of the Merlin and Daimler-Benz engines filled the
sky, he moved on. His demeanour ever-welcoming, his
personality exuding charisma but these days looking very tired.
Although his spirit was great his body was not as strong and
muscular as it had been. He was satisfied his life had been rich
and full and he was content. He valued each day left and
appreciated the gift of longevity bestowed upon him, particularly
as so many of his friends and colleagues had not made it
through the battle with him. . . .

Record of Service
Squadron Leader Basil Gerald Stapleton DFC (41879)

Date of Birth
12 May 1920

Previous Service

Pupil Pilot, Civil Flying School, White Waltham	23.1.39 to 31.3.39

Appointments and Promotions

Granted a Short Service Commission for 4 years Active Service as Acting Pilot Officer General Duties Branch Royal Air Force (with effect from 23.1.39)	1.4.39
Graded Pilot Officer on probation	21.10.39
Confirmed in appointment	23.1.40
Promoted Flying Officer	21.10.40
Appointed Acting Flight Lieutenant	22.5.41
Promoted War Substantive Flight Lieutenant	21.10.41
Transferred to the Reserve and retained on the Active List	23.1.43
Appointed Acting Squadron Leader	6.10.43
Relinquished Acting Squadron Leader	12.7.45
Appointed Acting Squadron Leader	1.8.45
Released	31.1.46
Last Day of Service	9.4.46
Relinquished Commission and permitted to retain the Rank of Squadron Leader	1.7.49

Postings

Civil Flying School White Waltham – Pupil Pilot	23.1.39
No.1 Depot – Supernumerary Disciplinary Course	1.4.39
No.13 Flying Training School – Flying Training	15.4.39
No.219 Squadron – Flying Duties	21.10.39
No.11 Group Pool (Attached) – Operational Training	22.10.39 to 20.11.39*
No.603 Squadron – Flying Duties	16.12.39
No.4 Delivery Flight – Flying Duties	27.3.41
Merchant Ship Fighter Unit – Flying Duties	22.6.41
Station Farnborough (Attached) – Temporary Duty	27.6.41
No.257 Squadron – Supernumerary Flying Duties	14.1.42
Flying Duties	21.2.42
No.2 Delivery Flight – Supernumerary Flying Duties	6.4.43
Station Kenley – Sector Gunnery Instructor	1.9.43
Central Gunnery School – Instructor	27.3.44
No.83 Group Support Unit – Flying Duties	25.7.44
No.247 Squadron – Flying Command	26.8.44
Missing (Flying Battle)	23.12.44
No.106 Personnel Reception Centre – Supernumerary (Ex Prisoner of War)	12.7.45
Air Ministry Unit – Supernumerary	1.8.45
Directorate of Personnel Services – P3	1.9.45
No.100 Personnel Despatch Centre – Class 'A' Release	31.1.46

*After leaving 11 Group Pool was with 32 Sqn before 603.

Honours and Awards
Distinguished Flying Cross – *London Gazette*   15.11.40
Flying Cross conferred by
  Her Majesty The Queen of the Netherlands – *London Gazette*   1.1.46

APPENDIX B

Aircraft Types Flown by Squadron Leader B.G. Stapleton DFC

Airspeed Oxford I & II
Avro Anson
Avro Mongoose
British Aerospace Harrier GR.7 (Simulator)
Bristol Beaufighter VIF
Bristol Blenheim IV
Douglas DC3 Dakota
de Havilland Dominie
de Havilland Tiger Moth
de Havilland Mosquito Mk.II
de Havilland Dove
de Havilland Heron
Fairey Battle

North American T6 Harvard
Hawker Audax
Hawker Hart
Hawker Hart Trainer
Hawker Hurricane Mk.II A, B & C
Hawker Typhoon IB
Junkers Ju52
Miles Master III
Miles Magister
Percival Proctor
Percival Q6
Supermarine Spitfire Mk.IA & IIA

APPENDIX C

Squadron Leader B.G. Stapleton's claims during the Battle of Britain: All claims were with No.603 Squadron, July – November 1940

Date	Enemy Aircraft		Aircraft Flown	Combat Area
3 July	Ju88A-2	$^1/_3$ share of 8/KG30	Spitfire Mk. I	10m north-west of Montrose
20 July	Do17P	$^1/_3$ share of I(F)/120	Spitfire Mk. I	30m east of Aberdeen
29 Aug	Bf109E	Probable	Spitfire Mk. I L1024 XT-R	Deal
29 Aug	Bf109E	Probable	Spitfire Mk. I L1040 XT-R	Manston
31 Aug	Bf109E	Probable of 3/JG3	Spitfire Mk. I L1020 XT-L	north of Southend
3 Sept	Do17	Destroyed	Spitfire Mk. I R6626	15m south-west of Harwich
5 Sept	Bf109E	Destroyed II/JG3	Spitfire Mk. I N3196	Biggin Hill
5 Sept	Bf109E	Probable	Spitfire Mk. I N3196	Biggin Hill
11 Sept	Bf110	Probable	Spitfire Mk. I X4348	South London
11 Sept	Bf109E	Damaged	Spitfire Mk. I X4348	South London
15 Sept	Do17Z	Destroyed 9/KG2	Spitfire Mk. I X4348	Over sea, 5m north-west Ramsgate

15 Sept	Bf109E	Damaged	Spitfire Mk. I X4348	Over sea, 5m north-west Ramsgate
17 Sept	Bf109E	Probable	Spitfire Mk. I X4348	Over Chatham
30 Sept	Bf109E	Destroyed	Spitfire Mk. I P9553	Ashford area
15 Oct	Bf109E	Destroyed	Spitfire Mk. I X4348	10-15m off Dungeness
17 Oct	Bf109E	Probable	Spitfire Mk. I P7324	Dungeness area
20 Oct	Bf109E	Probable	Spitfire Mk. I P7324	Canterbury/Dungeness
7 Nov	Bf110	Shared/ Destroyed	Spitfire Mk. I	Thames Estuary
11 Nov	Bf109E	Destroyed	Spitfire Mk. I P7528	20m north-east Ramsgate

Total: 6 Destroyed, 8 Probable, 3 Shared Destroyed, 2 Damaged

APPENDIX D

No.247 Squadron Bases

S/L Stapleton's movements with No.247 Squadron during his time as Commanding Officer1944/45, flying the Hawker Typhoon Mk.IB:

20 June 1944 to B.6/Coulombs
 (detachment at Hurn)
28 Aug to B.30/Creton

3 Sept to B.48/Amiens/Glisy
6 Sept to B.58/Melsbroek
22 Sept to B.78/Eindhoven

No.247 Squadron Typhoon Mk.Ib, ZY-Y, flown by Stapme. Illustration by Keith Mallen, presented to Stapme by the artist at Duxford in 1995.

APPENDIX E

No.247 (China-British) Squadron Commanding Officers

F/Lt F.M. Thomas	22 Nov 1939
F/Off T.W. Gillen	5 Dec 1939

F/Lt G.F. Chater	5 Jan 1940
S/Ldr P.G. St G. O'Brian DFC	24 Sep 1940
S/Ldr J.C. Melvill DFC	18 May1942
S/Ldr E. Haabjoern DFC	29 Aug 1943
S/Ldr J.R. McNair DFC	19 Jan 1944
S/Ldr B.G. Stapleton DFC	26 Aug 1944
F/Lt T. Tatham (temp)	25 Dec 1944
S/Ldr J.H. Bryant DFC	24 Jan 1945
S/Ldr C. Scott-Vos DFC	1 Dec 1945
S/Ldr D.M. Taylor DFC	18 Dec 1945
S/Ldr T. Balmforth DFC	17 Nov 1947
S/Ldr R.W. Oxspring DSO, DFC	18 Jan 1948
S/Ldr A.R.T. Beddow DFC	12 Jul 1948
S/Ldr P.E. Vaughan-Fowler DSO, DFC	5 Jul 1949
S/Ldr G.J. Gray DFC	18 May 1951
S/Ldr H.G. Pattison DFC	19 Nov 1952
S/Ldr L.S. Laughton OBE	25 Apr 1955
S/Ldr R.A. Carson	28 Jun 1957

APPENDIX F

Oberleutnant Franz von Werra
'The One That Got Away'

In the 1950s in the Archives of the Nobility in Vienna there existed a file marked 'Von Werra' which contained a deposition dated 1806 by Ferdinand von Werra of Leuk in the Republic of Wallis (Valais*) petitioning for recognition of his family's noble standing by the conferment on him of an Imperial title. Ferdinand von Werra refers to the loss of his family's records and deeds over the many years of wars and disturbances to which the district had been subjected. The document is witnessed by the Lord Lieutenant of Wallis who stated that the von Werras had never married beneath them, were traditionally regarded as hereditary nobility, had held high office and, in point of fact, a position of supreme honour in the Republic. Ferdinand von Werra also declared he was to be married to the Baroness von Storkalper, to hold the offices of Right Honourable Lord Steward and Chief Justice of the Worthy Council of Leuk, and to be the legitimate son of the Hereditary Junker Josef von Werra, the Standard Bearer to the aforementioned Council (In 1935, the population of Leuk was only 2,000). In response to this petition, Emperor Franz elevated Ferdinand von Werra to the rank of Imperial Freiherr.

François Gustave de Werra (formerly Werren) was born in Leuk (Loèche) in 1914 and was the eighth child and fourth son of Léo de Werra who, a short time after the birth of François, was financially ruined – this despite the honour bestowed on his family more than a hundred years before. In response the upbringing of François and the next youngest, a sister, was farmed out to Baroness Luisa von Haber, an old friend of the family, and the two youngsters went to live with her at Beuron, Kreis Sigmaringen, in Southern Germany. The

---

* Valais was formerly part of the German Empire. In 1802 Napoleon Bonaparte declared Valais a republic but later incorporated it with France. It was later liberated by Austria in 1813 and two hundred years later became a full member of the Swiss Confederation.

Baroness's husband was Major Oswald Carl, a cavalry officer. The couple had no children of their own and François and his sister grew up regarding the Baroness von Haber as their mother and, as far as he was concerned, the separation from his true family was terminal. Significantly, François became Franz and the 'de' was translated to 'von'. Franz's upbringing was considered abnormal with periods of unhappiness. He was vivacious and restless, two characteristics that remained with Franz into adulthood, but the Baroness was as strict and exacting as he was headstrong and high-spirited. The relationship between the Baroness and her husband became strained and she eventually divorced him.

During his early teens Franz ran away to Hamburg where he spent several days hungry and homeless trying to find work with a shipping company in need of a cabin-boy. His decision to leave home may have been prompted by a family row. He was taken on by the Hamburg-Amerika Line and just prior to sailing for New Orleans he wrote and told his foster-mother of his intentions. In response, the company's local shipping agent received a telegram from Franz's foster parents requesting he be held and looked after until he could be put onboard the first ship heading back to Germany. On arrival in the U.S. Franz was also passed a telegram by a representative of his employer's local agents in which his foster-parents expressed their concern. His time in New Orleans proved to be one of the happiest in Franz von Werra's life and probably played a significant part in developing his character. It was an adventure and he became independent and self-assured. Naturally, his return to Germany brought condemnation for his actions from his parents but at school he was a hero. Probably what could be considered his first taste of fame and popularity came when he was asked to recount his adventures in a lecture to the whole school. He left school shortly before the Nazis took control of Germany. At that time there was mass unemployment and the country boiled with political and industrial unrest. By this time he had left home for good and in order to make a living he took any casual work going. He became a jobbing gardener for some time before moving on to became a locksmith's mate, which he remained for about two years. This early employment was a far cry from his life of action as a fighter pilot in his country's air force. In 1933 Hitler and the Nazi Party had come to power and conscription was introduced the following year. In 1935 the formation of the Luftwaffe was announced by Hitler and Göring (which had been going on anyway, despite the Treaty of Versailles). The picture of the new air force, as painted by the Nazi propaganda machine, was chimeric to Franz von Werra at a time when the youth of Germany had known only hunger, hardship and frustration. Having volunteered as a private, Franz underwent two years of basic training at the completion of which he was selected as an officer candidate for flying duties. His enthusiasm, individualism and dare-devil attitude made him an ideal choice for further training as a fighter pilot. He was commissioned as a Leutnant in September 1938, and given his first operational posting to No.3 Fighter *Jadgeschwader* (JG.3), which was in the process of forming.

It would appear that having settled into life in the Luftwaffe, von Werra was keen to acquit himself well but impatient when it came to having his virtue recognised. He believed that dash, aggressiveness and flare were the qualities that would impress with perhaps a touch of dare-devilry but in peacetime there were only training exercises. Treating his girlfriend to an impromptu flying display over her home, flying under bridges, air-races (official and unofficial) or being towed across the airfield in a galvanised bath by a wealthy colleague in his sports car, were all things that served to get him noticed but things which many RAF pilots did themselves and, as a consequence, were 'ordinary'. After a while von Werra believed he knew what image the Luftwaffe wanted its fighter pilots to procure and did his best to exemplify the type. In order to do this he called in his noble antecedents. Leutnant Franz von Werra became Leutnant Baron Franz von Werra.

Although Hitler had an aversion to aristocratic titles and planned to replace the old German nobility, at that time it was still useful to have a title. Interestingly, neither the press nor German High Command ever accorded von Werra this title. This was not as a result of any ruling as hundreds of Luftwaffe officers genuinely entitled to use the title *Freiherr* were bestowed it in official communiqués. Baroness von Haber, von Werra's foster mother had actively encouraged him to believe in his nobility and to be proud of it. A coronet was embroidered above his initials on his linen and personal possessions, and embossed on his visiting card. However, he must have been aware that the use of *Freiherr*, bestowed more than a century before by a defunct monarchy on a citizen of a democratic republic (Switzerland has no noble titles) was highly questionable, to say the least – the more so as it was claimed by a descendant who had become an adopted citizen of National Socialist Germany.

Von Werra saw himself as an exceptional human being, a romantic figure who was destined to play a romantic role in life. This he undoubtedly achieved. The militarists may have trained him and produced a capable fighter pilot and a fine Luftwaffe officer, but the image was superficial, as years of political indoctrination and absorbing false ideals and values only helped to foster rather than cure von Werra's romanticism and conceit. To him it was only natural that such a figure should have a noble title, in fact it was indispensable. One of his commanding officers wrote: 'Werra has a mature personality with a degree of self-assurance that is quite remarkable. He is somewhat inclined to be arrogant and to have grandiose ideas, and therefore needs to be held in close check.' Whilst another wrote: 'He is the *Fighter Type*: extremely dashing, good-looking and humorous. Absolutely reliable. Some of his pranks misfire, but it is impossible to be mad with him. He would cut off his arm for his commanding officer.' In June 1939, one such 'prank' misfired so badly it nearly claimed his life. Whilst stunt-flying over JG.3's airfield at Koenigsberg he crashed his Me109. The nose of the aircraft was buried deep in the ground and von Werra found himself unable to move, fortunately the aircraft didn't catch fire. He was lifted from the cockpit and taken to hospital where it was discovered he had spinal injuries. Months of hospitalisation lay ahead and it seemed his Luftwaffe career was over.

The Commanding Officer of JG.3 was Oberleutnant Wilhelm Balthasar; although only just senior in years he had already achieved much that von Werra craved. Balthasar was already a national hero as a result of his record-breaking flight round Africa and as a fighter ace with the Legion Condor in the Spanish Civil War. The Franco decorations and the Spanish Cross in gold with diamonds on Balthasar's chest must have frustrated von Werra when he brought news of the squadron and his friends when he visited him in hospital. On another visit Balthasar brought with him a friend, a female he had met at a party. Von Werra fell in love with her immediately and later the couple were married.

With renewed motivation, von Werra improved rapidly and passed a medical in time to take part in the Polish campaign which began at the end of August 1939. By the time of the Battle of Britain, von Werra was seen as fairly typical of German fighter pilots of the period. The Luftwaffe had broken the Polish Air Force, the small Norwegian Air Force had been destroyed, the Dutch, Belgian and French Air Forces had also been defeated and the RAF driven back from the continent in just a few weeks. Von Werra went into combat in the Battle of Britain with a feeling of invincibility and a determination to achieve glory as Baron Franz von Werra, fighter ace, in the short time that was left before it was all over.

The most controversial event during this period of his life occurred on 28 August 1940 when he claimed to have shot down an RAF fighter over the Thames Estuary following which he became separated from his unit. Finding himself over an RAF airfield he latched onto a number of Hurricanes as they came in to land at their aerodrome and shot two down, claiming to have used the ploy of pretending to have been one of their number in order to carry out the attack. He then proceeded to destroy five more aircraft and a bowser on the ground. Using the last of his fuel von Werra made his way through the wall of anti-aircraft fire put up by the aerodrome defences, through a ring of attacking RAF fighters before eventually landing back at his airfield in Northern France, an hour overdue. Von Werra's five earlier victories had already brought him the Iron Cross, Class I & II and perhaps this ridiculous wild and vainglorious fabrication casts some doubt over his earlier claims. Early in January 1941, the German press announced the award of the Knight's Cross (*Ritterkreuz*) of the Iron Cross for his achievements on 28 August, at a time when the award was highly coveted. However, in this instance the strict criteria required for this award was not adhered to, one aspect being that an eyewitness to events was required. The citation reads:

> In the course of 47 operational flights von Werra has shot down 8 enemy aircraft and destroyed 5 more on the ground. On one occasion, flying along over England, he turned a tactically unfavourable situation to his own advantage, and successfully attacked a formation of Hawker Hurricane fighters going in to land on an airfield. He then made four low-level attacks on the airfield itself, destroying aircraft and a petrol tanker on the ground and firing into groups of enemy personnel. This attack is unique in the annals of fighter aviation in this war. Oberleutnant von Werra had proved himself to be an outstanding and courageous fighter pilot, worthy of the high honour bestowed on him.

There is no evidence to confirm von Werra's claims for 28 August 1940, and J.M. Spaight CB, CBE, former Principal Secretary of the Air Minstry, later recorded in his book *The Battle of Britain* that von Werra's claims 'could not be reconciled with any incidents of the air fighting known to the Royal Air Force.' Sadly, von Werra was not the first to 'shoot a line' in order to gain the Knight's Cross, nor was he the last.

His life story has since become legend, in part for his daring and obvious courage as a fighter pilot and then escapologist, but also for the fact that he was prepared to deceive to achieve. He cannot be criticised for deceiving the Allies during his captivity, he would have seen it as his duty to misinform his captors at every opportunity and probably took a pride in doing so. Deceiving his own colleagues in manufacturing an image to satisfy his own ego is another aspect to the legend of 'the one that got away' that has tempered the perception he had hoped to achieve.

APPENDIX G

Group Captain Charles Green DFC, DSO and Bar

(A Short Biography of S/L B.G. Stapleton's 124 Wing Commanding Officer,
while he was serving with No.247 Squadron.)

Charles Llewellyn Green was born on 23 September 1912 at Marandellas, South Rhodesia (now Zimbabwe). He was educated at Umtali High School and after a period farming with his father he joined Imperial Airways as a clerk and served at various southern Africa stations until he was appointed ground superintendent at Beira in Mozambique. In 1938, he applied for and was granted a short service commission in the RAF. Following training in November 1940, he was posted to No.500 (County of Kent) Squadron, AuxAF, in Coastal Command, flying Avro Ansons. Early in 1941, Green was posted to No.235 Squadron, another Coastal Command unit flying the Bristol Blenheim on operations against enemy shipping in the North Sea from their base at Bircham Newton, Norfolk. In 1942, after completing 51 sorties he was promoted to flight lieutenant and posted to 266 (Rhodesia) Squadron at Duxford, where he and his fellow pilots were introduced to the Hawker

Typhoon ('Tiffie') by Battle of Britain ace, Hugh 'Cocky' Dundas. Green developed skills which helped establish his reputation as a pilot of exceptional courage and determination and went on to play an important role in overcoming the early problems with the Typhoon and questioned the proposal to fit rockets to the Hurricane, winning his argument that the Typhoon not only performed better but also had a superior gun platform and was therefore better suited for rocket firing. With the unit, which included a number of other Rhodesian pilots, Green took part in sweeps over Northern France and in anti-shipping strikes off Holland in addition to intercepting Luftwaffe aircraft over RAF airfields.

After promotion to squadron leader and receiving command of 266 Squadron, Green led his unit alongside 56 Squadron in offensive sweeps by the Duxford Wing. All the while he was learning how best to handle what was a difficult aircraft to fly. During this period the Duxford squadrons shot down eleven enemy aircraft.

In May 1943, while serving at Duxford, Green married Betty Jean Bowden, a WAAF leading aircraftwoman. They had two sons, the second of whom died in infancy, and three daughters. That year Green was also mentioned in despatches and awarded a DFC for his 'outstanding leadership and intense desire to engage the enemy.' He then moved on to No.59 Operational Training Unit (OTU) where he served mainly as a flying instructor in the rank of wing commander.

In January 1944 he was appointed Wing Commander (Flying) of No.121 Wing, and was involved in attacks on the V-1 'doodlebug' launch sites and the operations to soften-up enemy installations in the run-up to the D-Day landings. He was awarded the DSO and Bar the same year. He mastered flying at low-level and destroyed enemy tanks, transport and concentrations of troops by 'hedge-hopping' in his rocket-firing Typhoon, helping clear the way for the advance of the Allied advance from the Normandy beachheads into north-west Europe. His brilliant leadership of 121 Wing (comprising 174, 175 and 245 Squadrons) resulted in the destruction of ammunition dumps and helped to destroy or demoralise enemy formations and positions. He led the Wing which helped to destroy vital German armour in the Falaise Pocket during August 1944. Following a counter-attack by two German Panzer Divisions on 7 August, Green returned from a reconnaissance of the battle to report that 300 enemy tanks were in the vicinity. Flying into battle with other elements of the 2nd Tactical Air Force (2nd TAF), 121 Wing halted progress of a column of 60 tanks and 200 other vehicles by attacking the lead and rear-most vehicles before attacking those caught in between. Green ran a 'shuttle service' of Typhoons with a squadron airborne every twenty minutes. By dusk, after some 300 sorties had been flown, it was believed that 119 tanks and 50 transport vehicles, including vital tank support vehicles and supplies, had been destroyed. He later recalled: 'At fifty feet over the fleeing columns I was so low I could see not only the black crosses on the vehicles but also the square heads of the drivers.' This action set the pattern for the battle in which Allied forces encircled the German 7th Army in the Falaise Pocket. In mid-August Green's and other 2nd TAF Typhoons devastated an enemy trapped in Normandy's narrow lanes, but this was not achieved without the loss of 151 pilots. As the offensive in Northern France and Holland continued, Green (by now a thirty-two-year-old group captain) commanded No.124 Wing with Wing Commander Kit North-Lewis as his wing leader.

Although group captains were discouraged from flying on operations, on Boxing Day 1944 Green announced that he would fly a weather reconnaissance. During the sortie he reported a build-up of enemy tanks and took the opportunity to attack. His canopy was shot off by return fire, his Typhoon caught fire, and he was forced to bale out, despite the dangerously low altitude of his aircraft. He was quickly captured and severely beaten by members of the SS before he was eventually taken to Oberursel for interrogation. There, he saw Stapme again (one of his squadron commanders) but the two did not let on to the enemy they knew each other. Stapme clearly recalls Green's face bore the legacy of his beating by the SS.

Green was moved to Stalag Luft I, near the village of Barth on the Baltic coast where he met Stapme again. Green was liberated from Barth when the Germans retreated in the face of the Russian advance. It has been inaccurately recorded that Green and Stapme swapped some Red Cross parcels for a small car and drove along the north German coast until they encountered Canadian troops, who then arranged for them to be flown home. Stapme did flee the camp in this way but with two Canadians, not Green.

Following his brief time as a POW, Green returned to Rhodesia and created a tobacco, maize and cattle farm from virgin soil, south-east of the capital, Salisbury. In 1961, as a group captain, he became the first post-war commanding officer of the Royal Rhodesian Air Force Volunteer Reserve. It was during this period that farming became less profitable and Green entered the tobacco trade. The Transcontinental Tobacco Company recognised his talents and sent him to Formosa (now Taiwan), and he continued to travel extensively to areas with substantial tobacco interests until his retirement in 1977. The following year he moved to Devon but after six years in Britain he, like Stapme, decided he would prefer life in South Africa and settled in Durban, where he joined the Virginia Wings flying club.

Charles Green died in September 2001, just short of his 89th birthday. After his death his flying club organised a flypast in his honour, during which his ashes were scattered on the airfield.

APPENDIX H

Programme of events from the Battle of Britain Fighter Pilots Reunion RAF Lakenheath 24 June 2000

(Due to the effects of time on the members of the Battle of Britain Fighter Association and the natural dwindling of numbers, it was decided that this was to be the last ever such function. It was a particularly enjoyable but poignant occasion):

Dear Battle of Britain Veterans and Friends of RAF Lakenheath,

The men and women of RAF Lakenheath warmly welcome you to the 2000 Battle of Britain Memorial Service and Fighter Association Reunion. The 48th Fighter Wing is once again honoured to host this distinguished event, and we sincerely hope you enjoy this year's service and festivities. Because this is planned to be the final reunion, it is our intent to make this the most memorable of all the previous reunions. Thank you for joining us once again to honour you and your comrades and for making this celebration a truly memorable occasion.

Order of Service

Posting of Colours
Honour Guard, RAF Lakenheath

The British National Anthem
The United States National Anthem
Sounds of Liberty

Welcoming Remarks
Captain Paul M. Johnson
493rd Fighter Squadron
Memorial Service Master of Ceremonies

Invocation
Chaplain, Major Paul Sherouse
48th Fighter Wing, RAF Lakenheath

Address
Commander, 48th Fighter Wing, RAF Lakenheath
Colonel Irving L. Halter, Jnr

Battle of Britain Fighter Association
Air Chief Marshal Sir Christopher Foxley-Norris, GCB, DSO, OBE

Plaque Dedication

Presentation of Floral Wreaths

Moment of Silence

Firing of Volleys
Honour Guard, RAF Lakenheath

Taps
Honour Guard, RAF Lakenheath

United States Air Force Fly-By
In 'Missing Man' Formation
F-15C Eagles from 493rd Fighter Squadron, RAF Lakenheath

Royal Air Force Fly-By
Supermarine Spitfire
Battle of Britain Memorial Flight, RAF Coningsby

Benediction
Chaplain, Major Paul Sherouse
48th Fighter Wing, RAF Lakenheath

Closing Remarks
Captain Paul M. Johnson
493rd Fighter Squadron

* * *

After the ceremony, please join us at the RAF Lakenheath flight line where there will be static displays of the F-15C/E and an aerial demonstration of the Battle of Britain Memorial Flight's Supermarine Spitfire.

Battle of Britain Veterans in Attendance
(as of 19 June 2000)

Rank	Name	Decorations	Sqn	Aircraft
Flt Lt	LH ALLEN		141	Defiant
Wg Cdr	AJM ALDWINKLE		601	Hurricane
A/Cdr	CCM BAKER	OBE	23	Blenheim
Wg Cdr	PPC BARTHROPP	DFC AFC	602	Spitfire
Sq Ldr	GH BENNIONS	DFC	41	Spitfire
Flt Lt	OV BURNS		235	Blenheim
Wt Off	RV COOK		219	Blcnheim
Gp Cpt	J CUNNINGHAM	CBE DSO DFC	604	Blenheim
Gp Cpt	TF DALTON-MORGAN	DSO OBE DFC	43	Hurricane
Flt Lt	JK DOWN		616	Spitfire
Wt Off	PH FOX		56	Hurricane
ACM	Sir C FOXLEY-NORRIS	GCB DSO OBE	3	Hurricane
Flt Lt	RC GOSLING		266	Spitfire
Wt Off	FW GREEN		600	Blenheim
Sqn Ldr	HE GREEN	MBE	141	Defiant
Flt Lt	PR HAIRS	MBE	501	Hurricane
Flt Lt	LW HARVEY		54	Spitfires
Flt Lt	RA HAYLOCK	AE	236	Blenheim
Flt Lt	RL JONES		64	Spitfire
Wg Cdr	TM KANE		234	Spitfire
Flt Sgt	J KEATINGS		219	Blenheim
Sqn Ldr	JGP MILLARD	AE KSG	1	Hurricane
Gp Capt	AD MURRAY	DFC	73	Hurricane
Wg Cdr	TF NEIL	DFC AFC	249	Hurricane
Sqn Ldr	D NICHOLLS	DFC	151	Hurricane
Flt Lt	DH NICHOLS		56	Hurricane
Flt Lt	EG PARKIN		501	Hurricane
Sqn Ldr	TG PICKERING		64	Spitfire
Sqn Ldr	GR PUSHMAN	DFC	23	Blenheim
Wg Cdr	JG SANDERS	DFC	615	Hurricane
Sqn Ldr	VC SIMMONDS		238	Hurricane
Wg Cdr	WM SIZER	DFC AFC	213	Hurricane
Flt Lt	RH SMITH	DFC	111	Hurricane
Sqn Ldr	BG STAPLETON	DFC	603	Spitfire
Wt Off	HG STEWART		236	Blenheim

Wg Cdr	JA THOMSON		302	Hurricane
Lt Cdr	RWM WALSH		111	Hurricane
Fg Off	KA WILKINSON		616	Spitfire
Wg Cdr	JRC YOUNG	AFC	249	Hurricane
A/Cdr	PM BROTHERS	CBE DSO DFC	32	Hurricane

Captain A.R.P. Reilly-Foull from the *Daily Mirror* cartoon strip, 'Just Jake', whose phrase gave Basil Stapleton his nickname.

A Selection of No.11 Group Intelligence Reports
& Stapme's Surviving Combat Reports
completed during his service with
No.603 (City of Edinburgh) Squadron, AuxAF

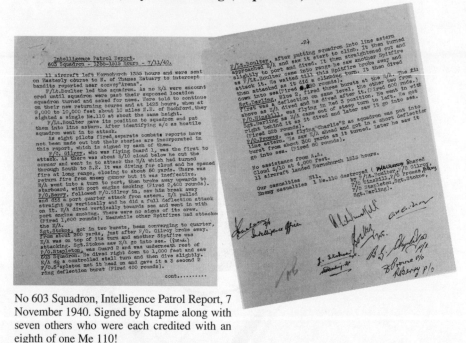

No 603 Squadron, Intelligence Patrol Report, 7
November 1940. Signed by Stapme along with
seven others who were each credited with an
eighth of one Me 110!

Intelligence Report from HQ, No 11 Group, showing confusion over Stapme's first patrol on 3
September 1940 when it states he took off with No 54 Squadron. During the patrol Richard
Hillary and Dudley Stewart-Clark were shot down.

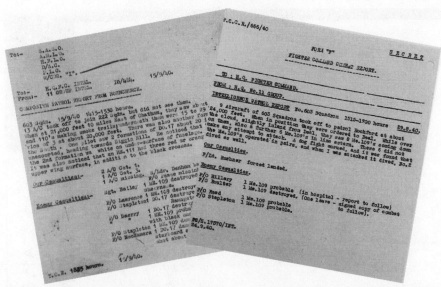

Intelligence Report from HQ No 11 Group to HQ Fighter Command on 15 September 1940, show's Stapme's part in the events on what later became known as 'Battle of Britain Day'.

Combat Report from HQ No 11 Group to HQ Fighter Command, 29 August 1940, recording Stapme's Me 109 probable.

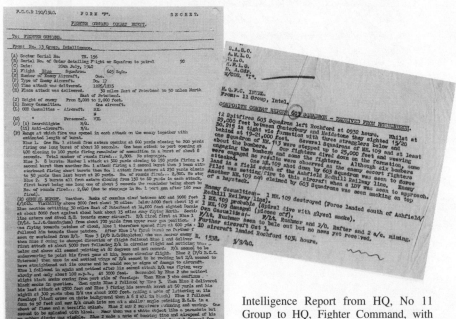

No 13 Group, HQ, Intelligence Patrol Report to HQ, Fighter Command, 20 July 1940, which shows Stapme's part in shooting down a Do 17 off the east coast of Scotland: 'The first time I fired my guns in anger'.

Intelligence Report from HQ, No 11 Group to HQ, Fighter Command, with details of Stapme's 'kill' on 5 September 1940 (Oberleutnant Franz von Werra).

Gun 3

93/3   424

SECRET   Form "F"

COMBAT REPORT

Sector Serial No. _____ (A)

Serial No. of Order detailing Flight or Squadron to
Patrol _____ (B)

Date _____ (C) July 3rd 1940

Flight, Squadron _____ (D) Flight : 3   Sqdn. : 103

Number of Enemy Aircraft _____ (E) One

Type of Enemy Aircraft _____ (F) Ju. 88.

Time Attack was delivered _____ (G) 14:10.

Place Attack was delivered _____ (H) 5 miles S.W. Montrose.

Height of Enemy _____ (J) 9,000'

Enemy Casualties _____ (K) 1 Ju. 88 in Sea.

Our Casualties _____ Aircraft _____ (L) Nil.

                 Personnel _____ (M) nil.

GENERAL REPORT _____ (R)

Green 2 sighted E/A after carrying out attack
Blue Green 1 attacked, then I attacked slightly
on the starboard quarter as E/A was turning to
Starboard I only had time for 1 short burst
after which the E/A entered cloud bank I lost
my section so I proceeded to patrol 20 miles
E of Montrose where there was no cloud.
Green 1 F/O Carbury Green 2 P/O Berry

                         Signature   B.G. Stapleton

           O.C. { Section Green
                      Flight B
                      Squadron 603 Squadron No.

R.A.F. Form 1151

Andrew Reid & Company Ltd., Newcastle-upon-Tyne 14974 H.

Blue 3

426

Form "F"

9207

<u>SE</u>CRET & IMMEDIATE.

COMBAT REPORT

Sector Serial No. .... (A) ....

Serial No. of Order detailing Flight or Squadron to
   Patrol .... (B) ....

Date .... (C) *20/7/40*

Flight, Squadron .... (D) Flight : *B* Sqdn. : *603*

Number of Enemy Aircraft .... (E) *1 (ONE)*

Type of Enemy Aircraft .... (F) *Do 17*

Time Attack was delivered .... (G) *12·05*

Place Attack was delivered .... (H) *30 MILES E. ABERDEEN*

Height of Enemy .... (J) *5,000'*

Enemy Casualties .... (K) *1 (ONE)*

Our Casualties .... Aircraft .... (L) *Nil*

                    Personnel .... (M) *Nil*

~~GENERAL REMARKS~~   (N)

Searchlights: Did they illuminate enemy? If
               not, were they in front of or   *N.A.*
               behind target?   (N)(i)   *N.A.*

A.A. GUns: Did shell bursts assist pilot in   *N.A.*
            intercepting enemy?   (N)(ii)

Range at which fire was opened and closed in
each attack and estimated length of burst
(also details of stoppages)   (P) *2 No1 attacks 300yds - 150yd*
3 beam attacks 3 no1 attacks closing to 20yds.

General Report   (R) *Enemy sighted when*
orbiting. Blue 1 gave line astern. I went into "no1 position"
because Blue 2 was behind. I opened fire at 300yds closed to 150.
Then followed 3 no beam attacks. After Blue 1+2 had finished their
ammunition, I did 3 more no 1 attacks closing to 20 yds. Noticing E.A.
letters were ~~at~~ H+6A.

               Signature   *B.J. Stapleton P/O.*

           XXX   { Section *BLUE*
                       { Flight *'B' FLT.*
                       { Squadron *603* ~~XXXXXXXXX~~

R.A.F. Form 1151

P/O STAPLETON   127/119   432

SECRET.   FORM "F"

C O M B A T R E P O R T.

Sector Serial No.	(a)	
Serial No. of order detailing Patrol.	(b)	
Date.	(c)	31. 8. 40
Flight, Squadron.	(d)	'A' 603 Squadron
No. & type of enemy aircraft.	(f)	5 ME 109's
Time attack was delivered.	(g)	1825 hours
Place attack was delivered.	(h)	North of Southend
Height of enemy.	(j)	25,000 feet
Enemy casualties.	(k)	Destroyed --
		Probable 1 HE 109
		Damaged --
Our casualties. Aircraft	(l)	--
Personnel	(m)	--
Searchlights.	(n) (i)	--
A.A. Guns. Assistance.	(ii)	--
Fire from fighters.	(p)	Range opened See attached report
		Length of burst
		Range closed
		No. of rounds fired.

—   433

P/O. STAPLETON.

When patrolling in line astern with the rest of the Squadron
I sighted bomber formation below us on the port.
With two other aircraft I climbed into the sun for a
favourable position, to make attack on the bombers out
of the sun, when 5 Me.109's engaged us.
These Me.109's came out of the bomber formations climbing
into the sun. F/O. Carbury engaged 3 Me.109's and I
engaged the other 2. These two were flying in tight line
astern. After giving the rear one a deflection burst of
3 seconds he pulled vertically upwards with white streams
pouring from his engine.

B. G. Stapleton

APPENDIX J

The bogus (Red Cross) Arrival Report Form given to POWs at *Auswertestelle-West*, Oberursel.

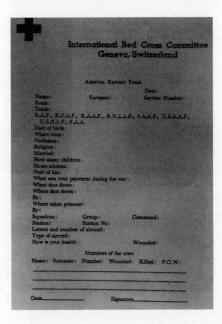

Line drawing of Stalag Luft I, Barth – April 1943

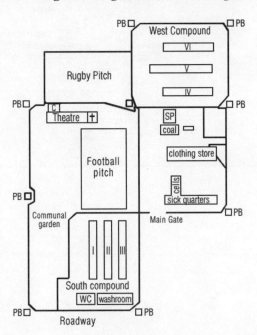

Map of Africa showing places Stapme, lived, worked and visited

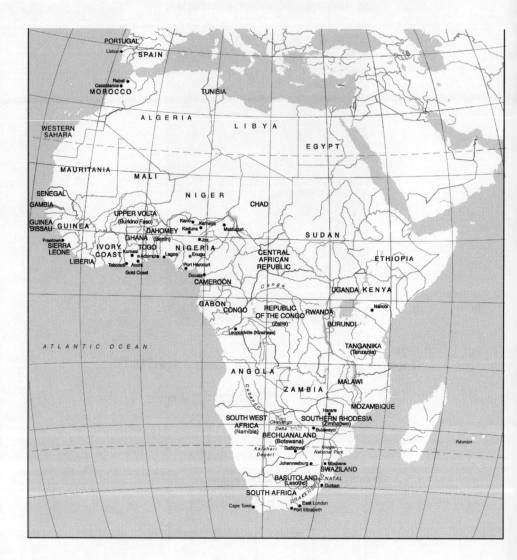

Map of South Africa including Botswana showing places Stapme lived, worked and visited

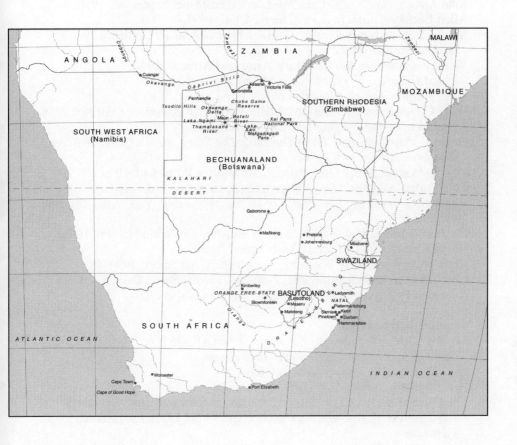

Published sources:
John Alcorn, *Battle of Britain Top Guns*, Aeroplane, September 1996.
Allen Bechky, *Southern Africa*, Sierra Club, 1997.
Kendal Burt & James Leasor, *The One That Got Away*, Collins with Michael Joseph, 1956.
Victor F. Gammon, *Not All Glory*, Arms and Armour, 1996.
Richard Hillary, *The Last Enemy*, Macmillan, 1942.
B.A. 'Jimmie' James, *Moonless Night*, Leo Cooper, 1983.
Wing Commander C.G. Jefford, MBE, RAF, *RAF Squadrons*, Airlife, 1988.
Alan Lake, *Flying Units of the RAF*, Airlife, 1999.
David J. Marchant, *Rise From The East. The Story of 247 (China-British) Squadron*, Air Britain, 1996.
Francis Mason, *Battle Over Britain*, McWhirter Twins Ltd, 1969.
Cole Porter, *Night and Day*, Warner/Chappell Music Ltd, London.
Winston G. Ramsey, *The Battle of Britain Then and Now*, After the Battle, 1980.
Charles Rollings, *Dulag Luft*, (Article in) After the Battle No.106, 1999.
David Ross, *Richard Hillary*, Grub Street, 2000.
Chris Shores and Clive Williams, *Aces High*, Grub Street, 1994.
Chris Thomas and Chris Shores, *Typhoon Tempest Story,* Cassell & Co.
Raymond F. Toliver, *The Interrogator*, Aero Publishers, 1978.

Unpublished Sources:
No.603 (City of Edinburgh) Squadron, RAuxAF, ORB & Combat Reports.
No.603 (City of Edinburgh) Squadron Archive.
No.247 (China-British) Squadron ORB.
No.257 (Burma) Squadron ORB.
The Flying Log Books of: Wing Commander George Gilroy, Squadron Leaders Jim Morton and Jack Stokoe and Flight Lieutenant Keith Lawrence.
Diary extracts, No.247 Squadron, by Michael Shirley (formerly Michael 'Crusher' Croft).
Stadtarchiv of Oberursel, Germany.